NEVER TURN BACK

NEVER TURN BACK

THE **RNLI** SINCE THE SECOND WORLD WAR

RAY AND SUSANNAH KIPLING

Lifeboats

SUTTON PUBLISHING

First published in the United Kingdom in 2006 by
Sutton Publishing Limited · Phoenix Mill
Thrupp · Stroud · Gloucestershire · GL5 2BU

In association with the Royal National Lifeboat Institution

Reprinted 2006

British Library Cataloguing in Publication Data
A catalogue record for this book is available from the British Library.

ISBN 0-7509-4307-6

RNLI name and logo are trademarks of RNLI used by Sutton Publishing
Limited under licence from RNLI (Enterprises) Ltd. Registered Charity
No. 209603.

Typeset in 11.5/15pt Garamond.
Typesetting and origination by
Sutton Publishing Limited.
Printed and bound in England by
J.H. Haynes & Co. Ltd, Sparkford.

Contents

Acknowledgements and Bibliography   vii

Introduction   ix

1. The Lifeboat VC   1

2. Reluctant Heroes   23

3. Triumph and Disaster   49

4. Designed for Danger   71

5. All at Sea   103

6. Pomp and Circumstance   127

7. Finding the Funds   143

8. Overseas Adventures   163

9. Why Do They Do It?   177

10. Diversification   197

Index   211

Acknowledgements

We have met hundreds of lifeboat crew members, station officials, fund-raisers, supporters and staff over the last thirty years. It is a privilege to number them among our friends and there is a part of every one of them in this book.

In particular, we are grateful for contributions and advice from Bernd Anders, Richard Barclay, Keith and Ros Bower, Hewitt and Margaret Clark, Susan Fernley, David Hudson, Brian Miles, Andrew Papworth, John Petit, Alan Tate, Zip Wiebenga and Alan Williams. Special thanks go to Joan Davies. Under her editorship *The Lifeboat* magazine celebrated the exploits of lifeboat crews in their own words, from which we have drawn material.

Derek King of the RNLI's image resource unit, gave enormous help with the photographs. We are grateful for the permission of the copyright holders who allow their images to be used for the benefit of the RNLI.

Bibliography

Bensley, Mick, *The Rescues of Henry Blogg and the Cromer Lifeboat Crew*, Bengunn, 2001

Kipling, R., *Rescue by Sail and Oar*, Sulhamstead, Tops'l Books, 1982

Kipling, R. and S., *Strong to Save*, Yeovil, Patrick Stephens, 1995

Skidmore, Ian, *Lifeboat VC*, London, Macmillan, 1980

Introduction

The achievements of the RNLI, often romanticised, depend on ordinary people doing extraordinary things. There is failure as well as success, pain as well as glory, humour as well as grim determination.

The period since the Second World War, particularly since the mid-1960s, has seen the most rapid change in the RNLI's long history. The transition from conventional to fast lifeboats, the introduction of inshore lifeboats and the expansion into beach rescue and sea safety have all dramatically changed the lifeboat service. This book describes the human stories behind the last fifty years of the RNLI, using the personal accounts of the people involved.

In spite of all the changes, there remains at the core of the RNLI the magnificent diversity of crews, nearly all volunteers, drawn from communities around the coasts of England, Scotland, Wales and Ireland. It is because of the crews that the RNLI has been described as the best club in the country, for there is a welcome to lifeboat people at any station they visit. The strong camaraderie, and a rich sense of humour, helps lifeboat crews to carry on in the face of adversity.

Their doggedness and perseverance was exemplified by a disaster more than a century ago. In 1901, the Caister lifeboat capsized, killing nine of her crew. The retired second coxswain, James Haylett, aged seventy-eight, had two sons, a son-in-law and two grandsons in the boat. He dashed into the surf, regardless of the danger and, with great difficulty, managed to pull two lifeboatmen to safety. He was awarded a gold medal for his outstanding bravery and at the formal inquest, he was questioned about his actions. It was then suggested that the lifeboat might have been returning to the beach after abandoning the rescue mission. Haylett's reply was bold and simple: 'Caister men never turn back.' It has been the unspoken motto of the lifeboat service ever since.

CHAPTER ONE

The Lifeboat VC

The gold medal is the highest bravery award of the RNLI. It is awarded for a rescue in which outstanding courage, skill and initiative have been shown. This medal has been awarded only nine times in the last half century, so it is hardly surprising that it is known as the lifeboatman's Victoria Cross. No lifeboatman would set out to win a gold medal, for the dividing line between extreme gallantry and death is thin indeed. And the medal has never been awarded unless all criteria are met. With the medal comes a welter of publicity, yet it can also foster jealousy and envy. All gold medal rescues, by any measure, are outstanding.

If he grew a beard, Brian Bevan would fit the archetypal image of a lifeboat coxswain. Dark hair, twinkling eyes, two gold earrings and a cheeky half smile meant that 32-year-old Bevan was swamped by women of a certain age when he was in London to have three bravery medals – a gold, a silver and a bronze – pinned to his chest. Suddenly, and uniquely, a lifeboatman turned pop star. The women were looking for kisses and autographs, while Bevan, embarrassed, was looking for the exit. His story is worth telling not only for the rescues that propelled him to prominence, but also to count the price of fame.

Brian Bevan was a Yorkshire fisherman who went to school with Fred Walkington, who later became the Bridlington coxswain. As young men Bevan and Walkington crewed the local Bridlington lifeboat. Then the Humber coxswain had to stand down as he was diagnosed with diabetes, a condition that has caused heated debate within the RNLI on the level of risk it poses to crew who are sufferers. Bevan applied for the job of running the Humber lifeboat and being the appointed village chief of the tiny community of seven lifeboat families stranded on a 4-mile spit of land, washed on one side by the powerful North Sea and on the other by the silt-laden River Humber.

Spurn Head, where the promontory widens slightly, has no other permanent residents, though Humber pilots work there and hundreds of seabirds visit.

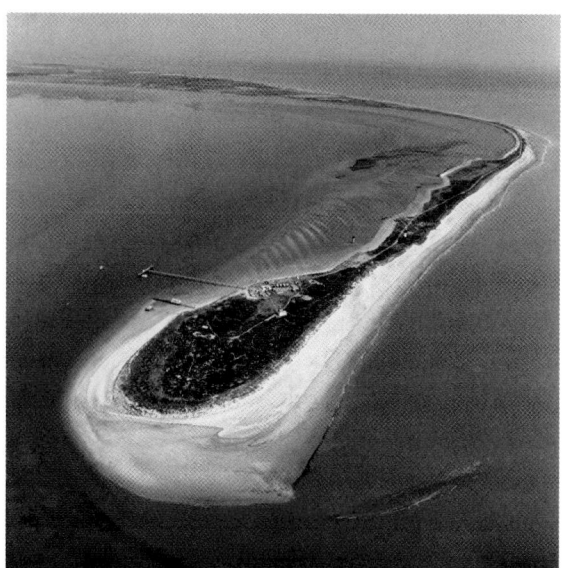

Spurn Point, home to the Humber lifeboat crew.
(Hunting Aerofilms Ltd)

Ruins of Second World War fortifications remain, as do traces of the railway that took supplies along the point. Between the land and the end of the point, the spit narrows to a few yards, and is constantly battered by the sea in a cycle of erosion and deposition that is fully chronicled by academics at nearby Hull University. They contend that nature should be allowed to take her course and turn Spurn into an island; the families living on the end disagree. The existence at Humber lifeboat station is, then, only for the hardy. The men must stay on station, but women and children are free to come and go as they please, travelling for 6 miles to schools, shops and the nearest community. The current Superintendent Coxswain (there is only one holder of this grand title in the whole RNLI), Dave Steenvorden, says that for those who can stand the isolation, the place is idyllic – safe for children, good for families who don't mind living in close proximity. 'The day I stop enjoying it is the day I'll hang up my lifejacket,' he says.

The men are on a strict roster for five days a week. The pub, a tempting 4 miles away, can only be visited on a day off. Humber is a busy station, averaging fifty calls a year. Weeks can go by without a call out, but then there can be more than one at a time.

In the grim winter of 1978/9 that is exactly what happened. Over a period of seven weeks, the men of the Humber were tested time and time again in the most extreme conditions. They emerged covered in glory.

Many seafarers were pleased to see the back of 1978. The Fastnet Race in August that year had been overwhelmed by hurricane force winds, with a fleet of 306 yachts strung out across the 150-mile stretch between Land's End and the Fastnet Rock. A massive rescue operation was mounted, involving ships at sea, coastguards, helicopters and thirteen lifeboats that spent a total of 170 hours at sea. Fifteen yachtsmen died, some needlessly abandoning their boats for life rafts that were overwhelmed, one tragically washed off a rescue ladder as he had forgotten to unclip his lifeline from the raft. It was a shocking loss of life.

NEW YEAR'S EVE RESCUE

Just as the year was drawing to a close, another gale whipped across the North Sea, which Rudyard Kipling called 'the cold, grey widow maker'. The intensity of the storm was a major threat to shipping. First caught was the Dutch coaster, *Diana V*, which was shaken and rolled until her cargo of maize shifted in the hold, pushing the ship into a dangerous list. Although she was 74 miles from Spurn Head, she was in acute distress and needed help desperately.

Watch how the time unfolds with this story. Imagine this. Leave the comfort of reading this book and put yourself in the cold, wet, stomach-churning storm. In front of you, in serried ranks, an endless line of waves as high as houses, steep and powerful. You start at 2 p.m. and all afternoon, evening and night, you do battle with the elements whose power will sap your energy, chill your bones, throw you about, damage and, potentially, kill you. Why do it? Because the call to action comes. The call to help complete strangers. The call to save seafarers.

Imagine, then, pushing on relentlessly at full speed into snow showers that give you only 100yds visibility. After nearly two hours, you have made only 25 miles. Everything depends on your skill, endurance, and your boat. Suddenly, the boat speed drops. The storm is beginning to take charge. An oil pipe has cracked under the violent battering. You cannot safely go on.

That is what faced Brian Bevan on his way to *Diana V* in the Humber lifeboat *City of Bradford IV*, but the Dutch ship was no longer on her own. The naval vessel *Lindisfarne* was heading for her, and Cromer lifeboat had been launched too. Bevan had an agonising choice – turn back for repairs or go on, risking his boat, his crew and the rescue. He did what coxswains hate to do, he turned back – a decision that was vindicated as the rescue unfolded, for if he had gone on with only one engine there was every chance that he and his crew would have been killed. Mechanics Bill and Ron Sayers hunkered down in the cramped engine room and, as the lifeboat battered its way back to Grimsby, somehow managed to strip down the pump, ready for fitting a new pipe.

By 5 p.m. *Lindisfarne* was on the scene and *Diana V* was able to get under way at 9 knots towards the River Humber. Cromer lifeboat was released. The Norfolk men made for Great Yarmouth as it was impossible to rehouse at Cromer. They spent eight hours – the equivalent of a whole working day – in the storm.

Bevan reached Grimsby, stopped just long enough to pick up the spares, and the new pipe was fitted as the lifeboat ran down the river to refuel at Spurn. Shortly before 9 p.m. things took a turn for the worse. The storm was still raging and water was now seeping slowly and treacherously into *Diana V*.

A helicopter reached the scene but had to turn back because of the weather. *Lindisfarne* was still there but she was much too big to get near enough to take people off *Diana V*. Humber lifeboat had to put out again, now with 28 miles to go to reach the crippled ship.

Once again, the *City of Bradford IV* took on the violence of the North Sea at full throttle. As she topped one wave, she would momentarily be airborne, crashing down into the hollow of the next. Then, still 8 miles from the casualty, she fell off a huge wave and the lights, wipers and fans failed. Lifeboatman Dennis Bailey Jnr (both father and son were on this mission) was thrown into a bulkhead, injuring his right eye, knee and elbow. Bevan reduced to half speed to allow the mechanics to fix the problem, but as soon as he did, the radio brought a terse message from *Lindisfarne*. The situation on *Diana V* was now critical. The four crew and two women had to be taken off – would Humber make best speed? Bevan put the throttles down again and briefed his crew. They would go alongside using their only illumination, two hand torches.

At 11.01 p.m., they reached the Dutch coaster. She was steering an erratic course of 5 knots, the maize and water making her list heavily to port. The wind was gusting to 56 knots, storm force 10 and the temperature was -4°C. Sea water was freezing on the lifeboat's deck and rails, making every move perilous. But Bevan needed his crew on the bow, to put out fenders and to catch the survivors. They clipped on their lifelines as Bevan radioed *Diana V*'s captain. *Lindisfarne* trained her powerful searchlight onto the coaster. Bevan made his first run in. As he edged into the coaster's stern, where the survivors were huddled, a wave broke over them, almost washing them away and smashing the two vessels into each other. The lifeboat was lifted 10ft above *Diana V*'s deck and crashed down, damaging her fendering. Throttles back, the lifeboat pulled away and tried again.

On the second run, the storm chose the lifeboat, a wave crashing her bow against the coaster, inflicting more damage. As he pulled back this time, Bevan's head was 3ft away from the cold steel of the ship.

The third try was lucky. The lifeboat hit the casualty 5ft below where the desperate people were waiting. A twelve-year-old girl was dropped into the arms of the lifeboat crew. As a wave pushed the lifeboat up the coaster's side, a woman and four men jumped to safety, the lifeboatmen breaking their fall. Cold, wet and severely shocked, but safe, the survivors were taken below. Now only the captain remained on *Diana V*. Twenty miles from the safety of the Humber, his ship being constantly washed by seas so that only the bridge could be seen, and with *Lindisfarne* and *City of Bradford IV* as close escorts, he managed to coax his ship to safety. Ambulances were waiting at Spurn, and, after landing the survivors and refuelling, the lifeboat was back on her moorings at 3.45 a.m. on New Year's Eve, after 13¾ hours on service – and ready to go again.

TWELVE HOURS IN FORCE 12

The New Year started as the old had finished, and at sea the winter continued to be cruel. On 4 January the Greek freighter *Cantonad*, with a crew of sixteen, was listing heavily near the Channel Light Vessel. Guernsey lifeboat set out in a storm which reached hurricane force 12. Coxswain John Petit and his crew were at sea for twelve hours, like Bevan making full speed in the most punishing conditions. An hour and a half after setting out, they were told that *Cantonad* had disappeared from radar screens; almost certainly she had sunk. Petit recalled,

> At full speed the lifeboat was falling off the top of waves and crashing into the hollow of the next wave following with juddering crashes. In the darkness over the Casquets Bank, the boat took off from one particular huge sea and fell down on her shoulder, causing four of us to be thrown into the corner of the wheelhouse. I fell on top of Chick Robilliard, knocking myself out on a fire extinguisher and activating its lever. Snowy Hamon fell on me and white foam discharged all over the wheelhouse and us. Eric Pattimore managed to pull the throttles back as he fell. The lifeboat straightened up and we dusted ourselves down and resumed course at full speed. I found out afterwards that by falling on him I had caused Chick Robilliard to sustain two cracked ribs. However, the fire extinguisher foam proved to be a fantastic cleanser for our clothes and for the wheelhouse carpet.

Helicopters from Culdrose beat the lifeboat to the position by about fifteen minutes and they started to drop flares. They managed to winch up one survivor who was in a life raft but the rest were in the sea. They sent a winchman down into breaking seas. By this time the ship had capsized.

> I went to the upper steering position with a lookout. It takes your breath away when you go on deck, the cold. You couldn't feel your hands after being up there five or ten minutes. When you get on top of a sea everything's flying – wind, snow, spume – then you go down into a trough and it is quite quiet. It's uncanny.
>
> The helicopters dropped flares and they helped a lot. We saw the two bodies we picked up in the light of the flares. They seemed to throw an orange light down into the sea and you could see the bodies silhouetted in

the water. We managed to pick up those two but only after a great deal of difficulty. It wasn't easy, in those seas, trying to manoeuvre to keep alongside. The crew, one moment they were up forward then they had to come aft, then they were halfway along the deck. They had to keep moving the whole time in order to keep the casualties in sight.

While the helicopters were away refuelling we were searching downwind for five hours; the tide was ebbing down channel and the wind was north easterly behind us. I was up on the bridge, rotating the lookout, but you couldn't see much. It was pitch black.

After a long search, the lifeboatmen eventually had to admit that there was no further hope. The sea had claimed fifteen more lives.

FIVE MINUTES FROM DEATH

January ran into February and the storms continued. In mid-February, the most remarkable series of rescues tested the North Sea crews to the very limits. So bad were the conditions that at one stage lifeboat inspector Tom Nutman held back the Humber lifeboat from going south on a rescue because he feared for the safety of the Bridlington lifeboat. If she capsized, Humber would have to go north to help.

The story unfolds far out in the North Sea on the night of 13/14 February. The 414-ton Panamanian ship *Revi* was sailing from France to Newcastle with a cargo of silver sand. The tough tarpaulins covering the hatches had been torn away by the storm and sea water was flooding into the hold. *Revi* was reported in distress 30 miles north-east of Spurn Light Vessel. At a quarter past midnight on St Valentine's Day, all eight men of the Humber lifeboat set out in *City of Bradford IV*. It was like a replay of the *Diana V* rescue: storm force 10, intense cold, snow showers, huge seas. As the lifeboat fell off a wave, the lights and wipers failed as the circuit breakers kicked in. The waves, if anything, were even bigger than those they had faced six weeks before.

Like *Diana V*, *Revi* was not alone. A dredger, *Deepstone*, was standing by. And uncannily, just as with *Diana V*, when the Humber men were still 8 miles from the scene, the situation worsened and *Revi* reported that she was slowly sinking. Her captain decided to try and reach the Humber. Unlike the *Diana V*, *Revi* never made it.

When *City of Bradford IV* reached *Revi*, she was steering at 6 knots and being completely buried by heavy seas. Brian Bevan recalls: 'The casualty was so low in the water, virtually covered by breaking seas, that we couldn't see her at first.

The *Deepstone*, though, was lit up like a small town. It was an unforgettable sight – there she was, lights blazing, rolling like a pig in very rough seas. She seemed so big, around 5,500 tons, yet at times the waves were breaking right over her. Then we saw *Revi*. She was very low in the water and taking a terrible hammering.'

The captain said he would slow down so that two of his crew could be taken off. Bevan judged it impossible and asked him to stop and assess the situation, for the seas sweeping across the deck would have carried the men away, so he asked *Revi* to steer south at slow speed.

The rescue of six weeks ago was repeating itself. The crew went forward, clipped on their lifelines and waited for Bevan to make his approach. The first run in came close to killing them, as *Revi* was swamped by a sea and pushed down towards the lifeboatmen. *City of Bradford IV*, engines full astern, clawed clear just in time, but nobody had been rescued. Again and again, twenty times, Bevan dodged in and out, pushing forward, pulling back as *Revi* rose up 20ft above his crew, threatening to obliterate them. This was why he had turned back on the *Diana V* rescue – without both powerful engines under immediate control he could never risk these daring dashes. Yet twice out of twenty runs, they managed to pluck a man to safety.

Within the next five minutes, the captain had to admit defeat. The cargo of sand was shifting, the ship heeling over 45 degrees. She could not be saved. To try to provide some shelter for the lifeboat's approach, the captain turned *Revi* to the west, his low port side dipping into the sea. Bevan takes up the story: 'It was soon plain that it didn't make a ha'porth of difference. There just wasn't any lee that night. Seas were coming at us from all sides without any rhyme or reason to them. Judging the right moment to go in was impossible – everything was too unpredictable. All I could do was aim for where the two officers were standing and hope that the right moment would come.'

Again, the first run in failed when a large wave broke right over both boats and forced the lifeboat away from the ship's side. Bevan returned twelve times, trying to get to the heaving deck, each time being swept away. Then, momentarily, he got close enough. The mate jumped 5ft into the lifeboatmen's arms. Only the captain was left. It was like the *Diana V* rescue all over again but worse, and now things turned critical. *Revi*'s bows were submerged, the no. 1 hatch was awash and the stern was clear of the water. She was sinking fast and the captain was still on board, hanging onto the outside of the stern rails, ready to jump. Try as he might, Bevan just couldn't reach him, but he couldn't leave him. Ten more times he drove the lifeboat in, the last time coming within a whisker of killing his crew. *Revi*'s stern rose 20ft in the air and began to crash down towards the lifeboat's foredeck where the crew were lashed to the rails with no chance of escape. Bevan's heart must have been in his mouth as he rammed the throttles full astern. *City of Bradford IV* scraped clear by inches.

The lifeboatmen barely had time to draw breath when they saw *Revi* completely swamped by three successive seas, condemning the brave captain to be tossed mercilessly into the waves for the chill water to freeze his body, fill his lungs and kill him. Yet as the water cleared away, they saw him there, bedraggled but still clinging like a limpet to the rails. His ship was going to roll over at any minute. Bevan had to get him.

In a trough between two waves, Bevan drove the lifeboat in under the port quarter with almost reckless abandon, hitting the ship's stern. The captain had no choice – he jumped. Landing, he almost fell overboard, but the lifeboatmen grabbed him and hauled him onto the deck. It was 2.33 a.m. Five minutes later, *Revi* rolled over and sank.

NORTH SEA BLIZZARD

Twenty-seven hours after the *Revi* rescue, Humber lifeboat was out again. The storm was unabated and blizzards were sweeping up the east coast. Two more merchant ships, the German *Sunnanhavan* and Romanian *Savinesti*, were in trouble. *Sunnanhavan* had broken down 8 miles north-east of Flamborough Head and was drifting towards the headland at 1½ knots. Brian Bevan's old school and fishing friend, Fred Walkington, was coxswain of the nearby Bridlington lifeboat, a 37ft Oakley class. The same type of boat was stationed 100 miles down the coast at Wells in Norfolk.

A safe, solid and slow boat, the Oakley afforded little protection or comfort for her crew. Although Flamborough was closer, the station only had a smaller, non self-righting Liverpool class boat with no radar, and they would have to risk launching directly into the storm. Lifeboat inspector Tom Nutman had some tough decisions to make. He instructed Flamborough not to launch, asked Wells coxswain David Cox to set out to *Savinesti*, Bridlington to *Sunnanhavan* and kept Humber in reserve, as either of the Oakleys could be overwhelmed. The official account says it all; no additions are needed.

In blizzard conditions with falling snow and ice reforming as quickly as it was cleared, Bridlington lifeboat was launched into heavy breaking seas with visibility only a few yards making it impossible to see the next breaker.

Bridlington's Oakley class lifeboat in rough seas.

A violent storm, force 10, was blowing from the north east. The temperature was minus four degrees centigrade. The sea was white over with drift and the lifeboat was heading into driving snow squalls during which the wind became even stronger and visibility was reduced. The main sea was easterly with a cross sea breaking from the north. The throttles had to be eased and the boat squared towards the frequent breaking waves. The boat was lifted and tossed round 40 degrees to starboard.

Down in Wells, things were just as grim. Again, the dry language of the official report needs no embellishment.

The lifeboat was confronted with heavy rolling seas and the full force of the wind. The lifeboat was being continually hit and filled by the sea and lost her radar, MF radio and echo sounder.

Fred Walkington in the Bridlington lifeboat also lost his radar as the huge sea lifted the boat and filled the cockpit. Both coxswains were now relying on their extensive skills in basic seamanship. A few minutes after losing his radar, Walkington was told by the coastguard that *Sunnanhavan* had regained full power and was heading for the River Humber. In huge seas and blizzards neither the Bridlington nor the Wells lifeboats could be seen on the radars of the big ships.

With no radar, visibility of 50yds and breaking seas of 30ft, Walkington now had to get his crew home safely: 'We went for the high cliffs because you stood a better chance of seeing the cliffs than you would have done the low land to the south. The seas were breaking full on Smithic Sands and it was high water. You would have had a job to come across the sands alone, but if you got across them you would never have seen the shore before you were atop of it. This is why I went for the higher land.'

Using his drogue to steady the boat, with seas breaking over the stern, he drove on for 2½ hours when cliffs were seen half a mile ahead. Suddenly, lifeboatman Dennis Atkins shouted out in alarm. Filey Brigg, a notorious outcrop of rocks, was just 100yds ahead. Walkington spun the wheel hard over to port. As the boat came beam onto the sea, she was hit and knocked over to starboard. The engine cut-out, designed to stop the engines in a capsize, activated. In a flash, Walkington put his controls to neutral, ordered the switches to be reset and fired up his engines; they started first time. Bridlington lifeboat had nearly capsized, and she was so close to the shore she might never have righted. The crew confirmed they were all well, and course was set for Flamborough Head. The lifeboat made it safely into Bridlington Harbour, coastguards with life-saving gear manning both piers in case they capsized on the way in.

As the lifeboat was refuelled, the diesel froze in the funnel. To keep the lifeboat operational, as she would become stranded in the harbour at low water, the crew sailed around to the beach to haul their boat back onto its launching carriage, skidding across the icy slipway as they did so. Walkington said: 'That is the thing, when you come back; the responsibility. With this February job there was no beach to re-carriage so we went into the harbour. I got the crew to go home and have a drink and change into warm clothing. I think everybody came back slightly refreshed before we went and re-carriaged. It was a difficult re-carriaging job but we couldn't have left her in harbour, because, at low water, she would have been off service. She had to go back on station because the weather was so bad that the boat might have had to go again.'

The Bridlington lifeboat crew finally went home thirteen hours after they were first called out.

WAIST DEEP IN WATER

A capsize was precisely what Tom Nutman had feared and it was why he had kept the Humber lifeboat back. Bridlington had come within a whisker of turning over and now that she was safe, Humber could be released to go south and help Wells. David Cox and his crew were taking a terrible battering. From leaving Wells harbour to getting home, the crew were up to their waists in sea water for eleven hours. As they stood by the *Savinesti* for two hours in their open, exposed boat, the wind was force 11, later increasing to hurricane force 12, there was a very heavy swell with breaking waves of 40ft, and continuous heavy snow. The penetrating chill of the air was so extreme that Graham Walker, mechanic on that rescue, later said, 'The sea water breaking over us was actually warmer than the air. We were so cold and the pain was so intense that I was thinking "I hope we capsize. That will stop the pain, the warm sea."'

By the time Humber lifeboat was 7 miles away, *Savinesti* was flanked by two other ships – the coastal tanker *Annuity* and the North Sea ferry *Norwave* – and the tug *Lady Moira* was on her way. Wells lifeboat was released to try and get home in the remaining daylight. Like Fred Walkington in Bridlington, David Cox had to guess where the nearest landfall was. He was hampered by finding that the only course achievable without violent movement was south-west, and by snow blowing directly into the cockpit, requiring one crewman constantly to clear the compass screen. David Cox said:

I will say this for the Oakley; although she was filling with seas all the time, the water was clearing very quickly. She was filling and emptying, as quick as that.

For us, the visibility was just about nil. Snow storms – blizzards, if you like – are worse than fog in an open boat when you are heading into it all the while.

When we started back for home, at 1500hr, I knew we had the worst to come. I know what our place is like. There are no lights. You couldn't see any landmarks at all. And I knew darkness was coming on. I was not very happy running in those seas. I wasn't sure where I would end up but I knew it would be west of Wells harbour somewhere.

We had to come over the top of the Race Bank. I have never seen the sea so piled up in my life, running and breaking on the bank. I eased her up a bit and she took it all right. By the time we got in that day it was after dark, round about six or seven o'clock. That was my most critical time because we had been out about nine hours. We were just about all in, I would say. Yet we still had the worst conditions to deal with. You see, when darkness came on we weren't quite sure, at times, whether we were running on to the main

Wells lifeboat batters through a wave. *(Campbell McCallum)*

shore or whether we were still at sea. The first thing we spotted was a glimmer of light, and when we spotted it we were nearly in Brancaster Water – we were nearly on the shore.

At 6.15 p.m. lights were seen on the shore. David Cox thought it was Brancaster. He fired a parachute flare and the auxiliary coastguard confirmed the lifeboat was just north of Brancaster golf club. Only 7 miles to go, but they took an agonising two hours as the lifeboat was constantly knocked off course by the breaking seas.

At 9.10 p.m., the lifeboat went over Wells bar, swept by three huge seas, and entered the safety of the harbour. The crew, frozen to the core, had to be lifted ashore. Most were unable to walk. Some had frostbite in their fingers that lasted three weeks. Knowing how cold the crew would be, local fishermen had lined up bottles of rum on the quayside. Some of the younger ones went to the pub, but the rest went home. And Graham Walker, who spoke for the whole crew about the agony they endured, later said, 'I wouldn't have missed it for anything.'

Meanwhile, the Humber lifeboat had taken a tremendous pasting to get to *Savinesti*. There was a 3in layer of ice across the whole boat. The radar, unable to penetrate the blizzard, could only just show Spurn Light Vessel a mere mile and a half away. The Decca Navigator was not working; checking the scanners, the crew found they were coated in thick ice, which they chipped away. At least the Humber men had the shelter of the Arun class lifeboat's cabin.

Brian Bevan could hardly believe how harsh the conditions were.

The snow and the frost that morning were the killers. It was freezing hard. At ten o'clock in the morning, at the coastguard station, 8 degrees of frost was recorded. That was at mid morning. Four hours prior to that it was 14 to 16 degrees of frost. The handrails on the boarding boat were iced inches thick all along.

When we got started our problem was navigating because of the banks down in David's area. The Decca was put out of action by the snow. We thought the radio was, too, at first. Then we found it was iced up. We chipped that off and the radar was all right. So we more or less went down on the radar.

Going to the job – I don't think you will ever see conditions worse. I have worked down there quite a bit, fishing, and been caught out, but I don't think I have ever seen such long broken seas for as long. As one petered out the next one was coming at you. You were even bringing the Arun round to meet them head to sea because you could see them coming at you like a house side. You were always frightened of the knock down. You were on course, then coming round to meet a sea, then back on your course even with the Arun.

I have spoken to the older fishermen and the older hands on the east coast and I don't think you will ever see any worse anywhere than it was that day. There were ships and fishing boats that had rode it out still coming to the river three days after with their masts, rigging and even their bows, where you would have thought it would have been washed off, thick with ice and snow. More like pictures that you see of deep-sea trawlers in Iceland – not the sort of thing we were accustomed to in the North Sea.

Bevan and his crew pressed on, stopping every now and then to chip away at the ice and fix their position. Around the *Savinesti* was a maelstrom. Nearby sandbanks were making the rollers run for several hundred feet. In the thick blizzard, even the large merchant ships were obscured, with only the tips of the masts visible at times. *Norwave* fired rocket lines to try and establish a tow, but all lines parted. When the tug *Lady Moira* arrived it was too dangerous to put men out on deck. *Savinesti* still had power and managed to limp along at 4 knots.

After all this drama, the storm started to abate and *Savinesti* managed to limp towards the River Humber. The rescue report now reaches an anticlimax: 'By 0035 on February 16, the snow had moderated to light showers and the wind to strong gale force 9. When in position 000 degrees Dowsing Light Vessel five miles, the casualty and her escorts turned before the sea on a course for the river. *Savinesti* entered the River Humber at 0303 escorted by *Norwave* and *Lady Moira* and was boarded by a pilot. Humber lifeboat returned to station and refuelled, reporting ready for service at 0425.'

TRYING TO UNWIND

Rescues in such extreme conditions do not simply finish when the men go home. Both Brian Bevan and David Cox were shattered but found it hard to unwind. Bevan said:

> After jobs like that you can't sit down to a dinner put in front of you. We find that you seem to be twelve or eighteen hours before you are back to normal. You can probably have a drink of tea or coffee. Everybody says you want a hot meal as soon as you get back but the blokes just can't seem to sit down and face that meal.
>
> You seem to come back off a job absolutely dog tired. All you want to do is drop into your bed, and within two minutes of being in bed you can't sleep. Everything is sort of wound up inside you.
>
> For my crew I think probably the job to *Diana V* was the worst in terms of endurance. We finished at breakfast time on New Year's Eve. I think for twenty-four hours or so I was so mentally and physically wound up that I was miles away – even during the New Year celebrations. I am in a world of my own for twenty-four hours after jobs like that.

It was a similar story for David Cox:

> A couple of young lads jumped aboard that morning, just kids. I just said 'Out!' because I knew the sort of day it was going to be. But I've got a young chap in my regular crew, he's twenty-five or twenty-six. He was the fittest one of all when we got home. He just went straight off the quay into the pub and had two or three rums. I'm afraid all I wanted to do was get home for a hot bath. So age does come into it.
>
> When I got home that night I just stripped off and got straight into a bath and even then it took me a long time to thaw out. When I got out of the bath, I stood there and my balance had gone. They all said the same thing the next morning. You are so tensed up through cold and concentration, you don't really sleep when you get to bed. I couldn't relax at all until the next day.
>
> It was the worst trip I've ever had. If my chaps weren't all fishermen, they might not have survived as well as they did. Even then, most of them were complaining about the weather – the intense cold and wet – by the time we got home.

Brian Bevan and the Humber lifeboat crew with other medal winners from 1979 to 1980. *(Peter Hadfield)*

The medal count that hard winter was spectacular. John Petit of Guernsey and Fred Walkington of Bridlington won bronze medals. David Cox of Wells won a silver medal. The crew of the Humber lifeboat, Dennis Bailey and his son Bill and Ron Sayers, Mike Storey, Pete Jordan and Sid Rollinson won bronze medals for the *Revi* rescue. Brian Bevan won, in the space of seven weeks, a gold (*Revi*), silver (*Diana V*) and bronze (*Savinesti*) medal. No man before or since has been presented with all three medals at once, as Bevan was the following May when the Duke of Kent pinned them to his chest to a standing ovation at the Royal Festival Hall.

BEING A HERO

The RNLI needs its heroes for publicity and fund-raising. No lifeboat crew member should seek a medal, and very few do. They do their job, and they do it superbly. Most join the crew, serve for years, then retire graciously and with little recognition. A tiny minority are thrust into the spotlight.

Shortly after Bevan won his medals, a north-east coxswain accused him of being a glory seeker. The coxswain had to be put right because Bevan was not seeking glory, but was simply saving lives. It was the RNLI which promoted his gallantry, thrust him in front of TV cameras on *This is Your Life*, and got him to open the London International Boat Show at Earls Court. Bevan kept his feet firmly on the ground. At the boat show his host was Lord Victor Matthews of Express Newspapers. A VIP lunch followed the opening ceremony and tour of the show. At the end of the lunch, a waiter appeared with a box of fine cigars, which he offered to his lordship.

'Coxswain,' Matthews asked, 'a cigar?'

'No, if you don't mind I'll have a roll up,' said Bevan, pulling a battered tobacco tin from his jacket. There was a very slight pause as Lord Matthews studied the tin. 'Would you mind rolling one for me?' he said with absolutely no condescension. 'I haven't had one for years.'

Some months later, a worried Bevan rang the lifeboat office in London. 'I think somebody's taking the mickey, only I've had this call from an admiral at Buckingham Palace asking me to lunch with the Queen.' Now if there is one thing the RNLI is good at, it is protocol. Dealings with royal households are handled centrally, but none of the departments could shed light on this invitation, so it was probably a hoax. As a last check, the London office decided to ring Buckingham Palace itself, easily done as it had a modest one-line entry in the London telephone directory. There was no problem in being put through to the admiral, who was rather frosty when asked whether he had been in touch with the lifeboat coxswain. 'Her Majesty holds a number of luncheons for distinguished people and chooses her own guests,' was his explanation, with a coded hint that RNLI officials might care to mind their own business.

Ann Bevan answered the phone when London rang back. 'Can I come too?' she asked. 'We have got corgis, you know.'

But the invitation was just for Brian. He was picked up by the RNLI at King's Cross station and driven past the palace to the lifeboat office for coffee. 'She's probably peeling the spuds,' he said as they drove past the palace. The official escorting him had, as befits a charity worker, a modest car, a Nissan Sunny, which he later drove to the palace gates. Bevan refused to get out. 'It says here you drive into the courtyard,' he said. 'Not in a battered Japanese car you don't,' answered the official. 'Those guards have bullets in their guns.' Bevan insisted, and the police waved them through and on into the inner courtyard. As the Nissan drove up under the glass canopy and Bevan saw the red carpet his nerve began to fail. 'What shall I say if they offer me a drink – I can't say a brown ale!' he protested.

Eamon Andrews surprises Brian Bevan for *This is Your Life*.

Later, he told of meeting the other guests – 'Some bloke who owned a newspaper gave me a lift back to King's Cross in his Roller' – and how the Queen kept a couple of savoury biscuits to feed her corgis. Ever modest, he made the Rolls-Royce chauffeur stop at the street before King's Cross, to avoid the chance that, however unlikely, someone he knew might see him stepping out of the car.

Brian and Ann Bevan stayed on at Spurn, Brian as the Humber coxswain, until he reached fifty-five, the RNLI's retirement age for crew. Retirement is a controversial point with crews, many of whom are fit and keen to carry on in their mid-fifties, and Brian felt he was not properly treated when he stood down. He continues to work at Spurn on the pilot boats and lives in nearby Easington in a house called Arun. Sadly, after his remarkable life-saving achievements and tremendous work as an ambassador for the lifeboat service, he felt unable to accept the invitation to join the other three living gold medallists when the Queen opened the new lifeboat college in Poole in 2004. He was missed, but his record stands as the proud achievement of a brave but modest man.

TORBAY RESCUE

The Humber rescues relied on the speed and power of their Arun class lifeboat whose sister ship at Torbay had proved herself two years before. Keith Bower was well aware of the hazards he faced when he was called out to take command of the Torbay lifeboat in storm force winds on 6 December 1976. He had been around the world in the merchant navy and was (and still is) a fisheries officer, working for the Devon Sea Fisheries Committee. His day job was coxswain of the 58ft twin screw fisheries patrol vessel patrolling the Devon waters from Rame Head to Lyme Regis on a daily basis. He had an intimate knowledge of boats, tides and weather. That December night Torbay lifeboat coxswain George Dyer was out at sea in a fishing boat off Plymouth, so Keith, the second coxswain, had to take the boat. The 475-ton Greek-owned cargo ship *Lyrma* was out in the storm with no steering, no radar and with ten men on board.

There were three Bower brothers, Keith, Stephen and Colin, in the crew. Thirty-year-old Keith had to go, to take command, and so did Stephen, the mechanic. Captain Barry Anderson, the honorary secretary, put his foot down and banned Colin, the youngest, from the boat that night. Three family members in such a bad storm was too big a risk. Colin is now one of the longest-serving members of the crew, as Keith had to retire after a bone graft to his heel and Stephen tragically died from a brain tumour in 1995.

Keith describes his thoughts as he made his way to the lifeboat station: 'It was like the old lottery advert when a hand reaches out from the sky and says, "It could be you," only in my case the voice would be saying, "It's down to you." I had a great feeling of responsibility, but was confident I could handle it.'

Setting out from the harbour at full speed, the lifeboat *Edward Bridges* was sheltered from the worst of the winds. As soon as she rounded Berry Head and took the full force of the southerly storm, the crew knew they were in for a beating. A local trawler, making for port, saw the lifeboat disappear in a big sea and reported to the coastguard that he thought the boat was lost. The coastguard told the fishermen they were still talking to the lifeboat and Keith was unperturbed:

> I remember at this time that I was in command of one of the best and most up-to-date vessels that money could buy. I had no fears whatsoever of the capabilities of the boat, which was of great reassurance to me. We battened down and plotted the course to the casualty. By this time we had hit three of these big seas and we were right in the teeth of it. We could hear the engines revving and dying as we left the tops of the crests and fell into the troughs. I estimated the boat to be airborne, practically, at times. You could actually see the white water coming over the bow, so we eased her down.

The lifeboat had set out at 1.15 a.m. and *Lyrma* was thought to be about 20 miles away. Huge seas, estimated at 40ft, were piling up in front of the lifeboat, the battering from them flinging the traditional navigational tools of parallel ruler and dividers into the air, so that the crew had to use Decca fixes for navigation. Four of the lifeboatmen were seasick, but all stuck to their tasks, John Dew navigating with skill as a ship appeared on the radar, only to be ruled out because it was heading in the wrong direction.

The men and the boat could not endure the punishment of the battering at full speed and Bower eased back the throttles on the largest seas, trying to avoid the white water rushing straight over the bow and burying the boat. Partly by accident, partly by design, he adopted yachting tactics, tacking to put the wind first on one side of the bow, then on the other to avoid the onslaught of going directly into the wind.

After an hour at sea, new information from the coastguard gave a more accurate position for *Lyrma* and her lights were soon spotted. The wind was now gusting to force 11. Bower wryly observed, 'Well, it's not going to get any better.' Pushing open the cabin door and climbing to the upper steering position on top of the cabin, Bower could now see *Lyrma* and had to come up with a plan. To reach the ship he would have to go broadside across the waves, risking knockdown or capsize. 'I thought, "Oh well, all or nothing," and just steered to her.'

THE BEST CIGAR I EVER SMOKED

On board *Lyrma*, Captain Donald Codd had to handle the ship's engines to give some steerage as the steering gear was broken and at the same time organise his crew on deck. He had only had command of the ship for ten days and was the only one who spoke English. *Lyrma* was listing and, with no rudder control, the captain was struggling to keep her safe. He would head into the wind, be pushed off course, then go round in a large circle to regain control.

Keith Bower assessed the chances of a rescue by lifeboat as close to impossible and asked for a Sea King helicopter. The coastguard checked and eventually told him there was none available. 'We were laying off the casualty, thinking the job through and trying to work out a plan of action and the thought went through my mind that if anyone was to drop out of the heavens and take over this job they would be very welcome.'

Bower edged towards *Lyrma*'s stern. His calm account makes it sound like a Sunday school outing. 'We had a little conflab – I always have a little conflab with the crew when we are doing a job if there's time. I like to say "this is what I'm trying to do", and if anybody has got any suggestions and I think they are valid, I listen to them. If you tell all the crew what you are trying to do, you are all working to one aim.' Management consultants would charge thousands of pounds for such advice.

Keith Bower of Torbay. *(J. Appel & Co.)*

During the 'conflab', it soon became clear that the options were very few. As *Lyrma* rose in the water, her propeller was thrashing in the air. If the lifeboat went in to the stern, *Lyrma* could crash down on her deck, smashing lifeboatmen and lifeboat. Bower radioed Donald Codd to get his crew into a life raft. In spite of their captain's urging, the crew refused. A Wessex helicopter, smaller than a Sea King, from the Royal Fleet Auxiliary ship *Engadine* took off and at 3.30 a.m. tried to reach the crew, but the winchman, swinging like a pendulum on 100ft of winch wire, got tangled up in the ship's rigging and smashed his leg. The helicopter's instruments showed the freighter's deck was rising and falling 30ft. It was too dangerous to carry on – unless the crew got into the life-raft. Still they refused.

Bower was stumped. 'I had a feeling of helplessness, you know. What the hell are we going to do? The helicopter can't do it. We can't do it without the possibility of serious damage to the lifeboat and *Lyrma*.'

Above the howl of the storm the lifeboatmen could hear the cargo on *Lyrma* smashing up and down. Drums of diesel oil had split open, drenching the chipboard cargo, weighing it down and gradually easing *Lyrma* over into an increasing list. Then Donald Codd left his wheel to deal with a problem on deck and *Lyrma* slewed broadside to the seas – the most dangerous position, vulnerable to being rolled over by the huge curling breakers.

Bower, eyes narrowed against the salt spray, spotted a chance. *Lyrma*'s motion had changed, and, even though it would be tricky, he might just get in on the starboard side, which was now in the lee, providing some protection from the storm. There was a risk, if he overshot, of driving straight onto *Lyrma*'s well deck, which was already awash, but if he could stay back, the lifeboat could ride up and down alongside the higher stern and pick off the crew. Bower had to try. 'We went in. I'm not sure whether we touched or not, but we got pretty close. I was surprised how quietly she went in and came out. We wouldn't have broken an egg, even in those conditions. I said to John, "I think we could have had one then," and he said, "Yes."'

Bower told Codd to get his crew assembled and sent his own crew, seasick or not, forwards to the exposed open foredeck of *Edward Bridges*. Now the power and manoeuvrability of the Arun came into its own. On the first run in, the only woman passenger was pulled aboard. Bower then backed away, went in for a second try but had to abort at the last minute as the two vessels crashed towards each other.

Undaunted, Bower drove *Edward Bridges* in again and two more were pulled aboard. One more was saved on the next run, then another fruitless try. The rescue was going well, but it didn't last. Bower said later that at the back of his mind was the thought that if the ship rolled over on them he would have to use the sheer power of the Arun to pull her out. On the sixth approach, just as the lifeboat came in, *Lyrma* rolled heavily and smashed into the lifeboat's guard rails. The crew standing right by them leapt inboard as bolts snapped and shot off like rifle bullets. Momentarily, the *Edward Bridges* was trapped by the *Lyrma* and the ship's lifeboat swung towards Keith Bower and John Hunkin on top of the *Edward Bridges*. It came so close that Hunkin had to fend it off. Bower was now only a few feet from the captain on his bridge and was talking to him face to face.

As the engines, full astern, pulled the lifeboat free, another man jumped and was grabbed by lifeboatman John Dew. The foredeck of *Edward Bridges* now had loose guard rails, bent over to 45 degrees, protruding into the deck space and hindering rather than protecting the crew. Another run was made, another man rescued. Only the captain remained on board. He told Bower that two of his crew had finally taken to the life raft.

It took two more runs in to get the captain and the rescue now took a comic turn. The life raft was tied alongside the *Lyrma* and to persuade the men to cut it free, the lifeboat crew mimed cutting their throats. The men in the raft looked puzzled at these antics but eventually got the message and cut the rope. The lifeboat backed off to let the raft drift down but the men in it thought they were being abandoned and started waving furiously, so to reassure them that he was on his way, Bower went straight for them, down wind, rather than circling around to come up, under control, into the wind.

Just then a curling wave caught the *Edward Bridges* and carried all 32 tons of her, like a surfboard, at 15 knots towards the life raft. In fact, if they had collided, the lifeboat would simply have bounced the raft away, but Bower had taken enough risks for the day and once again rammed his throttles into reverse. The propellers bit, the lifeboat stopped and then went astern, the impressive power making her rise up against the breaking roller. When the sea had passed through, the lifeboat settled about 2ft from the raft. After the stint of comic miming, the lifeboatman on the foredeck was thrown backwards as the boat reared up, adding a touch of slapstick to the rescue.

Ten men had been saved and *Edward Bridges* turned for home. Confident now, Bower stayed in the exposed upper steering position, later being told off by

Torbay lifeboat *Edward Bridges*.

lifeboat inspector Roy Portchmouth. He felt safe, even though the lifeboat did 'lean over a couple of times', but the job was done, and 'the cigar I had then was one of the best I ever smoked'.

Alongside at Brixham, the survivors were landed without even saying thank you, though lifeboat station people were there to say well done.

The night was not over, for the lifeboat had to be refuelled and, by 6 a.m., the crew were in the boathouse for a welcome mug of pea soup.

It was early on Monday morning, the start of the working week, so Keith Bower went home, got changed, had a proper breakfast, and went to work.

THE MORNING AFTER

Keith read about the rescue in the local paper that evening. Ros, his wife, had woken when he was called out and again at 3 a.m., when, hearing the ferocity of the wind howling around their house, she assumed that the crew could not possibly be out at sea but must be in the boathouse, talking.

The storm had its domestic consequences. When Keith came home he found his 10ft-square greenhouse had been shifted over a foot by the force of the wind.

It was not until the weeks following the event that Ros realised the enormity of the rescue, and it really hit home as Keith and his crew stood nervously in the Royal Festival Hall, listening to the dramatic citation before Keith received his gold medal, and the crew their bronze ones.

CHAPTER TWO

Reluctant Heroes

The story of the RNLI is a remarkable one, spanning almost two centuries. It was set up as a voluntary service only because the Admiralty refused to become involved. Its core values, of people volunteering as rescuers supported by funds freely given, are largely intact today, though they are slowly changing. And while the lifeboat service has evolved throughout its history, the last fifty years have seen huge changes, the origins of which can be traced to the 1950s. At that time, all lifeboats were the shape they had always been, pointed at both ends; all were slow, with a top speed of about 9 knots, and almost all were manned by fishermen, often with generations of the same families crewing the boat – and they were all men.

The boats offered very little shelter, and if they capsized, would stay upside down, drowning their crews. The busiest lifeboat stations would have a dozen rescues a year, and the most arduous rescues could last twenty-four hours or more.

Today all big lifeboats are fast, enclosed and self-righting. Fewer than 10 per cent of the crews are seafarers, and many are women. Fast inshore lifeboats have absorbed much of the ten-fold increase in calls of the past fifty years and the RNLI has expanded into sea safety, inland rescue and beach lifeguarding. Local government money pays for some of these new services, and there are many more full-time lifeboat crew members and lifeguards than there used to be.

What has not changed is the sea, which remains wild, unpredictable and beyond any control. The people facing the challenge of the sea, although they are more highly trained than ever before, are still completely at its mercy on the rare occasion when the rescues are really dangerous. In the worst conditions, they have to take risks that experienced seafarers would instinctively avoid, taking their boats out into raging seas when others seek shelter, slamming into the sides of vessels to pluck off survivors, going perilously close to the shore with no sea room to escape.

This is not romantic hyperbole. Captains of merchant ships and round-the-world yacht crews may encounter fearsome storms but they can batten down and ride them out. Lifeboat crews are called to action in these storms, to put their own lives at risk for the sake of complete strangers.

The people of the RNLI have always been its greatest strength, but they do not see themselves as heroes. They are ordinary people prepared to do extraordinary things. While technology has given them new and better tools, and the increasing use of the sea for leisure has brought more and diverse challenges, the spirit of the lifeboat service is constant. It has no better exemplar than Henry Blogg of Cromer, in Norfolk.

THE GREATEST LIFEBOATMAN WHO EVER LIVED

Lifeboat crews had been busy throughout the Second World War, facing extra dangers of unlit coasts and floating mines and, on several occasions, even coming under fire. There were scores of heroic acts, with dozens of gallantry medals awarded. The man who emerged as a national hero was Henry Blogg, coxswain of the Cromer lifeboat. He also acts as a reminder that the public

Henry Blogg of Cromer (centre without cap). *(Associated Press)*

façade of heroism can hide a private life filled with sadness. Heroes are usually presented as one-dimensional; we know them only by their heroic acts. Yet they are all people, with emotions, relationships and human failings, and understanding them as people makes their heroism all the more remarkable.

Blogg's exploits spanned two of the great eras of lifeboating, the first when horses launched the boats and the men rowed them, the second when engines took over from muscle power, creating the solid traditional lifeboats that have been seen around the coasts for the last ninety years.

He was a remarkable man who lived in interesting times, cinema newsreels and early television stations bringing his exploits direct to a huge audience. That he was courageous is beyond doubt. Indeed, his adventures were so extreme that, had any one of them failed, he could have been labelled foolhardy or reckless. He took big risks – calculating his chances, backed by years of experience and an intimate knowledge of his local waters and the capability of his crew and his boats. The crew often took a terrible punishment from long, harsh rescues. The boats fared even worse, for Blogg would smash his lifeboat into, and even on top of, stranded ships to rescue their desperate sailors. Time and again, Blogg would save all survivors against all odds and limp back to Cromer beach with gaping gashes in the hull of his lifeboat. The rescues are so dramatic that they surpass fiction.

Blogg, dubbed 'the greatest lifeboatman who ever lived' barely scrapes into this book, as he retired as coxswain of the Cromer lifeboat in 1947. His story is, however, worth telling, as it sets in context the work of the RNLI during the Second World War and the state it had reached at the beginning of the 1950s. It demonstrates how a lifeboatman could become a household name across the nation, something never since achieved and unlikely to be repeated. Blogg also shows where the pre-war generation of lifeboatmen came from; fishing villages, open boats and harsh physical exposure shaped the crews of the 1950s, the start of our story. When we reach contemporary times, none of these conditions will be in place. Blogg would recognise the spirit of today's life-savers but would be amazed to see lawyers and bus drivers in charge of highly sophisticated, powerful boats, bristling with high-tech equipment.

Blogg started in heavy, open, rowing lifeboats and, during the First World War when the young men were sent away to fight, his crew included two in their seventies. In January 1917 they were called out to a Greek steamer and rowed for three hours to rescue sixteen men. As they returned to the shore, there was a huge explosion. The Swedish ship *Fernebo* had hit a mine and broke in two. Each half of the ship stayed afloat, as she was carrying timber. Blogg rallied his exhausted crew and they put out again, taking half an hour just to get

Cromer's motor and sail lifeboat. *(P.A. Vicary)*

through the surf. The RNLI's lifeboat inspector was in Cromer and gave an eyewitness account: 'Over and over again the boat was swept back into the shallow water inshore, but each time they succeeded in keeping her head on to the sea and pulling her out again into deeper water. I would not have believed it possible for even a strong and young crew to do so much with this heavy boat. It was not until five oars had been broken and three more washed ashore, while the boat was approaching dangerously the end of the groyne, that the coxswain gave up and allowed his boat to come ashore.'

Blogg was not finished though. He scoured the beach and found a point where the tide had begun to form a current sweeping out towards the wreck. Out went the Cromer men for the third time that day, this time reaching the wreck in the dark, picking off eleven men and coming back to the beach at 1 a.m. They had been working all day and most of the night on the two rescues, for which Henry Blogg won his first gold medal. His second was in 1927 for a 28-hour rescue, this time in a motor lifeboat, saving fifteen men from the Dutch tanker *Georgia* which had broken in two.

Blogg was still coxswain when the Second World War began and the North Sea convoys along the east coast made the Norfolk lifeboats among the busiest in the country as the strong tides, sandbanks and enemy mines took their toll. In one spectacular feat, Blogg went in turn to six ships from the same convoy, which had grounded in fog, and rescued eighty-eight men. Time and again he managed to find survivors on wrecks where there was no sign of life; time and again he drove his boat, mercilessly, across ship's decks and into their unforgiving hulls to take off the seamen, once losing one of his own crew in the endeavour.

There are few people alive who knew Blogg personally but one is Richard Barclay, whose boyhood years were spent in Cromer, where his father was vicar. Barclay's time in Cromer sparked a lifelong enthusiasm for the RNLI and he eventually went on to join the RNLI's committee of management, but as a thirteen-year-old boy, he cycled down to the church in the first air-raid warning on the morning of 3 August 1939 to tell his father that war had been declared so that he could pass the news to the congregation.

He remembers Blogg as heavily built, with a huge hooked nose and sparkling, piercing blue eyes. He was average height and would have blended into a crowd of fishermen, all in navy-blue serge trousers, brown jerkins over Guernsey sweaters and a brown peaked cap. Blogg was a quiet man, shunning attention, and Richard remembers long pauses as he gathered his thoughts to give terse replies to questions. But there was warmth combined with this aloofness, and a great sense of humour. It was Henry who gave Shrimp Davies his lifelong nickname. When the boy was born, he looked at him and said, 'Why he is only a little shrimp,' and 'Shrimp' he became.

As a teenager, Richard hung around the lifeboat house, went out in the crab boats and helped to polish the two lifeboats. He was not keen on being called 'Dick' by the lifeboatmen and mentioned this to Henry. 'Okay, Peter,' said Blogg, who called him Peter for the rest of his life, even writing to him as 'Dear Peter'!

PERSONAL SADNESS

Blogg's calm exterior shielded a difficult personal life. He had been born illegitimate in 1876, and he and his mother Ellen lived with her parents, Phoebe and Thomas, a fisherman. Henry was a withdrawn child who was bullied but would never join in fights. A school report described him as 'a spindle-shanked lad who never took part in games. He could not run and never learned to swim.' He was bright but left school to help his stepfather John James Davies on his fishing boat. John, who had warmly welcomed him into the Davies clan when he married Henry's mother, was second coxswain of the lifeboat, serving under his father James. The family firm, J.J. Davies, ran a hire business, renting out towels and bathing dresses for a penny. Young Henry also led the horses which drew the heavy bathing machines into the sea.

When he was twenty-five, Henry married Annie Brackenbury, a schoolteacher. They had a son who died aged two and a daughter, the much-loved Queenie, who died aged twenty-five. Having lost both their children, they were a lonely couple and they welcomed young Richard's visits to Swallow Cottage. Perhaps they recognised an equally lonely boy whose movements were limited by the vicarage being inside a wartime defence zone in the town, from which most children and visitors were banned. He remembers Annie as a quiet, wizened old lady, scurrying around her spotlessly clean cottage like a frightened mouse. She rarely spoke in front of her husband, and later Richard discovered that she not only had the strain of having Henry risking his life at sea, but there were stories of her fondness for drink, which was deeply upsetting to teetotaller Henry.

This national hero, who was honoured with a George Cross, three RNLI gold medals and four silver medals, was more decorated and celebrated than any lifeboatman before or since, but kept his personal sadness buried deep.

Blogg hated being in the public eye and became completely tongue-tied. He would never willingly talk about his rescues, and the only way to open him up was to ask about a technical point – perhaps something about the engines, or the boat handling. Even when he talked, there were long silences, caused by a mixture of reflection and modesty.

Henry Blogg was seventy when he retired from the Cromer lifeboat in 1947, having saved hundreds of lives. Shrimp succeeded him as coxswain, and eventually his nephew, Richard Davies, followed on. Henry died in June 1954 and over 2,500 people attended his funeral.

CHANNEL ISLAND GOLD MEDALS

Henry Blogg had seen the transition from the rowing lifeboats of the early 1920s to the motor lifeboats of the rest of the twentieth century. The 8- or 9-knot boats changed very little until the 1960s, even the equipment remaining relatively simple, with signalling lamps and flags being carried for communication even after radio was introduced. A fast patrol boat had been used as a lifeboat in Dover during the war to reach downed airmen speedily but there was no attempt to use speed again until the 1970s. So the rescues from the end of the war until then were in traditional slow boats, difficult to manoeuvre, but solid and seaworthy.

Thomas King of Jersey found himself in just such a boat on 13 September 1949. The building of new lifeboats had been suspended during the war, so although the first twin-engined boat had been introduced in 1923, there were still many in service with only single engines at the end of the 1940s.

The Guernsey and Jersey lifeboats had been called out on the afternoon of 13 September 1949 to look for a French military aircraft which was thought to have ditched in the sea. Although it was a hopeless task, they spent six hours in rough seas, heavy rain and fog, but by 9.30 p.m. there was no point in going on and the lifeboat was running low on fuel. King turned for home, still some 20 miles away and by midnight was within 2 miles of St Helier when the radio crackled into life. A light had been spotted out at sea, near the point the lifeboat had just passed. King had to retrace his route. A local yacht, the substantial 10-ton *Maurice George*, had left St Malo earlier in the day, using her engine to cross to Jersey. However, the engine failed as she neared Jersey at dusk and the crew dropped anchor. By now the storm had thrown up heavy seas; the anchor cable snapped and the yacht was swept into the rocky area just off St Helier harbour. The crew quickly dropped a second anchor but it was under tremendous strain.

The tide was ebbing, exposing more rocks by the minute and it was pitch dark. The lifeboat would have to go in among the rocks to save the *Maurice George*'s crew before the boat was dashed to pieces. Worse still, the lifeboatmen, exhausted after eight hours at sea, were in an unfamiliar relief boat with only a single engine and hardly any fuel. Gingerly, they edged forward, trying to pick out the tips of submerged rocks with their spotlight. Then a sudden surge took hold of the lifeboat and pushed it further into the rocks, washing her clean over a ledge. 'That's one of the buggers passed anyhow,' remarked a member of the crew.

Eventually a towline was passed and the lifeboat managed to save both the men and their boat. But when it came to the investigation of the rescue,

Thomas King of Jersey with the Queen Mother. *(Evening Post, Jersey)*

the lifeboat inspector asked Tom King to take him to the spot where they found the yacht. In broad daylight and flat calm, King refused, saying, 'I wouldn't like to go in there now, we might hit something.'

Thomas King was awarded a gold medal for his rescue, the only one given since the war for the rescue of a yacht, even though they now account for most rescues.

In 1963 it was Guernsey's turn to win a gold medal. Hubert Petit was coxswain and his son, John, was on the crew. John was to see the transition from slow to fast lifeboats and to realise the value of speed and power. When he joined Hubert on the crew in the early 1950s, the St Peter Port lifeboat was a 51ft Barnett *Queen Victoria*, which was powered by two fuel-hungry petrol engines. After a long service, as many as fifty red-painted 2-gallon petrol cans had to be taken from the lifeboat shed into a dinghy, ferried out to the lifeboat on her moorings and the petrol poured into a huge funnel.

The communication equipment was a transmitter and a morse key which threw a tremendous arc and spark every time the key was depressed. In spite of this spectacular discharge of electricity, the range of the signal was only a mile. The lifeboat station still had a shore signalman, a position harking back to the days of rowing lifeboats which could be recalled by flag signals from the shore. Although he no longer had any real function, Pat Hamon was as dedicated as any lifeboatman. One Sunday, he joined the crew of the *Queen Victoria* on a regular exercise. The boat still carried auxiliary sails and had a drop keel to provide stability if the sails were used. Out at sea, the order came to lower the keel. One crew member pulled out the correct pin to allow the keel to pivot downwards. Pat Hamon, not wishing to be left out, pulled out the other pin – the retainer. The keel dropped straight down to the seabed, never to be seen again. At the lifeboat's next refit a few weeks later, the sails and drop keel were declared redundant and dismantled.

John remembers the Barnetts as robust, heavily engineered boats. There was a 2½ins diameter shaft, which the coxswain had to straddle, running from wheel to rudder and a small yellow funnel which emitted a purring sound from the twin exhausts when the boat was at full speed. They were also wet boats, with a tiny windscreen providing only perfunctory protection from spray and waves, leading John to speculate that the RNLI's intention was to keep the crew awake during long services. The *Queen Victoria* was replaced by a new 52ft Barnett in 1954. She was fitted with MF direction finder and VHF radio in 1959, helping the crew to track down casualties.

The 1963 gold medal rescue was for saving nine men from a sinking freighter. The 1,995-ton Norwegian ship *Johan Collett* was bound from Tunis to Ghent, and her cargo of zinc concentrates had shifted, giving her a severe list to starboard. Six ships had picked up the distress message and made for the position, and Hubert Petit used all his local skill and knowledge to go close inshore, south of the island, to avoid the 3½-knot tide that would have almost halved the progress of the lifeboat. Inside the rocks, only 50yds from the shore, the lifeboat made good progress. As they came out into open seas, the lifeboatmen felt the force of the storm. The sea and swell were huge and it began to snow. The after cabin was battened down but about 4ins of sea water were sloshing around the cabin deck. Four of the crew sat huddled around the paraffin stove, which kept extinguishing, sending noxious fumes around the boat. In those days there were ingenious self-heating cans of oxtail soup, which warmed when a fuse was burned to heat the contents, and this added to the fumes, though the warm soup was welcome in the blizzard. However, the combination of the paraffin fumes with the smell of rising hot engine and diesel oil whenever the engine room door was opened caused queasy stomachs to churn unmercifully. The nausea was made worse by the intense cold, which John Petit said 'ate into our very bones. I have never felt so cold before or since.'

As the storm was worsening, the captain of the *Johan Collett* decided to lower his ship's boat while he still had a chance. Eleven men got away and were picked up by the SS *Bonnard*. Another three scrambled into a rubber life raft and reached the SS *Kaupanger*. Most useful of all, a South African frigate, *President Kruger*, arrived on the scene shortly before the lifeboat.

By 6.30 p.m. it was blowing a full gale, with a long low swell topped by seas of 15ft. Snow was turning to ice on the lifeboat's windscreen. Hubert Petit could not raise the *Johan Collett* by radio so he tried to communicate by using the signal lamp at the top of the mast, but the seas were so big it could not be seen. The South African naval vessel stepped in, receiving Petit's messages by radio and passing them on to the distressed ship with its own signalling lamp from the height and relative stability of her deck.

A tug was on its way from Cherbourg to tow the ship to safety, but the captain of the *Collett* wanted more men taken off, so the lifeboat tried to get in on the starboard side in the lee of the ship. However, the davits and ropes, now empty of the ship's lifeboat, were swinging around wildly, and Petit had to pull away to wait for them to be lashed back. Then, in three separate runs, he got a man off each time.

The lifeboat had been on scene for just over four hours when the tug *Abeille 10* arrived. The weather had grown steadily worse. A full gale gusting to force 10, with the tide now flooding, caused very rough, steep seas. By now the *Collett* was on her beam ends and the seas were sweeping over her exposed port side and her starboard bulwarks were under water. Several wooden doors leading to the accommodation quarters and engine room swung open each time she rolled, allowing tons of water in to flood the ship.

The tug pressed in and after seven sorties over an hour and a half eventually fixed a towrope. As soon as she started towing, *Collett*'s list increased to 40 degrees, very close to capsize as the seas swept her from stem to stern. After less than thirty minutes of towing, the six men left on the *Collett* decided it was too dangerous; they would have to abandon ship, even though she was still being towed at 3 knots.

There was now no shelter and Hubert Petit had to get alongside the higher port side, timing his runs so that the lifeboat would be on top of a wave, high enough to reach the men. The *President Kruger*, keeping a close eye on the lifeboat, lit up the scene with her powerful incandescent ice-blue searchlight.

On the first run in, a huge sea pushed the lifeboat's bow away, leaving Petit no option but to turn round and start again. The next run was better, getting one man off, and the next time two jumped. Run four got one man straight away but another hesitated. The lifeboat started dropping away and he fell 20ft into it.

Now only the captain remained. The lifeboat went in, he jumped but fell on the wrong side – the outside – of the guard rail. At the same moment a swell picked up the lifeboat and drove it towards the ship. In desperation, three lifeboatmen stretched out and hauled him in, seconds before the lifeboat crashed into the side of the *Collett*.

The lifeboat now turned for home and shortly afterwards the *Collett* sank. It took another 5½ hours to reach St Peter Port, and when the lifeboat arrived at 6.45 a.m. she had been at sea for fifteen hours.

Uniquely, Hubert Petit won two gold medals for the rescue, one from the RNLI and one from the Norwegian Lifeboat Institution, the first they ever awarded for bravery at sea.

LIKE FATHER, LIKE SON

John Petit, Hubert's son, had an equally distinguished lifeboat career, winning a silver and three bronze medals for his bravery. He was coxswain when the first Arun lifeboat was sent to Guernsey and the benefits of the fast lifeboat were illustrated within hours. The boat arrived during the day of 12 October 1972 in ideal weather conditions. By the evening, the weather had deteriorated and by midnight gale force winds were blowing. At 3 a.m. the French trawler *L'Esperance* sent out a Mayday. She was holed among rocks 20 miles off St Martins Point and the fishermen had had to take to their life raft. Even in the force 10 gale, John Petit was able to push the Arun to its full speed of 18 knots,

John Petit of Guernsey is interviewed for BBC's *Newsround. (Peter Hadfield)*

twice the speed of its predecessor, intercept the life raft and save the trawlermen before they were driven onto the shores of Brittany, with dire consequences. Speed had triumphed, but more severe tests were ahead.

It is hard to imagine the scale of the worst conditions at sea. John Petit was a sea captain, lifeboat coxswain and harbourmaster and is not prone to exaggeration. Indeed he is a quiet man, a broad grin never far from his face. So when John describes the service to the ship *Prosperity* in January 1974 as his most challenging, we can be sure conditions were appalling: 'The wind was hurricane force 11 to 12 and this was the first severe test that the lifeboat was to endure, so we were a little apprehensive as to how she would behave. We would not be disappointed.'

As they left the mooring, the crew double lashed the inflatable dinghy lest it get ripped away by the gale. John Petit pushed the throttles down to get maximum speed along the sheltered east coast of Guernsey. But even he, so familiar with these seas, was not prepared for the sight of the open waters around St Martins Point. There was a very high spring tide at full ebb, running westward against the wind at 4 knots:

This caused the heaviest seas I and the crew had ever seen. Fortunately the full moon had risen so that we were able to see the monsters being hurled at us.

As we rose over the top of a breaking sea, the fearsome noise also rose to a crescendo, the deafening wind shrieking like a thousand banshees, performing a duet with the moaning of the superstructure. As the boat plunged into the trough perhaps 40 or 50ft below, the noise ceased into an uncanny silence except for the purring of the engines. On the crest of a wave, the radar set depicted an awesome scene. Normal seas are shown on the centre of the screen as a solid mass of dots but now solid bars of echoes, 3 or 4mm thick filled the display, like a series of hedgerows. These were the echoes received back from the tops of the swells and the breaking seas.

The boat ploughed on, at 10 knots, with absolutely no visibility through the heavy spray being flung at it. Eventually the lifeboat was recalled as a plane had circled the position given in the Mayday broadcast and had seen nothing. The aircraft was reporting heavy spray even at a height of 400ft. Now John Petit faced another problem, to turn across the sea and run eastward with the seas behind him. It turned into a roller coaster ride. A particularly high wave came towards the lifeboat. Petit put the helm hard to port and pushed the throttles down but the sea took control: 'The lifeboat spun round and steadied on the easterly heading, surfing wildly. She overtook one wave at 20 knots, dived down into the trough and continued going down. I was convinced that the propellers were driving the vessel downward at a steep angle.'

The lifeboat was buried nose down in the wave, the cabin surrounded by solid water, lit up by the eerie glow of the navigation lights. Petit grabbed his controls and yanked them back to the stop position. His next remark is a masterpiece of understatement: 'The lifeboat popped upward like a cork and I was able to proceed at a more respectable speed, without any further ado.'

Later one of the crew reported that his fingers had been badly bruised as the water pressure on the wheelhouse window squashed them into the reinforcing bar to which he was clinging.

Another rescue by the Guernsey boat showed how local knowledge and experience are just as important as technological aids. A Belgian trawler with four men and a boy on board transmitted a Mayday on MF radio. She had a substantial leak and, as the engine started to become submerged, no longer had power to use her pumps. The sea was calm but visibility was poor, down to about half a mile. The trawler was unsure of her position but, judging from the strength of the radio signal, St Peter Port and Jersey Radio estimated she was north of Jersey, as did a ferry in the vicinity.

The Guernsey lifeboat set out and soon Eric Pattimore got a bearing of the trawler on the MF direction finder. A direction finder can give two bearings of a radio signal: a true bearing or its reciprocal. In this case, one of the bearings showed a position to the north of Jersey, as judged by the shore radio stations. The other was to the north-west of Guernsey. The true bearing is normally the weaker of the two, but in this case they were almost identical in strength. Eric Pattimore was convinced that the vessel was to the north-west and the lifeboat defied the authorities to go north of the island to search. However, Eric's frequent bearings showed that the strength of the trawler's radio signalling was steadily getting weaker. The obvious explanation was that the Guernsey men had made the wrong decision and were actually heading away from the trawler. Eric stuck to his guns: 'I think it's getting weaker because his battery is running down. I'm convinced we're on the right track.'

Then the trawler's radio failed completely. No more bearings could be taken. The lifeboat swept on through the fog, the crew unsure that they would find anything. Suddenly, the low outline of the trawler appeared out of the gloom. John Petit looked across at Eric and both broke out in broad grins of relief. The trawler's decks were awash and the fishermen were about to launch their leaky old dinghy to abandon ship. The dinghy looked as if it would sink at any moment. As the lifeboat took off the Belgians, the trawler started to sink under their feet. But for John Petit backing Eric Pattimore's hunch, four men and a boy would have drowned.

Oil Rig Rescue

John Petit's most bizarre rescue was on 1 February 1978 from the oil rig *Orion*, which was being towed from Rotterdam to Brazil. The rig consisted of four retractable legs and a drilling platform which had been mounted on a tanker hull for the journey. It towered 275ft above the waterline, and when the rig broke free from its tug, the legs acted like giant sails and whisked the powerless contraption along at 6 knots. Guernsey's Arun was away for refit so they had a Barnett, the slower lifeboat capable of only 9 knots, to chase the rig, catching up at around 10.30 p.m. Petit told the rig's skipper he would be aground in half an hour so he decided to get his men off. The rig platform was 30ft above the water so they dropped a scrambling net off the helicopter landing platform that jutted out 50ft. The net was huge and hung down in the water, threatening to tangle the lifeboat propellers.

Two men started down the net and John Petit drove the lifeboat in. It took four lifeboatmen to drag the first man on board as the lifeboat rose and fell in the swell. As the lifeboat dropped away, the anchor caught in the net, which suddenly went tight and catapulted the second man into the sea while throwing

Guernsey lifeboat and the oil rig *Orion*.

the lifeboat towards the tanker hull. Petit went full ahead, and another huge swell lifted the lifeboat. Snowy Hamon untangled the net, but the lifeboat was still rising and her mast was smashed on the underside of the helicopter platform. The mast came crashing down, the MF aerials tangled round the radar scanner and its fibreglass cover flipped over the side. One of the lifeboat crew, though, had not taken his eyes off the man in the water and, as Petit shrugged the boat clear, they picked up the shivering survivor with great difficulty. As the noise of breaking equipment faded, crew member Mike Scales, scratching his head Laurel and Hardy style, looked into the wheelhouse and said to Petit, 'And that's another fine mess you've gotten me into, Stanley.'

A few minutes later the rig lurched to one side as it hit a rock, then it came to a grinding halt, hard aground on an even keel. The immediate danger to the crew was over. Although he had lost his mast, Petit still had VHF radio communication, so he advised *Orion*'s master to sit tight and wait for the Sea King helicopters, which were on their way, to be guided in by parachute flares from the lifeboat. The helicopter crews took huge risks, flying within feet of the rig's legs in winds gusting to force 9. Winchmen were swung up to 45 degrees away from the platform in the gusts and had to swing back to reach survivors, who had to crawl on their hands and knees to meet them.

For three hours they worked, the lifeboat standing by, and twenty-five people were lifted off before conditions became too dangerous to do more.

John Petit won a silver medal for the rescue, but a few days later he was called out again to the rig. A salvage crew was on board and the wind had got up, so they needed to be evacuated. The whole episode was captured on film by Channel TV from the shore nearby. In the film, the Barnett lifeboat, notoriously difficult to manoeuvre in tight spaces, is seen wallowing in the narrow channel, carefully approaching the rig. The crew scurry around to tie the fenders to the starboard side. As the lifeboat comes closer, she starts to swing round and the crew rush across to port with the fenders, but hesitate while they consult the coxswain. 'Which side shall we rig the fenders, boss?' John Petit, master mariner, had a terse reply, 'When this bitch makes up her mind where she's going, I'll let you know.'

Neither Tom King nor Hubert or John Petit became well known outside the Channel Islands, partly because of their distance from the London news media and the difficulties of getting the men to the mainland to give talks and attend dinners. However, a coxswain from a remote community on Anglesey became much better known, eventually becoming the first lifeboatman to appear on television's *This is Your Life*.

LASHED TO THE WHEEL

You have to work hard to get to Moelfre. First, cross the Menai Strait to reach Anglesey, then keep on, past genteel Beaumaris and round towards Holyhead. Turn off to your right, down into the village, almost a dead end, and, sitting above the cliffs, you will find the lifeboat station which has been awarded five gold medals, two to one man.

Sea captains used to abound in Moelfre, either born and bred there, or settling down to have a view over the approaches to Liverpool, the port from which many sailed. But none has been the subject of sculptures and paintings like Moelfre's most famous son, Richard Evans. The paintings include a portrait by Jeff Stultiens, commissioned by the RNLI, and one of his *Hindlea* rescue by Tim Thompson.

The artists were captivated by Dick, whom they met when he was in his eighties. When Tim Thompson visited him, some thirty years after the *Hindlea* rescue, the retired coxswain's recall was crystal clear. He talked of a 'boiling cauldron of foam' and waves which were 'snarling mountains of fury': 'My little lifeboat was at one moment flat on her side with her mast under water, the next falling stern first off the coaster's deck. Then I gained control, only to find myself thrown under the thrashing propeller.'

Thompson loved the lyrical tales but needed other details for his painting. 'I asked Dick, "Was the *Hindlea* fouled with any particular weed or barnacles?" To which he replied, after a moment's thought, "Well, do you know Tim, I don't think I had time to look!"'

When Stultien's portrait was unveiled at a special ceremony in Beaumaris, Dick could hardly see the work because his sight was blighted by cataracts. He could, however, hear the eulogy delivered by the local council chairman, a slight man in a brown suit who read a script in English, obviously prepared for him by a council employee. It was accurate, worthy and dull and the chairman knew it. 'Right,' he said, 'I've said what I was meant to. I'll now address you in the language of angels.' And he delivered an oratory, swooping and diving like the seagulls off the cliffs, in fluent, singing Welsh. Dick, himself a public speaker of great renown, was visibly moved. The Englishmen in the audience were moved too by the spirit and obvious sincerity of the words, not one of which could they understand.

A fine bronze statue also commemorates Dick's courage. It overlooks the lifeboat station and gazes across the seas where he carried out his rescues, showing Dick gripping the wheel of a lifeboat. In his speeches, he always said, 'There I was,

Dick Evans of Moelfre.

lashed to the wheel, thinking of Nancy and my boys at home by the fireside.' Although he was a risk taker as well as an ingenious seafarer and a caring, soft-spoken man, one of his constant themes was the weight of responsibility he felt not only for his own family but also for the families of all his crew.

Dick was born in 1905, the son of a sea captain, William Evans, who was also in the lifeboat crew, as was his brother, Dick's Uncle John. As a boy, Dick was often at sea in his grandfather Matthew's sailing boat, catching fish. He left school to go to sea on a coal-carrying coaster, and by twenty-three was a captain himself, master of the motor vessel *Colin*, a 320-ton coaster. Dick loved the life and was delighted when Uncle John was made full-time lifeboat coxswain, until he learned that it meant that he would have to come ashore to take over the family butcher's shop. However, he was not away from the sea for long. Dick had been on his first lifeboat launch aged sixteen and was voted coxswain when John retired in 1954. Ironically, having left the butchery behind, his first rescue was of a cow that had fallen down a cliff into the sea. The farmer, backed by the RSPCA, demanded that the lifeboat launch. The honorary secretary of the lifeboat was away, so Dick decided to go. He towed a punt behind the lifeboat, got the cow alongside after a considerable struggle and landed her on a sandy beach. A fortnight later she calved and the calf later won a prize at Smithfield Show.

Dick was worried about the reaction of the honorary secretary, Colonel Williams, to his decision to save an animal. He need not have been, as Williams played a gentle joke on him. Congratulating him on a good effort, the colonel urged Dick to make a drawing to send to head office as guidance to any coxswain faced with rescuing a cow in the future. Dick spent hours on his sketch and was convinced that the cow looked more like a monkey. Head office entered into the spirit and wrote to congratulate him on his drawing.

THE *HINDLEA* RESCUE

The next compliment was the highest the RNLI can pay – a gold medal. On 27 October 1959, in a gale gusting to 104mph, the ship *Hindlea* was being driven towards the rocks of Anglesey. The lifeboat had to go. Telephone lines were down, maroons would be useless and time was running out. A few men had been rounded up, but only three of the regular crew were available: Murley Francis, Evan Owen and Hugh Owen – plus one extra, Hugh Jones, who had never been on the lifeboat before. On such a night, a coxswain would want to take experienced men, and extra hands – perhaps himself plus seven – but Dick couldn't wait – he launched.

The *Hindlea* was less than half a mile from the station, but it was almost an hour before they got to her. She had an anchor down and, although she was being battered by the seas, Captain Roland Chipchase would not abandon ship. The lifeboat had to stand by and watch for an hour and a half until *Hindlea*'s captain gave the order to abandon ship. Now *Hindlea* was only 200yds from the rocks. As Dick drove the lifeboat in, *Hindlea* reared up, her thrashing propeller a mere 4ft above head height. The lifeboat swung around, a seaman jumped and Hugh Owen grabbed him. However dangerous, going into the stern had worked and Dick knew he would have to try again. Ten times the Moelfre lifeboat went in. Three of them were abortive attempts but on the seventh a man was snatched into the lifeboat. Only one man was left, hanging onto the *Hindlea*'s rail. Dick made his final run in but a wave lifted the lifeboat as *Hindlea* bucked away. With his boat completely unresponsive, Dick had no idea what was going on until a sudden crash wrenched the wheel from his hands. As he looked up, he saw to his horror that the lifeboat had been tossed onto *Hindlea*'s deck. The boat was out of the water and he had no way of getting off. Then another wave struck *Hindlea*, which shifted uneasily under the lifeboat. The water rushed over the deck, refloated the stranded lifeboat and washed it back into the sea. As the lifeboat rushed past the rail, Hugh Owen and Hugh Jones stretched out to pull the last man to safety.

The actual rescue had taken only sixteen minutes but the battered lifeboat was still not safe as she was only 100yds from the shore and surrounded by rocks, and the storm was still raging in the open sea.

Dick remembered little about the passage home, but recalled reaching shore: 'I sat on the slipway utterly exhausted. Suddenly I realised that tears were streaming down my face. They were tears of joy. My crew and I had saved eight men from certain death and I felt very happy about it.'

Dick had to report to RNLI head office. The boat was badly damaged and he was told not to take her out until there had been a full inspection. Yet twenty-five minutes later, breaking all the rules, the Moelfre lifeboat launched again. A ship had a flooded engine room and her anchor was dragging. Moelfre went out and stood by until the Beaumaris boat arrived to take over, the Beaumaris men taking a real pasting as they came around Anglesey into the teeth of the hurricane. Even then, Dick could not go home. He despatched the crew home to their families but he and mechanic Evan Owen stayed up all night, trying to patch up the lifeboat. At 6 a.m. he got a call to go out and take over from Beaumaris. He fired the maroons and the same four men who had been out to the *Hindlea* came pounding down the path again.

Finally, at 5 p.m. that day, the Moelfre boat was hauled back into the boathouse and this time Dick went home. 'I live about half a mile from the station but I was so tired I couldn't walk,' he remembered. 'I had to stop every few yards to rest. I got into the house at last and I slumped into the old armchair. I'm not a good sleeper usually but I fell asleep, or unconscious, I don't know. Anyway, my wife told me afterwards that I had her very frightened because every so often I was leaping out of the chair. Probably I was dreaming.'

On the day of the *Hindlea* rescue, Dick's son, David, was chief officer on a tanker, sheltering from the storm in the Bristol Channel. Suddenly, the airwaves

Hindlea anchored near Moelfre lifeboat station, around the headland. *(London Express News and Features)*

Hindlea breaks up after the rescue.

were alive with news of a lifeboat out, on a lee shore, in the hurricane. David could hardly believe that a lifeboat would attempt a rescue in those conditions, but his captain assured him that was the message. One ship's radio operator said, 'I'm sorry for those lifeboatmen, they'll never get out of that,' and shortly afterwards another ship broadcast, 'The lifeboat's got the crew off – it's Moelfre.'

David leapt down to the captain's cabin three steps at a time, 'Captain, it's my old man that's out in that lifeboat!'

THE WEIGHT OF RESPONSIBILITY

If David had been worried about the lifeboat, his father often had occasion to worry about his sons, all of whom served on the lifeboat and were outstanding life-savers, David and Derek winning Royal Humane Society awards for acts of individual bravery.

Dick had to treat them like any other crew member, but the decisions were hard. On a Sunday in July 1957, strong winds and currents were carrying a girl out to sea, and as the lifeboat approached her, the crew saw two more heads in the water some distance away. Two men had gone out to rescue the girl and their small boat had capsized. All had been in the water some time and were weak, cold and vulnerable. Dick had to work out how to save them all, so he asked David if he could dive in and keep the girl afloat while he went for the men.

Dick couldn't help worrying: 'You can imagine my feeling. Trying to rescue those men and thinking maybe I have sent my son to his death.' David, however, was made of strong stuff and reached the girl; by floating on his back and supporting her on his chest, he kept her safe. The lifeboat pulled in the exhausted men then went across to David and the girl. By now she had been in the sea almost an hour and was in very poor shape. Her eyes were wide open and staring and her heart was pounding. One of the rescued men came out of the lifeboat's shelter and told Dick to give her some rum. Dick knew that was against the rules, but then realised that the instructions were coming from the village doctor who had attempted the rescue, so he reluctantly got out the rum bottle.

The doctor wanted to get the girl ashore as soon as possible, but Moelfre was half an hour away and he gave her only ten minutes to live. The lifeboat was only a year old and Dick was in unfamiliar territory, but if he wanted to save the girl he had only one option – to beach the boat. A jeep was driving down to meet them so he drove the lifeboat up on the shore. The crew rushed the girl and the doctor to the jeep, which took them to the nearest house.

Dick was stuck with his lifeboat on the sand. Once again, he feared the reaction of Colonel Williams: 'I was in hiding when he came down. I was ashamed of the lifeboat being high and dry. I need not have worried. It would not have mattered if I had run that lifeboat onto rocks, possibly causing damage costing thousands of pounds, provided we saved life. One life. This is what makes the RNLI such a wonderful organisation. It's life-saving that's their only concern.'

THE INSPECTOR'S JOB

Lieutenant-Commander Harold Harvey VRD, RNR, had the fine features, penetrating eyes and smooth voice of a star from black and white films, which was appropriate as he ended his RNLI career running the stores depot at Borehamwood, just down the road from the Elstree film studios, where, looking like a cross between Kenneth More and Dirk Bogarde, he might have felt at home.

His was the era of the traditional lifeboat; he mixed with crews of fishermen and was a man for his time. Leaving the Navy in 1952, aged thirty-two, as a young lieutenant to become a lifeboat inspector, he was told, 'Here you are, Harvey, it's all yours – the responsibility of an admiral and the authority of a midshipman.' The crews then were more independent minded and less involved with training and support from the RNLI. It was not too fanciful to say that they could step from their fishing boats onto the lifeboat and notice little difference, so the lifeboat inspector had to be prepared to learn from them. His job is to ensure that everything at a lifeboat station – the crew, boat, building and equipment – is ready for action.

Harvey wrote in the *Lifeboat Journal*, 'Here was a man's world where newcomers had to forge out their own relationships; to stand up and be counted; to get some sea time in and be recognised for what they were.' He was posted all around the coast, as he vividly described: 'Each district, and indeed county, had its own character; not simply of the communities themselves, though perhaps this was the area of most variety, but each lifeboat station had its own special variation of ground and sea conditions. Aboard ships the sea often rolled over you but I found a vast difference when I changed my height of eye from 50ft and more to just 10ft. Seas and horizons took on very different dimensions.' He summed up the life well by describing a lifeboat passage; sailing the boat to its station after a refit:

Twelve hours at sea in a gale of wind in coastal waters is a tiring day. Once ashore and cleaned up, and after an evening meal, a chat and meeting with local crews rounds off the evening. A jug of beer or two puts us all in a cheerful mood and we get up to a variety of activities; bar football with men from Filey, Flamborough and Runswick, darts with the Walton crew, feats of strength with the Rhyl chaps, Irish jigs with those from Valentia, male voice choir antics with the Cornishmen of Mousehole and the Lizard.

Harvey said of the lifeboat inspector:

He looks for the opportunity to get to sea on a service, preferably a lively one. Sometimes it happens that the maroons go off after he has left a station; many times the maroons are put up when he is at home typing or interviewing. Occasionally he is on the spot. Such an event was the launch to *Nafsiporos* on 2 December 1966 when I got to sea with the Holyhead crew. There was a wind that day – well in excess of 100 knots at times – and a big sea.

It was Harvey's involvement in this rescue that put him into the RNLI's records as one of its gold medal heroes.

A SEVENTEEN-MEDAL RESCUE

The *Nafsiporos* rescue unfolded over twenty-four hours, involved three lifeboats and resulted in a haul of seventeen bravery medals. The 1,287-ton Greek freighter had unloaded her cargo in Liverpool and was on her return passage, with little ballast, across the Irish Sea to Belfast. It was the first command for 28-year-old Captain Angelo Katsovufis and, almost as soon as he left the River Mersey, he lost control of his ship as her propellers and rudders were lifted clear of the water in a full storm. In such conditions, a prudent skipper seeks shelter, so Katsovufis set course, as best he could, for the Isle of Man, hoping to anchor off Ramsey. The plan was sensible and seemed to be going well, as *Nafsiporos* rode to her anchor for two nights and a day, but on the morning of the second day the anchor started to drag. The power of the engines was no match for the storm, and as the propellers again churned uselessly in the air, the engines overheated and eventually broke down. *Nafsiporos* was now completely out of control.

She first reported trouble early on the morning of 2 December when she was 12 miles south of Douglas Bay. Winds of over 100mph were blowing and the sea conditions were horrendous. Coxswain Robert Lee and the Douglas lifeboat crew set out at 8.30 a.m. to chase the *Nafsiporos* as the storm drove her back across the Irish Sea towards North Wales. Although a Shackleton aircraft,

Nafsiporos powerless in the Irish Sea.

circling above the ship, gave a position quite close to the Douglas boat, the crew never saw *Nafsiporos* because the force 11 hurricane reduced the visibility to under 500yds.

Meanwhile the Holyhead lifeboat, with Harvey aboard, had been launched at 10.30 a.m. and found the ship, so Douglas turned for home, reaching harbour after a gruelling ten hours at sea. Holyhead had rendezvoused with *Nafsiporos* at 1.38 p.m. and found her being escorted by two other ships, so the lifeboat joined in to escort her as she was driven before the storm.

While all this was going on, the Moelfre lifeboat was also busy with two ships in distress at the same time. First, the *Vinland* reported engine trouble and Moelfre launched at 7.40 a.m., ploughing on for 2½ hours to reach her off Point Lynas. Then a new message came through from the coastguard. The ship *Grit* was now 3½ miles away and had broken steering gear. Coxswain Dick Evans had to choose which ship to help. Instinctively, he knew it had to be *Grit*, which had much less sea room and was nearer to his position. He soon found the ship and stayed with her until midday, when she reported that temporary repairs had been made and she no longer needed help. In the meantime, a tug had been despatched for the *Vinland*, so Evans turned for home, getting his boat back on the slipway at 1.40 p.m. – a six-hour stretch. Just half an hour later, Moelfre was asked to launch again as *Nafsiporos* was now drifting towards Point Lynas, the very place Evans had just left.

For *Nafsiporos*, events were unfolding rather too fast. She had now been driven to within 8 miles of the Anglesey coast and was still moving at 3½ knots. In just over two hours, she would be ashore in Bull Bay. She was rolling alarmingly and oscillating to and fro, first burying her bow as the propeller lifted clear, then rising up to push her forefoot clear of the water. Her rudder gave no steerage to put her into the wind; she was completely at the mercy of the storm.

Shortly before 3 p.m. a Russian ship, *Kungurles*, got a towline across but it snapped twenty minutes later, and as *Nafsiporos* scraped past the Ethel Rock Buoy, her captain dropped his starboard anchor. It failed to hold until the ship was only a quarter of a mile from the notorious West Mouse Rock where there was 6 fathoms (about 40ft) depth of turbulent sea, with waves 35ft high.

On the Holyhead lifeboat Coxswain Thomas Alcock came round the stern of the ship to see how close he could get. *Nafsiporos* rewarded him by crashing down onto his boat, inflicting severe damage. If things were looking bad, they were about to get worse. The seamen had started to prepare the ship's lifeboat to make their escape, and swung it round over the hand rails. Lowering a lifeboat obviously requires the bow and stern ropes to be released at the same speed, but the crew only let go of the bow rope, so the lifeboat dangled vertically, her keel facing forward, a heavy, dangerous and manically swinging pendulum that was only a few feet from the rescue ladder hanging over the ship's side.

Will Jones, who was second coxswain of Holyhead, remembers the tortuous search for a way to reach the Greek seamen: 'A wave slammed us against the steel plates of the *Nafsiporos* and we had to sheer away. As we circled, all of us were looking for a safe approach but that lifeboat was always in the way. We shouted through the loudhailer for the crew to cut it away, but either they could not hear or they could not understand our Welsh accents. In any case, that lifeboat remained where it was.'

The Moelfre men were having no better time of it. Dick Evans and his crew, already cold, wet and exhausted after a whole morning at sea, had to go out again. Dick had on board Captain David Jeavons, a deep-sea captain who had been master of six different Canadian Pacific ships, the largest 27,500 tons. Moelfre lifeboat was a mere 17 tons. 'I daren't open the chart room', said Dick, 'in case the sea flooded in. A cox on those old lifeboats couldn't look at the charts; he had to carry them in his head. I knew the rocks, the set and drift of tides, the currents. But that day the sea was like a foreign country. It was being blown into clouds of spray and visibility was nil. I could see nothing.'

Dick had a marvellous tale of Captain Jeavon's reaction. Sheltering with the rest of the crew on the benches in the canopy just in front of the coxswain, the captain three times poked his head up and asked Dick if he knew where he was going.

Finally, Dick told him, 'Look, you're captain when you're on the *Empress of England*, and I'm captain of this lifeboat. Now sit down and let me get on with it.'

As they ploughed on, Dick was concerned for his crew and ordered Murley Francis to go below and fetch the rum. In those days it was rough stuff, said to burn the skin off the inside of your cheeks but at least it produced a welcome warm glow inside. Down in the cabin it was warm and cosy but the bottle jumped out of Murley's hand and smashed. He put the second bottle inside his lifejacket for protection but as he came up the boat reared, the ladder slipped out of its fittings and Murley and the rum landed in a heap on the cabin floor. To add insult to injury, when he came back up the smell was so terrible that all the crew were seasick.

Meanwhile, back on board the Holyhead lifeboat, according to the official account of the rescue, Thomas Alcock now decided to hand over the wheel of his lifeboat to Harold Harvey, 'a wise decision, demanding both physical and moral courage', explained by the absence of his regular bowman and the need for extra supervision on deck. The RNLI can no longer find the full report of the incident and the unofficial version, recalled by Patrick Howarth, who was public relations officer at the time, is somewhat different. Howarth knew Harvey well and his account was that, for whatever reason, Alcock could not or would not take his lifeboat in again. He hesitated, unsure of how to tackle the situation. Harvey seized the moment – and the wheel – to take charge and be awarded a gold medal for gallantry. Some weeks later Alcock was summoned by the RNLI, anticipating a reprimand but receiving a silver medal for his part in the rescue.

What is certain is that the swinging ship's lifeboat nearly did for the Holyhead crew. As darkness fell Moelfre made a couple of runs in but to no avail. Then Holyhead, with Harvey at the helm, had a go. A man was hanging over the ship's side on the ladder, the lifeboat ranging up and down so that at one moment he was below the guard rails then hanging overhead. As Harvey pressed the lifeboat forward, the Holyhead men prised the seaman from the ladder by force. With Alcock and Jones on the foredeck more of the *Nafsiporos* crew clambered to safety, their dangling ship's boat scraping Holyhead's bow. Just as the fifth man was rescued, the rope holding the boat snapped, sending it crashing down onto the lifeboat. Harvey reacted like lightning, barking out a command for the crew to get clear and putting full throttle astern. The boat landed upside down on the deck, spilling out its contents and scattering oars, which poked through the wheelhouse windows, only inches from Harvey's head. His sharp reactions saved the day as the lifeboat's backward momentum made the ship's boat roll away and slide clear. Remarkable teamwork was at play because in these old lifeboats, the coxswain only had direct control of the steering. He shouted orders to the mechanics who ran the engines from the canopy just ahead of him. Harvey knew the danger posed by the boat, but to get the lifeboat clear by commands shouted above the noise of the storm was in itself a remarkable feat. The lifeboat was damaged but still Harvey pressed on, preparing for another run in as the crew cleared away the debris.

However, Moelfre took over, staying alongside long enough to take ten men aboard. The captain and four men were left and decided not to abandon ship, so both lifeboats returned to Holyhead to land the survivors, four of whom were injured. With only a pause for a cup of tea, Holyhead put out again to stand by *Nafsiporos* throughout the night until a Dutch tug got her in tow and took her back to where she started – Liverpool.

Harvey was as modest afterwards as any lifeboatman: 'That day, I hope, I won my spurs. We were all exhausted after twenty-two hours at sea, and during the night following the rescue many thoughts and silent prayers occupied our minds. After this, once ashore, the rum came out. We were all proud and grateful men, speaking little, thinking deep and bound by the experience of such extreme lifeboat drama and action.'

CHAPTER THREE

Triumph and Disaster

No merchant seaman will leave his ship until he knows the situation is hopeless. Ship's lifeboats and rubber life rafts are no match for a storm that can overwhelm a well-found vessel. So when coastguards received a Mayday from the motor vessel *Lovat* in January 1975, reporting the crew were abandoning ship, they knew the outlook was grim.

The Penlee lifeboat, *Solomon Browne*, launched just before 7 a.m. It was dark, there were heavy rain squalls and the wind was gusting to hurricane force 12. The *Lovat* was 24 miles south-west of Lizard Point. Aboard the lifeboat the crew were in extreme discomfort as *Solomon Browne* rolled in the beam seas, but Coxswain Trevelyan Richards pressed on at full speed, 9 knots, knowing he had to get to *Lovat* with all urgency.

After two dreadful hours, the lifeboat reached the scene where a car ferry was standing by and a Sea King helicopter hovered above a life raft. Passing an upturned ship's lifeboat, Richards made for the life raft. The crew lashed it alongside and, while the lifeboat rolled violently, threatening to catapult them into the sea, managed with great difficulty to haul on board two bodies, one of them a teenager.

Five more bodies were floating in the sea, and helicopter divers, in immense danger as the vicious seas kept washing them away on the end of their winch wires, eventually managed to recover two of them. Meanwhile, the lifeboat crew went even further into danger. The only way they could reach the bodies was to drop the guard rail, the only thing stopping them plunging into the water. As the lifeboat rolled over 60 degrees, her decks under water, four lifeboatmen leaned into the waves to lift the waterlogged bodies aboard. All they could do was lash them to the deck for a distressing journey home. Only now, their sad task completed, could Trevelyan Richards reduce speed to bring some relief for the passage back to Newlyn where a physically and emotionally drained crew landed five bodies at 2.40 p.m.

The crew that day was Trevelyan Richards, Edward Wallis, Nigel Brockman, Stephen Madron, Phillip Wallis, Alan Treganza, Kevin Smith and Barrie Torrie.

Penlee lifeboat *Solomon Browne*.

Just under six years later, five of that storm-seasoned crew were killed as the same lifeboat, *Solomon Browne*, was smashed to pieces in the most dreadful lifeboat disaster of modern times.

PENLEE LIFEBOAT DISASTER

The loss of the Penlee lifeboat with all her crew in December 1981 brought an immediate outpouring of sympathy from the whole nation; but an early reaction from parts of the media was to portray the volunteer crew as plucky amateurs, overwhelmed in circumstances which were, perhaps, beyond their competence. The RNLI had to act quickly to get out the real story, for the *Lovat* incident had proved the skill, courage and hardened determination of the Penlee crew.

Trevelyan Richards was a fisherman. A towering figure with a kindly, rounded face, he was a man of few words in public. Among his crew on the fateful day were a telephone engineer, a publican, and a Cunard seaman, all long-serving lifeboatmen. Trevelyan had time to hand-pick his crew as the evening unfolded. Young Neil Brockman, aged seventeen, was there but Trevelyan was not taking a father and son together – he picked Neil's father, Nigel. Denis Leslie, the local doctor, robust but past retirement age, offered to go but Trevelyan gently turned him back.

The hindsight provided by the official enquiry posed some questions about the events leading up to the lifeboat launch.

The story starts with the coaster *Union Star*, on passage to Dublin, with a new captain, Henry Morton, on his first command. He had made an unauthorised stop on the east coast of England to pick up his wife and two stepchildren before *Union Star*'s engines failed off the Cornish coast. Morton was now under severe pressure as he had his family on board and he knew his ship was in danger. A salvage tug was close by and although salvage payments work on no cure, no pay, if the tug had managed to tow *Union Star* to safety, there would have been a hefty bill for the owners. Captain Morton probably did not want to have to explain extra passengers and extra cost. He decided to try and fix the engine. Throughout the whole saga, which led to the destruction of his family, crew and ship, Captain Morton never issued a Mayday. Piecing together the evidence, the thoughts of the various parties probably ran along the following lines.

Henry Morton, on his first command, wanted to save his ship, wife and children without a salvage bill. The coastguards may well have been reluctant to ask the lifeboat to launch in the dreadful conditions, and even though they were plotting *Union Star*'s fateful course towards the hard granite Cornish cliffs, they probably believed the powerful Sea King helicopter could manage the rescue. The RNLI's normal chain of command failed, as lifeboat secretary Del Johnson could not be contacted and his deputy, Mike Sutherland, was checking harbour moorings in his capacity as deputy harbourmaster. Trevelyan Richards was contacted, as was Denis Leslie, but they relied on the coastguard for information on the urgency of the situation.

Having noted, 'We must all avoid judging anyone else's conduct with the benefit of hindsight, but when actions have been so closely analysed, as during an investigation, it is of value to note those actions which could have been done differently,' one of the inquiry's more diplomatic recommendations was 'That HM Coastguard and the RNLI consider jointly: (i) the phraseology and procedures for requesting a lifeboat launch or anticipate (ii) further improving liaison between personnel of the two organisations and between HM Coastguard and others with local knowledge.'

The earlier launch of the lifeboat would have been 'advantageous', though it could not be proved it would have prevented the losses, and the absence of a

Mayday broadcast 'may also have led to restraint in asking for the lifeboat to launch'.

So what exactly happened on that terrible night? Put simply, the facts are these. *Union Star*, a well-built and maintained ship, was caught in a storm off the Cornish coast. Sea water got into her fuel, probably through vent pipes, and the engines failed as the contaminated fuel fed through. While the captain and his engineer struggled to restart the engines, *Union Star* drifted towards the coast, watched by a salvage tug and a helicopter. The helicopter crew, in a reckless display of outstanding skill and courage, repeatedly tried but failed to rescue those on the *Union Star*. Penlee lifeboat, having been put on standby ashore, was eventually launched. Incredibly, in the maelstrom only yards from the foot of the cliffs, Trevelyan Richards drove the *Solomon Browne* alongside the *Union Star* and his crew snatched the woman, two children and one man to safety.

In a hushed session of the inquiry, the last radio transmission from the lifeboat was played: 'We've got four off.' Then there was a clunk – and silence.

What happened next, nobody knows, for nobody saw. The helicopter in the turbulence of the hurricane force winds was almost dashed against the cliffs and had to withdraw. The *Union Star* was found the next morning, upside down in a cove near Tater Du lighthouse. The lifeboat was smashed to tiny pieces, most no bigger than a person's arm. And the lifeboatmen themselves were killed, some never recovered from the sea, others smashed into tiny pieces like their lifeboat.

The RNLI disaster plan swung into action as the nation awoke to the news of a major tragedy just six days before Christmas. For the headquarters staff, some of them hardened by previous experience of lifeboat disasters, this was like nothing before. Denis Leslie, Penlee station chairman, later wrote about the aftermath:

Come back with me, if you will, to that wild grey Sunday morning in December – the storm of the last night having moderated to perhaps force 8, still with heavy rain, and at just about nine in the morning a completely shattered group of men and women are making their way towards the office of our honorary secretary, Del Johnson. As many as possible of the Penlee branch committee had been contacted in the small hours – that is, those who had not already been up all night visiting families or searching the coastline west of Mousehole.

I called a meeting with an utter sense of being alone. Coming into the office, in a daze really, I noticed that the room was almost uncomfortably full and the sudden appreciation began to grow that we were not so alone.

The room had the lifeboat inspector, coast staff, regional fund-raisers and a team from Poole with senior operational, technical and welfare staff.

As the loneliness began to evaporate, there came the realisation that the whole weight of the RNLI secretariat and inspectorate had come to help us and our endeavours were strengthened by the news that Rear Admiral Graham, the Director, had been extracted from a foreign-bound aircraft at Gatwick airport and was on his way.

Messages of sympathy came from the Queen, the Duke of Kent, the Duke of Cornwall (Prince Charles) and the Prime Minister. Over 200 people, life-boatmen and fishermen, were at sea, searching in waves that were still being thrown 30ft into the air against Penzance promenade.

Then came more local support, the local authority and bank running the disaster appeal and the post office, already coping with the Christmas rush, handling so many extra letters that the lifeboat committee, now working sixteen hours a day, had to ask them to hold back the mail bags. Over 1,000 letters came from other parts of the RNLI, including the stations of Longhope, Fraserburgh, Broughty Ferry, the Mumbles, St Ives and Rye Harbour, all of which had suffered disasters in the past.

Every country in Europe wrote, including Russia and Czechoslovakia: also lifeboat people in Canada, New Zealand and South Africa and Cornish ex-patriots from as far away as Diego Garcia, the Falklands, Malaysia and the Pacific Islands.

YOU'VE GOT TO CARRY ON

Mousehole, the home of the lifeboat crew, is famous for its display of Christmas lights around the picturesque harbour. Two nights before he died, Charlie Greenhaugh, as chairman of the local licensed victuallers association, had switched them on. After the disaster, the harbour stayed dark. But the spirit of Mousehole and Penlee was exemplified by Charlie's widow, Mary. Three nights after the disaster she asked that the lights, unlit since the previous Saturday, should be repaired and relit. That spirit, said Denis Leslie, showed what lifeboating was all about.

But deep emotional scars were left on everybody involved. The pieces of *Solomon Browne* were taken, first, to the Trinity House depot in Penzance for safety and then to a warehouse at the RNLI in Poole where they were laid out to see if they revealed any clues. One propeller shaft had a thick rope loosely draped around it, but this proved nothing. To stop the shaft turning, the rope would have to be bound tight. It could simply have wound round in the days before the salvage divers retrieved the wreckage. In the end, the pieces of the *Solomon Browne* were burned. Before that, Barry Bright, a senior fund-raiser in Poole, stood in the warehouse and said, 'All RNLI staff should be made to see this – then they'll know what they're working for.'

The Wreck Commissioner's Inquiry concluded:

The loss of the *Union Star* and those on board was caused by:

(i)   the irreparable failure of the ship's engines due to contamination of fuel by sea water while off a dangerous lee shore

(ii)   the extreme severity of the weather, wind and sea

(iii) the capsize of the vessel on or shortly after stranding.

The loss of the *Solomon Browne* and her crew was caused in the aforesaid circumstances in consequence of the persistent and heroic endeavours by the coxswain and his crew to save the lives of all from the *Union Star*. Such heroism enhances the highest traditions of the Royal National Lifeboat Institution in whose service they gave their lives.

The dreadful nature of the disaster and the timing, so close to Christmas, led to an uncontrolled outpouring of public sympathy and cash, and a messy aftermath. Whitehall bureaucrats said the disaster fund had to be taxed. The public reacted angrily and the new lifeboat crew, formed within a day, stopped training. Lord Goodman intervened and the fund was distributed untaxed. Unscrupulous tricksters travelled to Penzance to try and ingratiate themselves with the bereaved families and some reporters intruded too far into the families' grief, though most behaved well. Relationships were placed under great strain – some broke and others managed to rebuild. Inevitably, the families were never the same again. Some people moved away, others managed to move on, but none forgot.

Pat Smith, Kevin's mother, later campaigned to set up a safety reporting system for local fishermen. On the anniversary of the disaster, Kevin's sister turned up, unannounced, at the lifeboat station nearest to where she was living, miles away from Cornwall and was taken in, given a cup of tea and a silent space to remember her brother. Janet Madron, Stephen's wife, renewed her fund-raising efforts for the RNLI and remains a dedicated volunteer.

The Penlee disaster had another unique aspect. The RNLI had never awarded medals to whole crews who had perished in disasters. This was because the criteria for medals require a combination of factors. Earlier crews who had perished were undoubtedly as brave and as determined as the men of Penlee.

Mary Richards with her son's posthumous gold medal, alongside gold medallist Mike Scales of Guernsey. *(Guernsey Press)*

The difference lay in the rescue. Four people had been taken onto the Penlee lifeboat, in the most extreme conditions, minutes before she was overwhelmed. If Trevelyan Richards had turned for home and abandoned the four left on the *Union Star* as a task too dangerous to contemplate, then he would have lived to have a medal pinned to his chest for a gallant rescue. Perhaps Trevelyan knew the old saying 'Lifeboatmen never turn back'. More likely, having rescued four, having weighed up the risks and being acutely aware of the danger, he could not bring himself to abandon Captain Henry Morton, his engineer and two crewmen, leaving them to certain death.

The RNLI made posthumous awards of a gold medal to Trevelyan and bronze medals to his crew. Next came the issue of how to present them. A meeting was convened in the Methodist church hall in Mousehole to chat to the families. They were warned that, while they would be warmly welcome at the RNLI AGM in London to receive the medals, they would be under intense media attention and a huge emotional outpouring from the audience. Some decided that a quiet, private, handing over of the medal would be better. Three women made the trip to London. The resilience of all the families was summed up by Mary Richards, Trevelyan's elderly mother, as she poured tea at the church hall meeting, 'You've got to carry on, my love.'

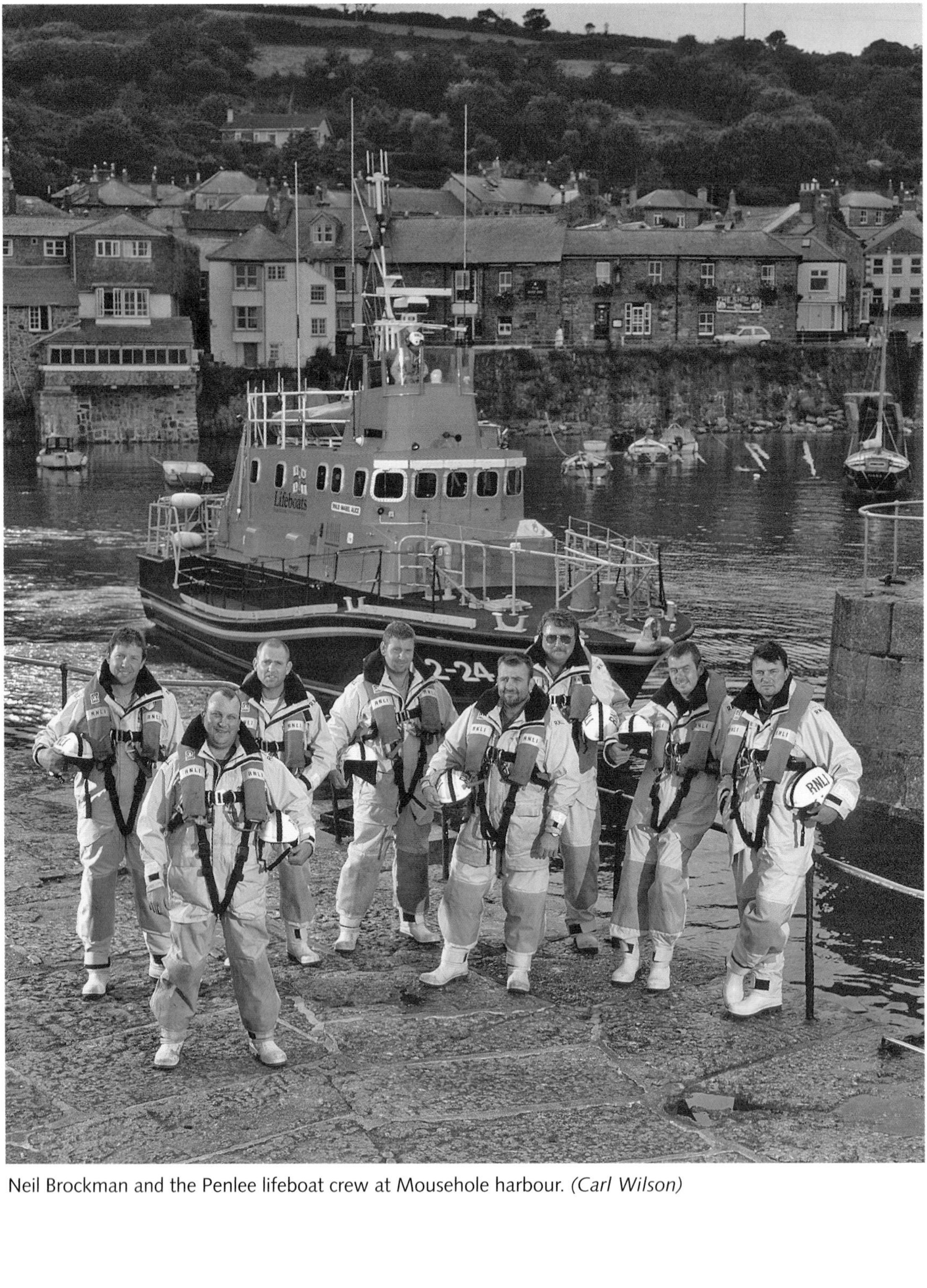

Neil Brockman and the Penlee lifeboat crew at Mousehole harbour. *(Carl Wilson)*

MEN OF CORNWALL

However, just as the families could never carry on quite as before, some lifeboatmen found the same. As concern for the Penlee boat mounted through the night, the neighbouring stations of Lizard, Sennen Cove and St Mary's launched their boats to search. Maurice Hutchens of Sennen, a tower of strength to Penlee people in the months that followed, found his lifeboat thrown back as he tried to round Land's End. The Lizard crew and their boat took a terrible pounding and when they finally returned and were winched up the slipway, they saw that their bilge keel had been wrenched askew by the pounding seas and gallons of water poured out of the damaged hull.

Returning to their families, a few crew members made the dignified decision to step down – a decision nobody questioned.

The new Penlee crew, under Coxswain Kenny Thomas, flourished as media and public attention waned. Gradually, Mousehole, Newlyn and Penzance were left to get on with their business. When Kenny resigned, Neil, Nigel Brockman's son, took over as coxswain.

A few years later, a spectacular concert was organised in Truro Cathedral to raise money for the RNLI. Englishmen in the audience trembled with fear as the Cornish Male Voice Choir thundered out the Cornish anthem 'Trelawny'. Jonathan Trelawny was one of seven bishops imprisoned in the Tower of London by James II in 1688. He was Bishop of Bristol and came from an old Cornish family, and his fellow countymen were enraged by his imprisonment. The anthem celebrates the threat to march on London to secure his freedom with the chorus 'And shall Trelawny live, / And shall Trelawny die, / Here's twenty thousand Cornishmen, / Will know the reason why'. The whole congregation had a lump in their throat as the coxswains from every Cornish lifeboat station marched down the aisle led by Neil Brockman carrying a flag on a pole crafted out of the only pieces of the *Solomon Browne* that had been saved. They stood, stock-still, before the altar as the final strains of 'Trelawny' died away. Flushed red, sweating and blinking, Neil was asked afterwards if the emotion of the occasion had got to him. 'No,' he said. 'That bloody flagstaff was made by the RNLI depot. They do everything double size and double strength and it wouldn't fit in the holster.' The stout wooden pole, held so rigidly aloft, had dug a hole in Neil's stomach, hence his discomfort!

SHETLAND SAVIOURS

Almost a thousand miles north of Penlee, sixteen years after the lifeboat disaster there, an uncannily similar set of circumstances unfolded in the wild seas off the north coast of Scotland.

Lerwick lifeboat saves the crew of a fishing vessel.

All the elements were the same. A cargo ship, *Green Lily*, with engine trouble, was being driven by a storm into rocky cliffs. An ocean-going tug and a robust search and rescue helicopter were on scene. The lifeboat was on stand-by and, as the other options evaporated, she was called out as the ultimate life-saver.

Even the outcome, though not as horrendous as Penlee, was marked with a singular tragedy arising from stupendous bravery. All were saved from the *Green Lily* and the lifeboat crew came home safe but helicopter winchman Bill Deacon, during an act of supreme selflessness, was swept to his death.

The most significant difference was that Coxswain Hewitt Clark had the RNLI's strongest and most powerful lifeboat under his feet, 2,400hp as opposed to the meagre 120hp available to Trevelyan Richards. Even then, Hewitt and his crew were in the utmost danger.

Captain Ezio Abram had put to sea on 19 November 1997 from Lerwick in *Green Lily* knowing there was a tremendous storm blowing. His ship was a

3,000-ton refrigerated cargo vessel. A south-easterly gale of up to force 11 had been battering Shetland for three days, giving the seas time to build up to giant rollers, pushing in to batter the cliffs. Ferry sailings had been cancelled but *Green Lily* was a good-size ship built to cross the oceans. However, when her engines started to malfunction, just as *Union Star*'s had done off Cornwall, tugs and a rig supply ship were called to the scene. The supply ship managed to get a line across and started towing *Green Lily*. Lifeboat secretary Magnus Shearer was kept in the picture but with large powerful specialist vessels – the supply ship *Gargano* at 210ft and the tug *Tystie* at 225ft – coastguards felt that the lifeboat would not be needed.

Then the storm took control. *Gargano*'s towline broke and her captain said it would take at least an hour to reconnect it. *Green Lily* was drifting towards the menacing cliffs of Bressay at 2 knots. Soon she would hit. The situation was now critical. The coastguards scrambled the twin-engined Sikorsky helicopter *Rescue Lima Charlie* and Magnus Shearer launched Lerwick lifeboat, the Severn class *Michael and Jane Vernon*.

To understand the magnitude of this rescue, a little context is needed. Lerwick is a relatively quiet lifeboat station but its location means that most of

Survivors from the fish factory ship *Pionersk*. (*G. Storey*)

the calls are hard and long in tough conditions. Lerwick coxswain Hewitt Clark became a frequent visitor to London to pick up bravery medals for his outstanding courage and superb boat handling. He joined the RNLI in 1966 as a crew member on one of the new 70ft cruising lifeboats, while it was still being built on the Clyde. Brian Miles, later to become Director of the RNLI, was in command and he remembers Hewitt arriving, a shy youngster who had never left Shetland before: 'From day one I knew I had a real seaman on my hands. Whatever he did, he did it well and he did it quietly. He soon became a damn fine lifeboatman.'

Hewitt and his crew have faced extreme hazards, including, in 1994, flying suitcases flung at them in the dark from the Russian fish factory ship *Pionersk*, when they rescued sixty-seven people, which won Hewitt a silver medal. Even more unpleasant was that a week later they were called out again, and, as one of the crew pulled on his sea boot, it felt wet. He was mildly annoyed that the boot had not dried out properly, until he found out that one of the Russians had used it as a seasickness bag the week before!

HELICOPTER HERO

Setting out to the *Green Lily*, coxswain Hewitt Clark and his crew strapped themselves in, acclimatising themselves in Bressay Sound to a mere force 9 to 10 gale and seas of 15ft before turning into the open ocean to meet the full severity of the hurricane. As the huge waves rolled in, Clark had to pull back the throttles to climb seas over 40ft high. *Green Lily* was now 1½ miles from shore. There was less than an hour before she would run aground. The *Michael and Jane Vernon* came into her own, managing 20 knots in the massive waves.

The full rescue team was now assembled. The helicopter hovered overhead, impotent as *Green Lily* rolled violently beam on to the seas. The tug *Tystie* was already in action, her skipper showing immense skill, getting close enough for a heaving line to be thrown across, but with only two men on *Green Lily* hauling in – by hand, even though a powered windlass was nearby – there was a huge struggle. Eventually a third man joined them, the rope was connected and *Tystie* gingerly took up the strain.

By now, *Green Lily* was so close to the shore that she was caught in waves bouncing back off the cliffs, welling up into 50ft towers of powerful breaking water. Suddenly, *Green Lily* was thrown to port and *Tystie* to starboard at the same moment. The towline pulled taut, started to unravel and finally broke.

Green Lily was minutes from the cliffs, powerless, with no towline aboard and rolling so violently that the helicopter could not help. Hewitt Clark and the

Lerwick lifeboat were the last chance. Clark asked Captain Abram to drop his anchors to slow the drift while he racked his brains to see what the lifeboat could do. 'It was extremely frustrating not being able to help at first and this was brought about mainly by the delay in dropping the anchors,' Hewitt recalls. The *Green Lily* crew were slow to act but did get one anchor down, slowing the ship and swinging her 45 degrees into the wind. Clark reassessed the dangers. He knew he had to act.

The only possible approach was on the port side, taking advantage of the slight shelter on the lee side, but this meant going between the ship and the rocks, with very little sea room. It is a situation that seasoned seafarers instinctively avoid, for in a storm the one thing you need is open sea in which to manoeuvre. Clark had none, but he had to go in.

He ordered his crew to man the starboard deck of the lifeboat, told Abram to get his crew assembled for rescue and climbed to the exposed upper steering position on the lifeboat. In went the *Michael and Jane Vernon*, rocks to the left, ship to the right, the lifeboat ranging up above the *Green Lily*'s deck then dropping below her waterline in a trough. Clark managed to get within 20ft but there was no sign of life on the ship. Eventually her crew emerged on the port deck, carrying their luggage. 'Everything happened so quickly – the crew was on deck and in a very dangerous situation.' Drawing on every ounce of his long experience, and knowing he must rely on an instant response from his two 1,200hp engines, Clark went in again. As both vessels rolled, the lifeboat was in acute danger of being crushed or capsized, just as the Penlee lifeboat had been all those years before. The Severn was lifted to deck level, crazily dancing towards *Green Lily* and Clark had to abort, pull back, hard astern on both engines, and start all over again.

As the inexorable drift shorewards continued, the space for the lifeboat grew steadily tighter. Clark made repeated attempts to get alongside, but was confounded every time by the seas and the violent motion of the boats. Whenever the decks of the *Green Lily* and the lifeboat were level, the lifeboatmen grabbed a survivor and manhandled him roughly over the ship's rail and onto the lifeboat. That would normally have been a safe haven but as the minutes ticked away, *Michael and Jane Vernon* was getting into more and more danger, as she was in a seething mass of water between the ship and the rocks.

Every time a man was plucked off, Clark had to get out, swinging the stern out on one engine then going hard astern on both to pull clear. And every time he made another run in the lifeboat was slammed into the solid slab side of the ship, the lifeboatmen on deck convinced that their boat was taking terrible damage beneath their feet.

Lerwick lifeboat *Michael and Jane Vernon*. (Johnnie Simpson)

Then the nightmare scenario happened. The lifeboat was trapped beneath *Green Lily*, 3,000 tons of ship looming over 41 tons of lifeboat and threatening to roll her over. This time the only way out was to drive forwards into potentially even greater danger. Clark pushed one throttle down. The stern swung out, as planned, but suddenly the trapped guard rail stanchion was ripped out, almost taking lifeboatman Michael Grant, whose lifeline was attached at that very point, with it. Ian Leask leapt across to pull the stanchion inboard, release Grant's line and re-secure it further aft.

Having almost lost a man, Clark must have been even more worried but still he pressed on. Sometimes there was nobody at *Green Lily*'s rail, and on one run a man had such a firm grip on his luggage that the lifeboatmen could not haul him across.

Unknown to the lifeboatmen, another amazing display of seamanship was taking place on the other side of the ship, daringly calculated to save her, but unwittingly almost finishing off the lifeboat. A second rig supply ship, *Maersk Champion*, drove right across *Green Lily*'s bow, managed to grapple her anchor cable and began to tow her out to sea. It was a desperate last attempt and as her bow began to swing into the wind, the slight shelter on the port side, which had allowed the lifeboat to get in, disappeared. Hewitt Clark could do no more. Just 200yds from the shore, with five people rescued, he broke clear and stood by. There were still ten men on the *Green Lily*.

Amazingly, the move that had rendered the lifeboat impotent made it possible for the helicopter to take over. The ship was now head to wind and rolling much less. Pilot Norman Leask, with two decades of search and rescue helicopter experience, spotted his chance and went straight into action. In spite of the acute danger, winchman Bill Deacon descended into the maelstrom, urging the survivors into the winch strop. To get them off more quickly, he stayed on the deck, cajoling them until all ten were taken into the belly of the hovering Sikorsky. Suddenly, *Green Lily*'s anchor cable snapped. In a flash, her bow swung round and she was driven ashore, pounded by the huge breakers. Bill Deacon, professional to the last, had seen all the survivors to safety and was the last man on the deck – the next to be lifted. He was washed overboard by a huge breaking wave and killed. The helicopter's winch wire caught up in the wreck as it swung round and it had to be cut lest it bring the aircraft down. The lifeboat could not contemplate going in to the boiling cauldron that engulfed the brave winchman. After twenty-seven years of helicopter rescues, Bill Deacon had given his own life to save others.

Hewitt Clark had the lives of his crew and survivors to consider: 'I always put the safety of my crew first and that is why, immediately after we had completed our part of the rescue, I disobeyed coastguard instructions and returned to Lerwick to land survivors before returning to search for the missing winchman, Bill Deacon – there were just too many lives at risk.' Having landed the survivors, the lifeboat put out again and swept along the coast, desperate for any sign of Deacon. It was a hopeless quest, as the lifeboatmen must have known, but they had to look for their rescue comrade. As darkness fell, *Green Lily* started to break up, scattering oil, steel hatches and cargo across the sea. *Michael and Jane Vernon* took a huge wave, which peppered debris and smeared oil all over her. There was no point in carrying on, Hewitt decided. 'When I called off the lifeboat search for Bill Deacon that night it was because we had almost pitch poled, and I was very aware that my crew were on deck in very dangerous conditions.' In the back of his mind was an incident from a few years earlier: 'One of my crew went overboard during a service and the first thing that came to mind as I saw him go over was, "What shall I tell his widow?" Thankfully I didn't have to tell her anything! I'm sure all coxswains are more conscious of the safety of their crews rather than their own.'

The next day, all that remained of *Green Lily* was a slab of flat steel on the rocks. The lifeboat was given a thorough examination. Part of the toe rail and the fendering had been ripped away but even at the point of greatest impact the hull showed only a tiny patch of damage, 5cm by 22cm. It is impossible to know whether Lerwick's previous lifeboat, a fibreglass Arun with half the engine power, could have coped with this rescue, but both coxswain and headquarters were sure that she would have

Hewitt and Margaret Clark are welcomed aboard QE2.

sustained heavy damage. As Hewitt Clark, not a man to make a fuss, said of his lifeboat, 'She did well, she's amazingly strong.'

Like most coxswains who face severe pressure Hewitt always found it took time to wind down. 'I did find it hard to relax particularly after a big rescue. When I came home, I very often didn't speak about it until a few days later and Margaret was aware of this and would never ask too much detail.'

The RNLI acted quickly to evaluate the rescue, awarding Hewitt a gold medal to add to his collection of one silver and three bronzes. His crew all received bronze medals and there was a joint vellum award for the helicopter crew. Bill Deacon was awarded a posthumous vellum by the RNLI and, much later, after a welter of bureaucracy, received official recognition from the government.

A SURVIVOR'S STORY

It is extremely rare to have a full account of a rescue from a professional merchant seaman who has been saved. While the story of the rescue from the Ecuadorian ship *Bonita* is well documented by the RNLI, the survivor's side has never been recorded. But John Aicher, Norwegian chief engineer of the *Bonita*, wrote down his recollections some fourteen years after the rescue and they were translated into English in 2001. Uniquely, we can tell the story from both sides.

Bonita was an 8,400-ton refrigerated ship, built in 1971 and capable of 22 knots. She was registered in Ecuador and most of the crew were Ecuadorians except for the officers, who were Norwegian, and the Spanish refrigeration engineer. The captain had his wife and two-year-old son with him, and the first engineer had his wife and two teenage daughters. Altogether, there were thirty-six people on board.

Bonita was loaded with sacks of fertiliser in Hamburg and left the River Elbe, bound for Panama, on 12 December 1981. She would then go on to Ecuador to take on bananas and return via Cork, Antwerp and Bremerhaven. She never even made it to the Atlantic.

As *Bonita* made her way down the English Channel on Sunday 13 December the wind strengthened, reaching hurricane force with driving snow. Aicher was familiar with the vessel and knew her to be in good condition so although she started rolling heavily, he was not unduly concerned, merely trying to lash down his belongings as they fell off the shelves in his cabin. The captain reduced speed in the storm but around midday, 40 miles north of the Channel Islands, *Bonita* was hit by two giant waves on the port side, making her list heavily to starboard. A third wave then struck the exposed underside of the hull and *Bonita* was heeled over, with no chance of rolling back as her cargo had shifted.

The engineer and the electrician clambered down to the engine room to keep the generators running, then went up to the bridge, where chaos reigned. The captain was doing his best to steer a course while his wife and the rest of the watch lay in a heap on the starboard side of the bridge. He needed full power so Aicher struggled back to the engine room. Meanwhile the second engineer had slipped on the sloping deck, hit the rail at great speed and crushed both legs beneath the knees. It later transpired that he had forty-eight fractures and a collapsed lung, and he spent seven months in traction.

Aicher, in the engine room, was making his way to the controls to give 18,000hp of thrust to maintain steerageway on the ship. Suddenly, the auxiliary engines stopped, the lights went out and the main engine also stopped, as it was designed to do in a power failure. Almost immediately the ship turned beam on to the seas and the rolling motion became even worse. The engine room door, now under water, gave way and tons of seawater poured in. Lubrication oil spilled out and Aicher was convinced that the main engine, weighing several hundred tons, was moving on its mounts as the flat bottom of the hull was battered by the sea. His account states baldly, 'The situation was far from ideal.' Wiping the oil from his eyes, he realised he was likely 'to drown like a rat down there'. This drove him to struggle out of the engine room to his cabin, where he grabbed his life jacket.

Shock and panic were spreading around the ship. Some of the Ecuadorians were so stunned they would not move. The radio operator had disappeared, so the electrician was trying to send out a Mayday.

As the list increased to 40 degrees it was incredibly difficult to get around the ship, but Aicher hauled himself up to the bridge to tell the captain the main engine had failed. There was no way to save the ship and no chance of launching the lifeboats in such weather. The captain broadcast a Mayday on the portable VHF radio. The people on the bridge were shaking from the cold and Aicher, with the electrician, wrapped them in flags. The injured second engineer kept passing out from pain. His legs swelled and his shoes had to be cut off.

By now, several ships were standing by and, although they could do nothing, their presence boosted morale on *Bonita*. An hour later, a Sea King helicopter arrived. Incredibly, in the 100mph gusting winds, the pilot managed to keep his winchman clear of the masts and swinging cargo crane and lowered him through the blizzard. It took several attempts but eventually the helicopter had the captain's wife, little boy and two others on board. The rotor blades were now icing up. The helicopter had to return to base.

As soon as Captain Moran knew his wife and child were safe, Aicher saw a burden lift from him and the captain swung back into action. A pilot ladder was hung over the starboard side of the hull, ready for the lifeboat's arrival.

Guernsey lifeboat coxswain Mike Scales and his crew had put out from St Peter Port at 2 p.m. John Petit, former coxswain and now both harbourmaster and lifeboat secretary, told them that the weather was atrocious, but the crew cannot have imagined the enormity of the task that faced them. From the early afternoon to the depths of the winter night they suffered slamming seas, bone-chilling cold and constant danger. When Scales arrived on the scene at about 4.30 p.m. the light was fading rapidly. He could see *Bonita*, listing heavily, her wing bridge actually in the water:

> I stuck the lifeboat's nose across the deck but I quickly abandoned that approach. One of *Bonita*'s two masts could have come crashing down on top of us on the roll and there was debris in the water. I thought, 'If we lose an engine, we've had it.' I went round the other side of the ship, the windward side where her bilge keel was out of the water. The seas were now very heavy. There was a pilot ladder hanging down with a chap halfway down it but it fell short of the water by 30ft and the man would have had to climb over the bilge keel. If he had dropped in the water he would have gone right under with the suction and we could not have got anywhere near him.

On *Bonita*, everybody was suffering from hypothermia, extreme shock and exhaustion. They were then told that rescue from the pilot ladder was impossible; they would have to crawl along the upper side of the ship, outside the guard rails, to reach the stern. The prospect was frightening in the extreme. The first engineer still had his wife and daughters on board, so he led them and some of the crew down to the main deck, through the guard rail and then on hands and knees on the outside of the hull to the back of the ship. Then Aicher and the electrician hauled the second engineer, with both legs broken, down ladders and along companionways which were drunkenly tipped over to 60 degrees.

Along the main deck a crew member was clinging to a hatch cover, his thigh broken and his foot pointing up towards his shoulder at a bizarre angle. Next to him the steward, still in white gloves, stood paralysed with fear. Seas were battering the hatches and the decks were awash. Aicher threw loose cables to the men but the steward lost his grip, fell into the sea and was killed as he hit the bulwark. His body, floating below them, was a grim sight for the remaining crew, lined up waiting for rescue.

Guernsey lifeboat *Sir William Arnold*. *(Brian Green)*

With helicopters illuminating the stern, Mike Scales drove the lifeboat, *Sir William Arnold*, in as close as he dared, the lifeboat rising and falling 50ft; at one moment it was level with the top of *Bonita*'s stern, the next below the propeller and rudder. It was impossible to get alongside so the plan was for the lifeboat crew, perilously exposed in the bow, to throw a line to the *Bonita* and for two people to grab hold of it together and jump as the lifeboat pulled back, to avoid the propeller and rudder.

As the first line landed, some of the Ecuadorians panicked. The engineer, his wife and children were stampeded, and as one teenage daughter jumped off the stern, one of the crew hung onto her leg and did not let go until they were pulled into the lifeboat. There was such a tangle of bodies that the second time the line was thrown nobody caught it and the engineer, holding his other daughter's hand, jumped straight into the sea. Once in the water, they were forced apart. The girl was picked up first and a helicopter, ever vigilant, picked out the engineer in its spotlight; if they had not, he would have disappeared into the inky black night.

Aicher takes up the account again:

The wind had backed northerly and the waves were 15m high when the children jumped. The captain, second engineer, electrician and myself were last in the line, clinging to the hull and we had no way of advancing to the stern in order to clear up the confusion that reigned there. Some did not dare to jump; others caused the heaving line from the lifeboat to part by making it fast. Many times, a new line had to be prepared on the lifeboat, which was rolling so heavily that the aerials touched the water. The lifeboat crew were professional in every way.

After many hours clinging to the hull I was so exhausted and frozen that I felt the urge just to let go and slide into the raging sea to get away from this nightmare. The thin boiler suit had been ripped to shreds by the wind and even my socks were gone. I shall never know completely how I avoided freezing to death before it was my turn to jump.

If Aicher was worried, so was Scales:

With that force of wind, the line was just being blown away. I had to get within about six feet of the vessel and even then it was only the sheer physical effort of the second coxswain, Peter Bougourd, which got the heaving line across to the people. We didn't have time for them to tie it round; it was just a matter of getting in there, contact and pull away for them to jump. Having something in their hands gave them confidence to jump in the water. And I had to control the lifeboat so that we were not picked up by the waves and driven into the stern of the ship.

Scales made fifty approaches, which took over 3½ hours. After rescuing sixteen people, he had to pull away for the frozen lifeboat crew to restore circulation to their chilled limbs. On *Bonita*, it was obvious that the injured second engineer could not jump so the officers signalled to a helicopter to lift him. They first had to assure the pilot, who had seen the lifeboat's line being tied to the rails, that they would not do the same with the winch wire. Then the helicopter came in low, so close that Aicher says he could have touched the wheels. The lifting strop was blown back in the wind and it took three attempts, even at such close quarters, for the electrician to grab it, get the second engineer in and see him lifted away.

When they saw *Sir William Arnold* draw away, the *Bonita* crew thought they had been abandoned. But Scales came back into the face of danger. Aicher describes how the lifeboat was driven by a sea right under the stern of the ship, and on another run in both of the lifeboat's engines seemed to stall, restarting just as the lifeboat was about to be smashed to pieces. He described that moment as 'heart-stopping'. Scales never reported it.

There were now only five left on *Bonita*. Aicher's account reaches a Butch Cassidy moment. Those who know the film *Butch Cassidy and the Sundance Kid* will know the memorable scene when Robert Redford and Paul Newman jump off a cliff into a river. Newman hesitates, as he cannot swim. Redford reassures him, 'Don't worry, the fall will kill you,' and they jump. Aicher's rallying cry to the electrician was, 'See you in Liverpool!' – then they jumped.

Aicher takes up the story again: 'We flew about 15 metres through the air before performing a belly flop in the trough of a wave. Although the water temperature was 3°C, it felt wonderfully warm. In the water, I heard Nils say, "Are you going to hang around, chief?" I replied, "I'll give you three guesses" before we were hauled on board the lifeboat.'

Captain Moran made his jump but there was still a petrified crew member at the rail, literally frozen with fear. Ten times the lifeboat went in for him until finally he fastened the heaving line round his wrists and was pulled off the ship and onto the lifeboat.

The survivors were in a terrible condition, piled into the lifeboat cabin among their own excreta and vomit. They had severe hypothermia and one man, who had jumped straight onto the lifeboat's deck, was in a coma. He died later in hospital. The lifeboat set out for Brixham, the nearest port, and eventually, after nine hours at sea, they tied up at 11 p.m. The Torbay crew, who had themselves been out on a rescue, were there to meet them, and sent the Guernsey men off to bed while they cleaned up the mess.

One man had been left on *Bonita*, still clinging to the hatch. Aicher had asked the lifeboat to get a helicopter to him, but *Bonita* was now keeled over to 90 degrees, waves hitting her funnel and would not last much longer. The helicopter was away, refuelling, when the injured man was swept into the sea. Standing by was the Cherbourg tug, *Abeille 10*, which had featured in the *Johan Collett* rescue eighteen years earlier. Carefully avoiding the cargo crane, the French skipper edged his powerful ship towards the man and scooped him up alive. When lifeboat mechanic Bob Vowles told John Aicher the news, he burst into tears: 'It had been the greatest regret of my life to leave him lying there on that hatch, powerless to do anything about it. It was particularly painful as he had brought his family aboard two years earlier and I got to know his children. The joy I felt there and then was unbelievable.'

THE AFTERMATH

Michael Scales was awarded a gold medal for his outstanding achievements and all the crew won bronze medals. The rescue left scars on both survivors and rescuers. Just six days after the *Bonita* rescue, the Penlee lifeboat was lost. The following day, Mike Scales was in the BBC studios for a long-standing appointment to appear on *Jim'll Fix It*. He went through the programme in a daze, keeping up appearances but deeply troubled by one constant thought – it could have been his crew. The thought probably worries him still.

The *Bonita*'s crew had mixed fortunes. Many of the crew suffered psychological damage and were unable to put to sea again. Second engineer Knutsen spent eighteen months recovering and did get back to sea for a while but eventually he had to retire on welfare. Aicher carried on, as did the captain, first engineer and refrigeration engineer. Aicher ends his account by saying that all were going strong 'at least on the surface'. In the midst of stirring stories of gallant rescues, there is rarely space for the painful and often lingering after-effects.

CHAPTER FOUR

Designed for Danger

Speed is the most obvious difference between modern lifeboats and those of Henry Blogg and Dick Evans. For many mariners the faster boats have proved to be their salvation, but for the most extreme rescues it is the power of the boats (which of course gives them their speed) that has made all the difference.

The reason is that it is rare for merchant ships to sink suddenly, though it does happen. For instance, in 1987 the ferry *Herald of Free Enterprise* capsized in minutes off Zeebrugge because her bow door was not shut, and in 1994 the same happened to the ferry *Estonia* in the middle of the Baltic Sea when her bow door was wrenched off in a storm. It is more likely that a large ship will succumb gradually, either taking in water and slowly listing or losing power and being pushed towards the shore. Her captain will have time to put out a distress call and there will at least be the chance of a rescue.

For the rescuers, once they reach the stricken vessel, the hazards are the same as they always have been and that is when things get horribly dangerous.

A helicopter winchman on the end of his wire is a lonely and vulnerable figure, no matter how powerful the aircraft above him. He can be smashed into masts, rigging or the bucking ship itself, swept overboard, even have his wire cut by his own air crew if it snags.

Lifeboat crews are just as vulnerable. No matter how quickly they reach the scene, they need to come close in alongside the ship to take people off. Now they have the power to get in and out quickly.

Whereas the rescues of Evans and Blogg are characterised by their lifeboats being swept, out of control, onto the decks of ships or smashing into their sides, coxswains now have mighty engines twenty-five times more powerful. The change in the rescue techniques means that instead of making a careful run in and trying to keep the lifeboat alongside as long as possible then laboriously pulling clear, the modern boats can dash in and out in seconds, responding almost instantly to throttle changes. But the dangers – swinging ship's boats, powerful wave surges, sudden shifts of cargo – run in an uncannily familiar thread through the greatest rescues.

SAFETY FIRST

There will never be a perfect boat. Perhaps more than any form of transport, boat designs are riddled with contradictions. If you want to go fast, you need powerful engines. However, they need plenty of fuel, and the added weight reduces your speed. Greater strength will mean greater weight, and greater range and endurance means more fuel, hence more weight.

Designing a lifeboat with strength, speed, range and the ability to survive a capsize is a tough task and full of compromises. To see how designs have advanced with increasing rapidity in the last fifty years, we need to examine the three great ages of lifeboats.

The first, and longest, was the era of wind and muscle power. Boats were very basic and the shape, pointed at both ends, lasted for a century and a half, well into the period covered by this book. There were local variations but the basic lifeboat was an open wooden boat which launched off a beach over skids or from a carriage. This limited their weight, as they had to be hauled back up by winch, hand or horse power.

There were very few slipways. In the early days of the RNLI there was a flurry of building new boats but by the 1850s many were in such poor condition that crews would take their own fishing boats to sea. It is noteworthy that in the famous 1838 Grace Darling rescue, when she and her father set out from the lighthouse in their skiff, the rescue attempt from the land, in which her brother took part, was in a local fishing boat, not the lifeboat.

In 1851, revitalised under the leadership of the Duke of Northumberland, there was a grand competition for lifeboat designs and it was agreed that the standard lifeboat would be self-righting. This was achieved by fitting high end boxes – sealed compartments at bow and stern, buoyant because they were filled with air – and by making the boats narrow in beam and relatively light to allow the righting. They were very unpopular with many of the crews, who preferred a broader, heavier more seaworthy craft and were prepared to take their chances if it capsized. This resentment of being given 'lively' self-righters that bounced around more in a storm is relevant to our story because it built up a prejudice against self-righting that was only solved in the 1950s.

Engine power was introduced in 1888 when the first steam lifeboat was built. Sir William Hillary, the founder of the RNLI, had written a pamphlet proposing steam lifeboats in 1824, barely six months after the RNLI was founded. His letter to the RNLI committee survives in the Institution's archives: 'I have the honour of laying before you a small manuscript on the practicability of constructing a steam lifeboat – and also on the extinguishment of fire onboard of vessels at sea.' The committee did not take up his ideas, nor did the judges in the 1851 competition for new lifeboat designs. The RNLI was concerned that paddles or propellers would get tangled up with ropes and wreckage, so the first three steam lifeboats were jet-propelled. Water was drawn in, accelerated by a turbine wheel and ejected through nozzles. Although a harbour lifeboat in Poole used a similar system in the following century, jets were tried in the Medina and considered for the Tamar class but not used again by the RNLI until it stationed lifeboats on the River Thames in 2000. The early steam boats proved too cumbersome, needing the constant attention of two engineers to keep up steam, and only six were built by the RNLI. They were also much more expensive to build and maintain; a new steam lifeboat cost £5,000, with annual running costs of £800, as opposed to a sailing and pulling boat at £710, with free power from the wind and the crew's muscles.

THE ERA OF ENGINES

The second era was that of engine power in conventionally shaped boats. Still pointed at both ends, but powered first by petrol and then diesel engines, these lifeboats were still similar in performance to fishing vessels. The first petrol engine was fitted to a lifeboat in 1904. As usual, the RNLI was cautious, and sails were retained, with coxswains being told, 'The motor is an auxiliary to the sails which latter are the principal motive power.' To show that they were taking this new-fangled device seriously, the autumn 1905 edition of the *Lifeboat Journal* said, 'It will be satisfactory to the supporters of the Royal National Lifeboat Institution to know that the subject of placing motors in existing lifeboats and designing new lifeboats to carry them has occupied a very large part of the time of the Committee of Management and officers.'

The problems of fitting engines into the existing fleet were considerable, some real and some imagined. How could an engine be fitted without destroying the balance of the boat? How could the engine be prevented from racing when the propellers came out of the water as the boat pitched? How could a petrol fire be prevented? How could the propellers be protected to stop them catching on ropes or fishing nets? It was not long before the value of engines was recognised and the first custom-built motor lifeboat was completed in 1908. Diesel engines were introduced in 1932, and by 1936 even the smallest lifeboats had twin engines for both power and safety.

Their hulls, which sat in the water displacing the equivalent of their weight, were limited to a speed of around 9 knots. The speed of any displacement hull is limited by its waterline length. No amount of power can make it go faster than

1.3 times the square root of the waterline length in feet, which gives approximately 8 knots maximum for a 34ft boat. It is one of those wonderful arcane facts of boats and the sea. However, to get extra speed, a different form of hull is needed.

THE AGE OF SPEED

The third era has been that of speed. Top performance racing boats commonly reach speeds of over 60 knots and the world water speed record stands at 220mph for a propeller-driven boat and 317mph for a boat with jets. To achieve such speeds, very light structures are needed with enormous engines to push the planing hulls right out of the water so that at top speed only the tiniest amount of hull causes any resistance. These boats have very short endurance and are inherently unstable at speed. But the principle of a planing hull, which lifts out of the water to reduce resistance at speed, is the only way to make a boat go faster and was adopted to make the current generation of lifeboats.

The RNLI has always been cautious in adopting new designs. The admirable ambition of achieving high safety standards and ensuring every innovation is tried and tested before it is adopted slows the pace of change, and a new design now takes the best part of a decade to get from conception to working production models. It is a measured pace, forced by the conflict of embracing new technology but ensuring the highest safety standards for the crews.

It is not only technology but also increasing expectations that have forced design changes. Fifty years ago, lifeboats were expected to survive by avoiding trouble. If they capsized, it was likely that the crew would drown. Then came reliable self-righting boats which would come upright after a capsize and hopefully be able to limp back to safety. In the last two decades, the stakes have been raised again to equip lifeboats to survive a capsize and carry on with their rescue mission. There is even the aim to survive a pitch-pole, when the boat is thrown bow over stern. For a huge 40-ton boat, the stresses of such an event are enormous. No other boat or ship is expected to survive these conditions, which is why no other boat or ship is designed like a lifeboat.

Lifeboat capsizes were relatively frequent up to the 1950s. While the idea of self-righting went back a century, George Lennox Watson, appointed as the RNLI's consulting naval architect in 1887, had promoted larger, heavier, non-self-righting boats, and these and their successors were popular with the crews. By the early 1950s there were no self-righters in the fleet. Then in 1958 Watson's successor, Richard Oakley, came up with the answer. The idea of taking sea water into tanks in the boat to add weight and thus stability dated back over

The old and new – Bridlington swap an Oakley for a Mersey lifeboat.

a century. Oakley devised an ingenious way of using the water's mass to bring the boat upright if it capsized. He placed an empty tank in the superstructure of the boat and connected it to the ballast tanks by pipes and non-return valves. Now if the boat turned upside down the water rushed into the superstructure tank, set to one side of the boat. Unstable in this position, the boat quickly righted, shed water from the upper tank and took in more ballast water.

Oakley's design opened up the possibility of making the whole fleet self-righting though this was not achieved for another thirty years, during which time capsizes took thirty-five lifeboatmen's lives. There was a belief in some quarters that the ultimate heavy-weather boat, the 52ft Barnett, which was strategically placed at the wildest, most exposed lifeboat stations, would not capsize. So, while Oakley class lifeboats were gradually introduced, and a larger 48ft 6ins version was brought in, non-self-righters continued to be built for another five years, serving well into the 1980s.

Two dreadful disasters in Scotland changed the RNLI's mind about their boats.

London Lifeboat Day fell hours after the loss of the Longhope lifeboat. *(Syndication International)*

ORCADIAN TRAGEDY

The dramatic history of the RNLI is neatly encapsulated in a row of blue cloth-covered volumes in the peaceful setting of the headquarters library. Starting in 1852, the *Lifeboat Journal* has faithfully recorded the major events of the RNLI, rather formally, but by its very nature as a quarterly magazine it fails to make connections across the decades. Turn to volume 40, spanning the period March 1967 to September 1969. On page 531, there is a stirring account of Dan Kirkpatrick's 1968 rescue, in the Longhope lifeboat, of fifteen men from a Grimsby trawler which won him a silver medal, making him the only serving coxswain with three silvers. Just seventy-seven pages later, the deaths of Dan and his crew, eight in all, is told. Dan and his two sons died, along with mechanic Robert Johnston and his two sons, James Swanson and Eric McFadyan, who was only twenty-four years old.

Early in the next volume, news creeps in of another Scottish tragedy, the capsize of the Fraserburgh lifeboat: five dead, one survivor. It was a turning point for the RNLI. While Longhope had been accepted as brave men overwhelmed by terrible seas, something about Fraserburgh made the press and public angry and suspicious. It was partly that the two events were only ten months apart, and partly that at Fraserburgh there was a survivor, so perhaps there could have been more. The lifeboat had recently had new engines fitted, so questions were asked about her stability. Yet it was mainly an emotional response to the loss of thirteen lifeboatmen within a year that caused the competence and capability of a charity to run a vital emergency service to be questioned. The disasters were terrible, though it was almost accepted that there would be such catastrophes from time to time. The magazine noted, with some satisfaction, that it was seven years since the last major disaster, at Seaham, and later described 1969 as 'a year of triumph for the lifeboat service'.

Dan Kirkpatrick, whose bravery medals had won him respect throughout the RNLI, was a veteran of the Pentland Firth, one of the most notorious stretches of water in the British Isles. Tides and currents race through at up to 12 knots, throwing up fearsome seas. Dan also knew about rescues from ships aground on the treacherous rocks and skerries around the firth; his last silver medal rescue was for saving fifteen men from the trawler *Ross Puma*, aground on the Little Rackwick Shoals, at the base of 400ft cliffs.

Tragedy came on the night of 17 March 1969, when the Liberian ship *Irene* reported that she was in distress in a south-easterly gale. Her exact position was not known, but coastguards did know that the lifeboat would be needed and asked Longhope honorary secretary Jackie Groat to authorise a launch. On such a foul night, Dan Kirkpatrick decided to take seven men with him and the lifeboat *TGB* raced down the slipway at 8 p.m., meeting very rough seas, a heavy swell, rain and snow flurries. The lifeboat reported her position, and was seen by lighthouse keepers, until her last message at 9.28 p.m. Two minutes later the principal keeper of the Pentland Skerries lighthouse saw the lifeboat, and he watched as her stern light faded into the storm at 9.35 p.m.

Meanwhile *Irene* ran aground and the coastguard cliff-rescue team eventually reached her around midnight, rigging a breeches buoy to pull the crew across the chasm between ship and shore. All were saved.

Shortly after 10 p.m., Kirkwall coastguard passed a message that conditions alongside *Irene* were 'almost impossible'. Nobody knows if the Longhope men ever got the information, for there was no response. Coastguards, Jackie Groat and lifeboat inspector Brian Miles were getting increasingly worried and coastguards were sent to vantage points on the east coast of South Ronaldsay to search.

Kirkwall's 70ft lifeboat was also at sea and the coastguard asked her to close on the *Irene* and rendezvous with the Longhope boat, in the hope that she might be there. In the thick of the storm, it was virtually impossible to see another vessel, so the coastguard called out a Shackleton aircraft and a helicopter.

Through the night nothing was found and three more lifeboats, from Stronsay, Thurso and Stromness, put out in the morning, joining what was now a desperate search for the Longhope men. At 1.40 p.m., everybody's worst fears were confirmed. Thurso found the Longhope lifeboat upside down, 4 miles south-west of Tor Ness. She took her in tow, escorted by Stromness, and reached Scrabster harbour after seven agonising hours. There were seven bodies in the boat; James Swanson, either swept overboard before the capsize or washed out of the boat as she turned over, was never found.

The formal enquiry determined that the highly experienced and tough crew, afloat in a well-found lifeboat, probably met their fate shortly after 9.30 p.m. when the boat was overwhelmed by very high seas and maelstrom conditions. The flood tide, running south down the east side of South Ronaldsay, met the east-going stream north of the Pentland Skerries, which is roughly where the lifeboat was last seen. As the two masses of moving sea met, they would create huge, turbulent blocks of water. The damage to the lifeboat's metal super-structure was probably caused by these seas.

Brian Miles, only thirty-two, had to visit every family to confirm their loss. After a difficult trip to reach Longhope, he stood above the tiny hamlet of Brims. 'I looked down the hill and it suddenly struck me like a physical blow. We had taken someone out of virtually every house.'

Each family asked what had happened to the crew of the *Irene* and expressed gratitude that they had been saved. 'My husband would have been pleased to know that,' said one widow.

THEY WILL NOT LET FEAR BE THEIR MASTER

The Fraserburgh story of 21 January 1970 was no less dramatic. The lifeboat *Duchess of Kent* had been called out to a Danish fishing vessel *Opel*. She had a leak in her engine room, which pumps were failing to stem, and, although the situation was not urgent, her skipper's message to Denmark was passed on to the coastguards in Scotland. The Fraserburgh lifeboat honorary secretary, the man who authorised launches, was ill, so the coxswain took the decision to launch the lifeboat just after 6.30 a.m. Unlike at Longhope, there is no doubt about what happened; it was witnessed and the very moment of capsize was captured on film. As the morning wore on, the situation on *Opel* worsened, so the lifeboat's mission became more urgent and a Russian ship *Victor Kingisepp* also made for the *Opel*. Two other Russian trawlers, already on the scene, got a towline across to the *Opel* but the lifeboat was not informed and pressed on, now 36 miles off Fraserburgh. By around 11 a.m., she had reached *Opel*, but as the

Fraserburgh lifeboat (right), moments before capsize.

Fraserburgh lifeboat, actually capsizing.

coxswain closed in, the *Duchess of Kent* was hit by a huge breaking wave on the port bow. The lifeboat reared up, bow rising into the air to fall in a graceful arc over the stern as the boat plunged back into the water, upside down. John Buchan, William Hadden, James R.S. Buchan and James Buchan were drowned. Frederick Kirkness was never found. Jackson Buchan was pitched into the icy sea but managed to clamber onto the hull of the capsized lifeboat and twenty minutes later was picked up by the Russians. They lashed the lifeboat alongside and a cold war farce developed as lifeboat inspector Brian Miles was flown out to the *Victor Kingisepp* to negotiate the release of the lifeboat with the KGB man on the ship. The boat was not untied from the Russian ship until 5 p.m., some thirty-six hours after the capsize. It was towed back by Buckie lifeboat, the dead lifeboatmen sombrely laid on the deck.

The immediate aftermath of the Fraserburgh disaster was a massive outpouring of public sympathy – 10,000 people turned out for the funerals as Arctic winds roared around the bleak fishing port. In the church at the funeral, the convener of the Scottish Lifeboat Council, Lord Saltoun, said, 'I have never called lifeboatmen heroes. I have always felt that they are men who can appreciate the risks they run even better than I – but who strain their hearts to outstrip a comrade getting to the boat because they will not let fear be their master. Such were these men.'

There was also a frenzy of media criticism, questioning the competence of the RNLI, its procedures and its boats. The *Duchess of Kent* had recently been fitted with new engines, slightly altering her trim, so the waterline where the traditional lifeboat blue meets the white of the hull had had to be repainted. The press seized on this, speculating that the boat was unstable, adding to the sensation by claiming that the boat was overwhelmed by a 'freak' 60ft wave. The accusation was that RNLI lifeboats were too small and vulnerable for the wild waters off Scotland and should have restrictions placed on them. Lifeboatmen around Britain disagreed, though it is interesting that the *Lifeboat Journal* managed to get strong support from Welsh stations and none from Scotland. From Pembrokeshire, the Angle station, which also had a Watson class lifeboat, similar to Fraserburgh's, came a ringing endorsement of full confidence in their lifeboat, written not by their crew but by their treasurer, a retired colonel; from Fishguard, a more direct statement came from Coxswain Glyn Bateman, who said he had sailed in a Watson for twenty years and had always felt confident in it; in Beaumaris, Coxswain Harold Jones said, 'The lives of people at sea come before my fears.'

Nonetheless, the official enquiry posed some awkward questions for the RNLI. The report stated that too much was asked of the majority of lifeboats, which were expected to work both close inshore and out to sea. Could there not be more deep-sea boats, such as the 70ft type already in service at Kirkwall? Should not the RNLI take more external advice from government research facilities to improve lifeboat design and safety? Would not matters be clearer if there was better coordination between the coastguard and the RNLI (a question that resurfaced at the Penlee enquiry thirty years later) and if the RNLI had a formal system of deputies for authorising launches?

The RNLI reeled under the weight of scrutiny and criticism. The official enquiry was the most thorough examination of the RNLI since a select committee of the House of Commons investigated the lifeboat service in 1897. The conclusion was that the lifeboat *Duchess of Kent* was 'unfortunate' to encounter the very large wave which overwhelmed her. The coxswain, crew and the RNLI were blameless. The lifeboat was well equipped and seaworthy: 'No vessel can be guaranteed to survive all possible sea conditions . . . lifeboat rescue operations are, and always will be, extremely hazardous.'

Then the Chief Coastguard was highly critical in the national press and went on to hint that he might set up a fast rescue boat service. The RNLI committee, while noting that 'his comments were to be deplored', agreed that open confrontation with HM Coastguard should be avoided but that 'suitable reference to the article should be made in a press statement'.

Worst of all, senior officials at the Department of Trade and Industry wanted to bring the RNLI under government control, though the marine section of the department opposed this. The idea was strong enough to warrant an evasively worded denial at the first meeting of the government search and rescue committee, set up in 1971 to ensure better cooperation between the different rescue services. RNLI minutes record, 'Assurances had been given by the Department of Trade and Industry that at the present time and in the existing political climate, there were no plans to interfere with the independence of the RNLI nor were there any plans for the coastguard service to provide a rescue service afloat.' It took years to rebuild trust between the country's two main search and rescue organisations, the RNLI and HM Coastguard.

SELF-RIGHTING PROVED

The Longhope and Fraserburgh disasters led to the plan to make the whole fleet self-righting as soon as possible, though it took years to achieve as older designs still had plenty of life in them. While it was possible to design new boats to be inherently self-righting, an ingenious solution for converting many of the existing boats was also developed. This was to have a large air bag fixed, under a cover, to one side of the cabin. If the boat capsized, valves would automatically release compressed gas to inflate the bag and bring the boat back upright. The principle is a bit like safety air bags in cars (a much later development) on a grand scale, and though it seemed a bit Heath Robinson, it worked perfectly.

Barra lifeboat, air bag inflated, is towed home by a coaster.

Two later Scottish capsizes on the same day lost no men thanks in one case to the air bag and in the other to a modern design. They also brought the next step change in thinking about lifeboat safety.

On the night of 18 November 1979 the Thames class lifeboat at Islay and the Barnett at Barra both set out to the aid of a Danish coaster, *Lone Dania*. Winds were gusting to force 12, seas were 30ft and there was estimated to be a one in ten chance of catching a sixty-footer. *Lone Dania*'s cargo had shifted. She was 37 miles from Barra. Both lifeboats capsized and righted with only minor injuries to the crews. It was a particular triumph that the Barra boat came upright, as she had been fitted with the air bag conversion, designed to keep the older boats in the fleet while new inherently self-righting boats were built.

However, the lifeboat was left disabled as loose ropes became bound firmly around her propeller shafts, the crew unable to cut them away in spite of a massive effort over five hours. Eventually another coaster, *Sapphire*, reached them and towed the boat to safety. Meanwhile, *Lone Dania* limped into Barra escorted by another Danish ship, and actually arrived before the lifeboat. The ship owners sent a large donation to the RNLI.

The RNLI's reaction was to devise ways of thinking upside down. Once again, the difference between a lifeboat and a commercial boat becomes apparent. No sane boat builder would provide a superstructure so strong that it can support the weight of the boat upside down – it is just too expensive. The same boat builder would not contemplate the fate of the engine oils and coolants if the engines are inverted, for if a fishing or merchant vessel turns over, that is the end of her. Then came the equipment. What was needed was a series of ways of keeping everything on deck – ropes, axes, anchors and so on – in place if the boat capsized, yet accessible for use at short notice. Different fittings and stowages were added, the aim now being to make a lifeboat survive a capsize and be capable of continuing on her mission, which is just what the

Salcombe lifeboat *Baltic Exchange* did when she capsized and righted in 1983. *TGB* and *Baltic Exchange* were both 47ft Watson class lifeboats, built in the same year, 1962. But for the air bag, the Salcombe men, like the Longhope crew all those years before, would have drowned.

THE YANK

The Thames class boat at Islay was an RNLI design developed from a highly successful US Coast Guard 44ft steel surf boat, known as the 44. This was the boat that revolutionised the RNLI fleet and heralded the era of fast boats.

She was first seen by an RNLI delegation in a film shown at the 1963 International Lifeboat Conference in Edinburgh. Cautious as always, the RNLI decided to try out this strange boat in home waters. With characteristic generosity, the US Coast Guard made one available together with one of its officers, Bob Witter. The secret of the 44's extra speed was in the shape of the steel hull. A pointed, flared bow helped to break through the waves and a flat section to the hull at the stern lifted the boat to stop it squatting down in the water, reducing resistance. The 44 also had over twice the engine power of conventional lifeboats and, although she was heavier, almost twice the speed.

Many RNLI crews were scandalised. Their boats had propellers in tunnels to protect them from damage on rocks. While the turbulence in the tunnels reduced efficiency considerably, it kept the props safe. The 44 was lively, wobbly even, and its propellers, drive shafts and rudders were completely unprotected.

The new boat was taken on a tour around the coasts of Britain and Ireland. Sceptical old fishermen and lifeboatmen would sit on the quaysides, sucking their teeth as this bright upstart of a boat paraded in front of them. Conscious that they would only be convinced if they saw something different, lifeboat inspector Harry Teare decided to take a calculated risk outside Whitby harbour. He chose an area scattered with dangerous rocky outcrops washed by the swell and drove the 44 right in among the rocks. It would have been folly to go in there in a boat of any size, but Teare knew the 44's manoeuvrability should see him through. A skilled coxswain can spin a 44 on its own axis. Teare teased the boat through the broken waters, risking little more than a dent in the boat and his reputation, and then calmly brought the boat, unscathed, into Whitby harbour. The old cynics may never have praised the boat but they never again criticised her.

And so, around the coast, the Yank, as the boat became affectionately known, or the Spam Can (because of her metal hull) as she was less fondly named, won increasing approval. The RNLI adopted the design formally, naming it the

The Yank. *(Grahame Farr)*

Waveney, and gained permission from Washington to build the boat under a licence with no charge attached. It became the workhorse of the fleet.

Charlie Bowry was one of the first coxswains to get a Waveney, at Sheerness. The power and manoeuvrability were soon apparent to him. 'You have only got to stick her up a bit on one engine or the other and she will go wherever you want,' he said. 'But immediately you take the way off the boat, if the wind is too fresh it will get hold of the Waveney's high bow and the boat will want to slew down wind.' This meant that in confined spaces near a casualty, the coxswain was constantly playing his throttles, but the power was the compensating factor, enabling a safe retreat. Charlie also found that the Waveney could be driven aground on sandbanks to reach grounded vessels even with its unprotected props: 'A Waveney will give as hard a kick astern as she will ahead, so that if you really throttle her up when you are coming astern, her stern will whip up in the air.' The boat would not be very stable when aground: 'a bit tight-ropeish because she tends to roll each side of the little keel she's got.' Charlie had an unconventional way of finding how far he could go up a sandbank. As the echo sounder started to register zero, he would put a man in the aft compartment and tell him, 'Let me know if you hear any clunks.' He admitted, 'It's a bit frightening for the lad that's standing down there. He can hear the shingle and the stones and everything that's chucking up around her. With a conventional lifeboat, working sandy areas like ours, you would have a job to get yourself off. With a Waveney you have got so much power that you can go and think, "Right, I want to come off now," and off you come. I have my boat out of the water for a bottom scrape every six months and there has never been anything wrong with my propellers.'

Inspired by the success of the Waveney, the RNLI tried to develop a larger version, which it called the Thames. It never really worked, though Dover and Islay, who had the only two of the class ever built, liked their boats enormously. In scaling up the Waveney and adding 6ft to her length, designers also altered the shape of the bow, and the boat needed several sessions of the nautical equivalent of plastic surgery to make her nose right.

Meanwhile, the Glasgow firm of G.L. Watson had been commissioned to design a brand-new fast hull which became the Arun, overtaking the Thames to become one of the most successful lifeboats of all time.

The Thames was further blighted by a financial crisis which hit the RNLI in the early 1970s. Inflation was in double figures; there was industrial strife. Money had been lost on the stock markets and, just as the headquarters in London was sold for the move to Poole (a recommendation from management consultants who thought a lifeboat service should have its headquarters near the sea), property prices tumbled. Money became so tight that there were meetings each morning to decide which bills the Institution could afford to pay.

Six Thames lifeboats had been ordered from Brooke Marine in Lowestoft, who had ordered in the steel. The RNLI could not afford to go ahead with the build and had to meet cancellation costs.

The Arun was proving a great success and so the Thames project was abandoned. Aruns were built one at a time. The first was a great sea boat, though like the first of most new designs she needed improvement. J.A. McLachlan, the designer at Watsons, wanted the hull to have chines – long strips of wood running the length of the hull to throw the spray away, add stability and improve the boat's performance. McLachlan had already designed an 18ft inshore lifeboat with these chines and it handled well at sea. Unfortunately, it had a high freeboard and it was difficult to haul people in from sea level. The same problem cropped up in the first Arun.

The McLachlan inshore boat was overtaken by the Atlantic 21, lower in the water when stopped and with inflatable tubes cushioning the survivors as they were brought inboard. Inshore lifeboat crews even developed a rather alarming

Safe but soggy – hauling a survivor into an inshore lifeboat. *(John Periam)*

technique to do this that was particularly effective with heavy, waterlogged casualties. It is very difficult to pull a heavy weight vertically at arm's length, so the crew grab the person and push them down into the sea, and the buoyant reaction forces them back upwards, giving an immediate upward momentum which the crew use to pull the person into the boat. It's unsettling for the survivor, who might think they are being thrown back, but it works!

The RNLI rejected the chines on the Arun and put a gentle curving slope to the deck on the second boat to make it easier to get at survivors in the water. This boat, made of wood, was sent to St Peter Port in Guernsey and was arguably the most elegant of the whole class.

Not satisfied, the designers fiddled with Aruns for their whole life so that no two boats in the class were identical. The hull was extended by 2ft to give a round rather than square stern to reduce the risk of damage to right-angled stern quarters. The next Aruns were made of fibreglass, prompting more cynical crews to name them Tupperware. The RNLI experimented with this new material by buying a 40ft glass reinforced plastic (GRP) boat based on a successful pilot boat design by Keith Nelson. It was non-self-righting and far from a normal lifeboat fit out but served as a useful experiment on how GRP performed. The boat, *Ernest William and Elizabeth Ellen Hinde*, was stationed at Calshot, where Southampton Water meets the Solent. Although she was moulded at Halmatic's coastal boatyard, the materials for her hull were made by Scott Bader in the middle of the country in Northamptonshire, miles from the sea. Later, steel hulls for the Tyne class would be welded in Derby!

The GRP boats were a great success, though after a time they took up water into the fibreglass through osmosis, adding up to 2 tons to the boat's weight. This became critical when some of the boats could not get up enough speed to plane and perform properly. Senior coxswains were disgruntled, as they knew the boat's true capabilities. So did the RNLI technical staff, who found another contributing factor to their underperformance to be the extra gear, such as coils of heavy tow ropes, put on the boats by the crews.

Expensive remedial action included stripping off the outer, blue, layer of GRP, allowing the hull to dry out and then re-sheathing the boat with a fresh layer of GRP. The blue colouring was partly responsible for the osmosis, so later hulls were made with a less pretty but more functional clear gel, and a later experiment, introduced by technical chief David Hudson was to put copper-nickel into the mix to cut down on weed growth.

Different engines were tried in the Arun fleet; one was made of steel and equipment layouts varied. The Aruns ended up like a family, all from the same stable but all individuals. They took their crews on countless rescues, winning scores of medals. No Arun ever capsized on service and no lifeboat crews were ever lost from them.

They continue as lifeboats in Chile, Iceland and China.

WOOD GIVES WAY

The quest for new materials was accelerated when the Oakleys, heralds of a safer era of lifeboating, suffered an ignominious end that was brought about by their unique design. The metal water tank, snug in the wooden hull, was designed to take in sea water when the boat launched and jettison it when the boat was rehoused. This is exactly what happened but small residues of damp sand were left in the tank. Salt water conducts weak electrical currents between different metals, which will then gradually erode. Because of this, sacrificial anodes, made of base metals, are fitted to boat's hulls and linked to the main metal fittings. The anode rots away and can be replaced, sparing the other fittings. However, in the Oakley, thousands of copper nails held the wooden hull together and the electrolytic action, which was expected to take place only at sea, continued on shore because of the damp in the metal tanks. To add to the problems, the Oakley was made by placing one layer of planks onto a frame, then covering it with a layer of calico, finishing off with another layer of planks. Over the years, the calico absorbed moisture and the wood around the nails gradually softened, dangerously weakening the hulls. It took years to have any effect, and as soon as it was noticed in the late 1980s, all Oakleys were given thorough emergency surveys. The worst were withdrawn and for a few months a handful of stations were closed. Repairing the boats was horrendously expensive, as they had to be completely replanked.

There was in any case a need to replace the Oakleys and a complex set of design parameters called for a faster boat that could be launched from a beach across skids, from a slipway or carriage, or could lie afloat. She had to be robust enough for all weathers, light enough for manual manoeuvring ashore, small enough to fit existing launching carriages and not sink into the beach, and have protected propellers. The design brief also required the boat to have double the speed of her predecessor and a steel hull, as the aluminium water tanks in the Oakleys had condemned the material in many people's eyes. David Hudson remembers studying the brief and concluded, 'It was full of so many competing requirements that it would have been impossible to meet them all.' He knew that steel would be too heavy for this boat, and had to persuade colleagues to try aluminium alloy by building a full-sized 'model' – hardly a prototype as it was never intended to be used operationally. First trials were disappointing as there was not enough speed, but, with changes to the hull shape and different propellers, 18 knots were achieved. Traditionalists still preferred steel to aluminium, so the idea of using fibreglass for these boats was unwelcome in some quarters. Even a better 'plastic' – made from radically different materials – would be mistrusted, so extensive tests of fibre-reinforced composite (FRC) were carried out. These mixtures of different cloths, with carbon fibres and resins, were already common in ocean racing yachts, which are kept as light as possible for speed. Lifeboats have to be much stronger.

Research officer Stuart Welford concocted a trial rig and dropped a 12kg steel projectile down a drain pipe from a height of 8.5 metres onto panels of different materials. The projectile went straight through wood, dented steel and aluminium and disappeared when it hit the FRC. Perplexed, Welford jumped back, startled, when it came rattling back down the pipe, having bounced off the FRC leaving no mark at all. To test the new material further, a hull was moulded and driven on and off the harsh shingle of Dungeness beach 243 times, representing twenty years of launchings, and was also dragged for a mile over a surface of shingle, sand and mud. The only damage was to the paint. Not satisfied, the designers then dropped the whole boat from a height of 4m into the water. Again, there were no adverse effects other than a crowd of drenched spectators – including a delighted Hudson. A further test of strength took place in Oslo. At the 16th International Lifeboat Conference, David Hudson took a

The testing rig for materials. Inset shows steel projectile.

sample panel of FRC to show it to the delegates. The square metre of material was light enough to hold in one hand, but strong enough to take the weight of a person jumping on it. US Coast Guard naval architect, Steve Cohen, was impressed and was invited by Hudson to do the jumping test. The panel was placed across two blocks of wood on the quayside just as the Deputy Commandant of the US Coast Guards walked past. Cohen hailed him. 'We need a fat admiral to jump on some plastic,' he said. The admiral obliged, the panel was unscathed, but Cohen's promotion prospects seemed, to outsiders, to be limited! FRC, remarkably light and stunningly strong, had proved itself and was used for twenty-four of the new Mersey class and all designs thereafter.

Dragging a Mersey lifeboat across shingle.

Faster lifeboats raised the awkward question of how many lifeboat stations were needed. Originally each coastal village with a lifeboat had its own territory, defined by how long it took to row or sail to a wreck. But as engines came in, so those territories expanded and they grew bigger again with faster lifeboats.

While it is possible to draw neat circles on a chart and calculate the rescue cover provided, life at sea is not so simple. Some ports and harbours will be busy, others less so. Some will have huge passenger ferries, which would need more than one lifeboat if there was an accident. Tides, harbour bars, shoals and reefs can all restrict the time it takes a boat to reach a certain point. Planning rescue cover is far from easy.

In 1920 the plan was to build a fleet of motor lifeboats and station them at salient points round the coast, not, if possible, more than 50 miles apart. The policy was rather prosaically described by Admiral Cunninghame-Grahame when he said, 'It is not small boats, as at present stationed in the bights [centres of bays] but large ones in the horns of the bays which the future will see.'

The 1970s and 1980s saw much more detailed planning, trying to match patterns of declining fishing fleets with rising yachting activity, and to cover strategic risks on passenger ferry routes and at busy container ports. This led to targets for the year 2000 'to reach 95 per cent of casualties within 30 minutes of launch and to reach virtually any point out to 50 miles within two hours of launch in fair weather'. The targets were far from statements of good intent. They helped the massive lifesaving organisation work out what was needed where; what sort of boats to build, how to mix all weather and inshore coverage, where to open and where to close stations. The last is a difficult process which has been going on since engines were introduced. Before then, the range of lifeboats was quite small, the sailing boats having the capability of going further than the rowing ones but most not venturing out very far. Virtually every fishing village had its lifeboat and stations were only a few miles apart. Motor lifeboats had a far greater range, so fewer stations were needed. The trouble was that the great strength of the RNLI, which is that it is an integral part of coastal communities, makes it an emotional matter rather than a rational one if a station is to be closed. The north-east and south-west of England, with a fishing fleet in every cove, bore the brunt of closures but they go on to this day. The number of stations shrank from 295 in 1900 to 154 in 1950, until the inshore lifeboats came along, often resulting in the reopening of stations that had been closed for years. In addition, the clear definition of cover highlighted some huge gaps, particularly on the west coast of Ireland, which had only three stations along its entire length, these receiving second-hand boats. There are now twelve stations along the western Irish coast to give proper coverage, and the newer stations have already established formidable reputations with some outstanding rescues.

So the shape of the lifeboat service is constantly evolving, but some communities feel so strongly that they set up independent services when the RNLI pulls out. The classic example is Caister, with such a proud tradition, much celebrated by the RNLI and highlighted by the disaster which gave this book its title. The RNLI sent a 44ft Waveney to Gorleston in 1967. Caister is only 5 miles away by sea. The Waveney, backed by an inshore lifeboat, can adequately cover a wide area, including the waters off Caister. The logic of this is difficult to dispute, but the emotion and tradition told Caister men something different; these were, after all, descendants of the crew who never turn back. They watched with sadness as the RNLI boat was taken away and immediately set about raising the money for a replacement, which they would run themselves. With backing from such people as Norfolk turkey farmer Bernard Matthews and comedian Jim Davidson, they succeeded and the Caister lifeboat service runs a very fine offshore lifeboat, maintaining cordial relations with the RNLI.

There are scores of independent sea rescue stations, most operating inshore boats. While the majority are good, they all have different standards, making it difficult for coastguards to know quite what they will get if they call them out. As a result the RNLI has taken on the unenviable task of trying to establish a baseline of common standards, which is no easy job, given the fierce independence of the different services and their suspicions of their larger, better-resourced big brother.

MORE SPEED

The 1980s planning exercise gave the impetus to develop boats with a top speed of 25 knots. Once again, two designs were developed at the same time, but this time not in competition with each other. To simplify the process, the naval architects worked out that a single hull design could be used for boats of different sizes simply by scaling it up. Usually in boat design such an elegantly simple principle gets confounded, but this time it worked perfectly, creating the Severn and Trent classes. Of course, there were teething problems, as happens with any prototype.

Large skegs, underwater fins fitted towards the back of the boat, were provided to protect the propellers. They were designed to break off if the boat hit rocks, leaving the hull intact, but unfortunately they were a little too willing to leave the ship and kept breaking free on trials, leading to the suggestion that they carry a freepost address for return to the RNLI in Poole. A new keel design was

The prototype Trent and Severn lifeboats on trial.

quickly devised, with the help of Lloyd's Register of Shipping, with twice the strength of the originals. The RNLI pointed out that with so many variables, such as the speed of the boat, sea conditions, and the size of an obstruction, it was impossible to be precise about when the keel would break away but calculated that it could withstand a horizontal load of at least 27 tons on its base.

Much more seriously, the prototype Severn was damaged at its full speed of 25 knots when it crashed down off a large sea when on passage with the Stornoway crew. There was visible cracking inside the boat and both the crew and lifeboat inspector for Scotland, John Caldwell, lost confidence in her as a boat for all weathers. After much soul-searching in the design office, modifications to both the skegs and the hull strengtheners were made, and the Severns and Trents soon gained the respect of crews, being tested in conditions where even Aruns would have struggled.

One of the first prolonged services in harsh weather for the Severn was at Harwich, where, after the boat's eight hours at sea, honorary secretary Rod Shaw was able to report that the only complaint from the crew was an irritating rattle from the cabin lining. After the earlier problems, the designers were happy to mark this down as a minor modification.

INSHORE LIFEBOATS

Independence and bloody-mindedness, combined with the ability to turn a Nelsonian blind eye, marked the innovation which may well have kept the RNLI afloat.

The idea of using small inflatable boats for rescue came from France, or, to be more precise, Brittany. With traditional Celtic independence, the Bretons had their own lifeboat service, Hospitaliers Sauveteurs Bretons, and had used inflatables since the late 1940s. Richard Oakley, designer of conventional lifeboats, asked lifeboat inspector David Stogdon to look at an inflatable boat with rescue potential as early as 1959, but Stogdon thought it would be rejected by the RNLI. In the early 1960s the Jersey Fire Brigade bought an inflatable and Stogdon organised joint exercises with the St Helier lifeboat. He was so impressed that he decided to carry out trials on the south coast of England. He persuaded Captain Tony Wicksteed from head office in London to spend days at sea in all conditions, getting soaked to the skin, tipped over in the waves and tossed up on the beach. They then toured Brittany, learning all the time. Unsurprisingly, the RNLI was highly sceptical. Here was a tiny open boat that blew away conventional seamanship. For example, a 9-knot lifeboat in a following sea (waves rolling up and breaking behind the boat) would slow down and put out a drogue (sea anchor) for safety. The tiny inflatable had enough power and speed to run away from danger and dodge the waves simply by opening the throttle. There was also the problem that the RNLI viewed casualties near the beach as the responsibility of local councils – an attitude completely reversed four decades later when the RNLI took on beach lifeguarding. The RNLI remained to be convinced and Wicksteed later noted, rather wryly, 'David had, at that time, a quite undeserved reputation for scattiness at head office. I remember turning to him and saying, "You'll never get this idea past the Committee of Management but I think I might."' So Wicksteed and Stogdon invited the chief inspector, Gerrard Dutton, to see for himself.

Stogdon took the boat out of Littlehampton on a windy day. The throttle became disengaged and within a minute the engine stopped. The boat was now out of control and was thrust into the heavy breaking surf. The first wave tipped the crew member out of the boat. Stogdon hung on as the boat, now full of water, was pushed towards the stern-faced chief inspector on the beach. Although the trial had turned into a farce, an important lesson was learned that day – even full of water, the inflatable was safe and stable. Luckily for Stogdon, there was another inflatable at sea that day and the chief inspector turned his gaze away from the RNLI trial to see how well these rubber boats could perform.

Inflatables were still treated with great caution, though agreement was reached to send one to Aberystwyth in 1963. Harold 'Hurricane' Harvey was the lifeboat inspector who launched her on the first trip and almost immediately telephoned head office to say she had capsized. By coincidence the RNLI's Committee of Management was meeting in London and when the news reached them there was shock and dread. At that time capsize meant deaths, and a trustee asked, 'How many lives were lost?' But this was one of the first lifeboat capsizes when no lives at all were lost, as both crew members scrambled ashore unscathed through the surf quite happily and were ready to go to sea again. It was only because of that question and the answer, 'None,' that the inflatable lifeboats were allowed to go on.

In truth, Stogdon's south coast trials had seen all sorts of escapades of capsizes, engine failures and people in the sea, which never reached head office, or the whole project would have been abandoned.

PSYCHEDELIC IINFLATABLES

The next huge step forward for inshore lifeboats was the creation of the rigid inflatable. There are competing claims for this concept but the RNLI's version came from another distinctive and determined outsider looking in. Admiral Desmond Hoare, after a distinguished naval career, became headmaster of Atlantic College in South Wales. The college still has a very special ethos, combining outdoor challenge and community service with an imaginative curriculum and an international outlook. It even runs its own RNLI lifeboat station with the crew being drawn from the students.

Having sailed, and seen others sailing, in the Bristol Channel, Hoare decided that there was a need for a fast rescue craft that could be launched quickly from a beach. It would have to be tough to deal with abrasive sand and shingle, but light enough to be manhandled into the surf. He started with an inflatable, which was too weak, so he added marine plywood to the bottom to help with the abrasion, and deck boards inside to strengthen the hull. Hoare worked out that by combining the characteristics of a surfboard and an inflatable boat, the critical and often dangerous part of getting off the beach through the surf line could be made much safer. The key feature of a surfboard, the flat section at the back, sits on the water, keeping the front safely above the sea. Soon, the marine ply and deck boards were transformed into a hollow hull with a solid deck and an inflatable tube attached. The rigid inflatable was born. Hoare continued to experiment and made a 17ft boat which he entered in a round Britain powerboat race. The name 'Psychedelic Surfer' was hardly likely to appeal to his fellow admirals on the

RNLI's committee but the race proved the concept of the rigid inflatable – basically a surfboard glued to a rubber tube and initially entitled hard bottom inflatables, overcoming the disadvantage of previous inflatables whose slack bottom fabric could prevent planing and which carried only a single engine.

Rigid inflatable boats (RIBs) are now so commonplace, with thousands of them all around the world, that few realise they had their origins at an outdoor adventure college in Wales.

Constant technical advances have turned the rigid inflatable into a highly sophisticated craft, with the RNLI versions having a righting mechanism and inversion-proofed engines. Once again, these are features that make no commercial sense, so the RNLI had to invent them. David Stogdon gathered an ingenious team around him and established the Inshore Lifeboat Centre in Cowes on the Isle of Wight. Outboard engines proved a particular challenge. The engines use a straightforward internal combustion process; an air and petrol mixture is exploded by an electric spark in a cylinder producing expansion which drives a piston. However, as anybody who has had trouble starting a car on a damp morning will know, water is no friend to the electrics or the fuel mix. The RNLI not only wanted to use outboards in extreme sea conditions but also to keep them working after they had been dunked if the boat capsized. The air intakes and exhaust outlets of an immersed outboard engine will direct sea water straight into the carburettor and cylinder. The engine manufacturers thought that trying to prevent this was a fascinating but uncommercial concept. After all, their customers wanted to stay upright and would call a lifeboat if they capsized. So engineers at the RNLI's Cowes base came up with a series of ingenious solutions to keep the sea water away from the electrics and out of the air intakes and exhaust. As manufacturers changed their engine designs every few years, so the RNLI engineers had to invent new modifications, testing them in special workshops in Cowes. They not only worked out how to stop water getting into the engine but also how to make it restart at the touch of a button.

To get the boat upright after a capsize, an air bag on a frame over the stern was inflated with carbon dioxide, pushing the stern out of the water. Crews are trained in the technique in the magnificent sea survival training pool at RNLI headquarters, a distinct improvement on the River Medina in Cowes, which used to carry unpleasant discharges from visiting yachts. The righting of the boat is a dramatic display to watch and made a marvellous feature at the London Boat Show when it was held at Earls Court. There were always divers on standby for safety and, to add to the drama, the demonstration crew were told to wait for about a minute in the air pocket between the tubes under the capsized boat. The pool at Earls Court is huge and takes a couple of days to fill. At the start of the

January Boat Show, the water was only just above freezing. On the first righting demonstration, the boat was tipped over, the crew stayed under as instructed, and as tension mounted, swam out, pulled the pin to release the gas – and the boat stayed upside down. The water was so cold that the rapidly expanding carbon dioxide froze in its valve, leaving the righting bag half-inflated. Ever resourceful, the helmsman swam round to the starboard side of the stern, hidden from the watching crowd, pushed up the transom and the boat lazily rolled round to the upright position.

The first seating console for the boat put the three crew in line, one behind the other. This prompted a jocular correspondence in a medical journal when a lifeboat doctor in the Bristol Channel area described a problem faced by his male crew members. When the boat dropped down off a wave, the crew were left momentarily airborne, crashing down to meet the seat that they straddled. One man had complained of a very painful landing as certain parts of his anatomy became trapped in the manoeuvre. The doctor's advice, to give a quick forward thrust of the hips just before landing, was practical but caused some alarm to the crew member in front!

The RNLI soon moved to a different seat layout, a T shape with the helm in front and a crew member on either side. The official reason was that the crew strained to see where they were going in rough seas, though the Bristol Channel men were probably pleased for other, more personal, reasons.

The first RIB to be used as a lifeboat was at Atlantic College in 1970, and the Atlantic 21 soon followed as one of the RNLI's most successful boats ever. With the Arun, the Atlantic redefined lifeboating, requiring new skills from crews but giving them a much greater capability.

The speed and power of the Atlantic 21 often stopped dramas turning into crises. Rod James of Hayling Island observed: 'When we describe a call-out some people ask why couldn't the casualty have sorted itself out. But the Atlantic, and the faster large lifeboats, respond so quickly that they often resolve a problem before it has become serious. It can be misleading. We've often crossed the bar and reached a casualty within a matter of four or five minutes and found them drifting into a situation which if left for another five or ten minutes would have been very serious.'

Alan Clark of Hunstanton also spoke of the boat's versatility: 'The Atlantic is a rapid response boat. Her speed is one of her greatest assets and can be paramount in saving life – but she can only be driven as hard as the sea will allow.'

Constant improvements were made in the next twenty years, leading to a larger, slightly faster version, the Atlantic 75, in 1994. Tinkering and fiddling, adding extra equipment, bigger engines, more strengtheners in the hull, increased the Atlantic's weight by over 50 per cent from 900kg to 1,360kg in twenty years.

As demand for more equipment made boats heavier and slower, in 2005 a further development was made, the Atlantic 85. This boat was bigger again, with two huge 115hp engines (as opposed to 70hp on the Atlantic 75) giving her a speed of 35 knots. To achieve this, the boat's hull is made of FRP, stronger and lighter than GRP. The 85 carries radar, for working in poor visibility and to find targets more quickly. While the crew remain exposed, with no cabin, the 85 remains very much an inshore lifeboat, but its capabilities push it close to a concept that evolved in the early 1980s, that of the intermediate lifeboat.

THE BIGGEST RIB

Stogdon and his team saw that RIBs had huge potential. The rubber tube, seemingly vulnerable to damage, could be made virtually impregnable by dividing it into separate sections. They demonstrated that on a simple inflatable with sectioned tubes, even if both bow compartments were punctured, the crew simply had to hold up the limp rubber and the side tubes would keep the boat afloat and get her home safely, if slowly. The tubes also gave enormous benefit in rough seas, absorbing energy from the waves and throwing spray away from the boat. In the rigid inflatable their buoyancy was only needed if the boat took on the extra weight of a large number of survivors, when the boat would settle onto the tubes and be driven more slowly. All these features led the Cowes team to develop a new, much larger boat, the Medina. Finally, technology and politics combined to defeat Stogdon, though only partially.

The Medina was a robust, safe, stable, fast 35ft rigid inflatable. It was developed by Stogdon's team at Cowes, not the qualified naval architects at Poole. It hit problems in trying to find reliable propulsion, with outboards, jets and inboard/outboard systems all being tried and found wanting. As the project developed, three boats were built. The Dutch lifeboat service heard of the boats and was so impressed that they signed a formal agreement with the RNLI to share the development costs. Within the RNLI, however, there was significant opposition to the boat. Lifeboat inspector Roy Portchmouth, in charge of the trials, went so far as to produce a Medina tie as a way of staff showing their support for the boat. The fact that he made such a move shows just how divisive the project was becoming.

Meanwhile, another approach was being tried to find an 'intermediate' lifeboat. The concept was for a boat with greater capabilities than an inshore

The mighty Medina, carrying over sixty people on a test run.

lifeboat but not with the full equipment or sea-keeping qualities – or the huge cost – of an all weather boat. The Medina was one contender and the other approach was to take a commercial boat and adapt it.

The Medina's competitor, the Brede, initially fared better. The robust 33ft boat, based on a Lochin hull and adapted to be self-righting, was a good workhorse. She was never regarded as fit for the worst weather, a view confirmed by lifeboat inspector Michael Vlasto when he was delivering a Brede to Scotland. Running up the Irish Sea in gale force winds and darkness, nobody on the crew could see where the waves were coming from. The seasoned inspector and crew were alarmed by the prospect, in the wild conditions, of their small boat being overtaken and swung round by the huge, invisible seas.

Later in their lives, surveys of some Brede hulls cast doubts on their structural strength, and the whole class was gradually phased out, though they continue to live on as lifeboats in South Africa.

As the Medina struggled to meet all its requirements, the RNLI decided to abandon development of the boat. The Dutch carried on working with David Stogdon, making bigger and better boats and now rigid inflatables of different sizes make up their entire fleet – and they swear by them.

RECENT DEVELOPMENTS

Modern lifeboats have a planned life of around twenty years, though this is flexible and it is usually the ability to get higher performance, rather than strength, that hastens replacement.

It takes five to seven years to get a modern lifeboat from the drawing board (or, nowadays, computer screen) to the water. This may seem strange, given that boats have been used for thousands of years and there are now millions around the world. It might be thought that by now every shape and size has been tried. It is also true that commercial craft, such the pilot boats and tugs that David Hudson used to work on before he joined the RNLI, can be designed and built in under two years. But lifeboats are unique; they are required to do things that no other boats can. There is a secondary reason, which is that the boats are approved by committees and crews alike and it is impossible to accommodate everyone's desires in a compact lifeboat.

Take the baby of the fleet, the humble 16ft inflatable. The material of the tubes is much tougher than most commercial inflatables. The tubes are subdivided into compartments so that if one is punctured the rest remain inflated. There is a tube under the deck boards to shape the hull and the boat can be tuned for optimum performance. The boat carries flares, a conventional anchor and a drogue, a spare propeller and tool kit, first-aid gear, a torch, an emergency aerial, heaving line, towing bridle, resuscitator, survival sheet, pressure gauge, bellows, survivor's life jackets, sheath knife and compass. The engine is protected against inversion by capsize or swamping. As inflatables go, it's up at the top end of the range for utility – and price.

That complexity multiplies as the boats get bigger and the demand for more power, speed and equipment grows, so the design process must be thorough. First, a specification is developed of what is required from the boat, the equipment it must carry, what might change over the boat's life, what the crews think. Then, what compromises can be made, for it is unlikely that the boat can encapsulate all views. The old competing enemies of weight and speed will enter the fray. The array of electronics, requiring power and space, will fight against seats, fire extinguishers, stretchers and a host of other equipment. Most important of all, will there be a boiler that can heat water for tea before the rescue is over!

Curiously, on one weight-saving exercise, a list of all loose equipment on the Severns and Trents was drawn with the aim of identifying heavy items that were not absolutely essential and could be removed. After thorough consultation, the only agreement was to take off a spare kettle – weight about 1kg!

Hull shapes are tested with scale models in long water tanks, performance being recorded by sensors and video cameras. The models are then fitted with motors and tested in open water. Then a prototype hull, barely fitted out, and ballasted to give the weight of equipment, will be built and trialled at sea, with different engines, propellers, rudder and keel arrangements. There are so many variables that it takes time to find the optimum combination.

Then production begins and often the first boat of the run still needs modification. The first 48ft 6ins Oakley had the steering position too far forward; the first Arun's decks were too high to reach survivors in the water and her wooden hull was holed on trials; the first Mersey did not steer well; the first Trent shed her skegs rather too readily. Trials, modifications and further trials keep going in a cycle until the boat is safe and seaworthy to a higher standard than any other boat at sea. A lifeboat takes an age to develop because it has to be as strong and reliable at the end of its life as at the beginning.

The latest boat in production, the Tamar, shows just how difficult the whole process has become. It needs to launch down a slipway, then be hauled back up again (which no commercial craft do), carry a daughter boat, be fitted with a complex set of electronics for communication and navigation, and incorporate, in a hull limited in size and weight by the fact of living in a boathouse with a slipway, equipment for a wide range of rescues, from fires to flooded engine rooms. The ingenious design of the stern copies the concept developed by the Germans, and followed by the Norwegians, of launching a small boat from the stern. However, those nations do not have the variations in coastline that bless our islands with a wonderful variety of scenery but blight the lifeboat designer's life as he tries to work out how to make one boat accommodate so many conflicting requirements. The RNLI has now managed to reduce the number of these spectacular slipway launches to the minimum, preferring the option of having boats afloat in harbours wherever possible.

The Tamar can do both – lie afloat or rattle down a slipway to create the perfect image of the lifeboat splashing into the sea in spume of spray. Hardly anybody thinks about the reverse of the process – how the lifeboat gets back up into the boathouse. It's a potentially very dangerous procedure, as the boat picks up lines from buoys either side of the slipway, edges in backwards to put the toe of her stern on the slip. Then one of the launching crew has to go down with the huge hook that will fit into the boat to pull her back up. It's a dangerous task if the boat is ranging up and down in a sea, so attempts were made to find an automatic system where the boat would drive back and slot into a haul-up system, but it just didn't work. So a man must still go down to the bottom of the slip, which is greased up to take the boat, and make a physical connection.

The Tamar slipway boat carries an inflatable in her stern. *(Derek King)*

It is remarkable that few lives have been lost from this perilous procedure – men have been knocked from the slipway onto rocks, to their death – and it emphasises that the whole team is needed to get a boat to sea and back safely, for there is a point at which the coxswain is suddenly powerless and completely in the hands of his recovery crew.

The other factor that is eclipsed by the drama of a lifeboat launch is that the slipway and carriage boats live in houses. The great advantage of having a boat out of the water is that she will stay weed free and not suffer from osmosis. The disadvantage is that she has to be launched and recovered, unlike a boat afloat, which is quick to get away and to moor on her return. The coasts of Britain and Ireland, so varied in their geography, do not allow a choice in most locations, which is why some boats are in harbours, while others are launched across beaches and sent down slipways.

The boathouses have been enlarged and modernised extensively in the last thirty years. Major changes were needed to accommodate drying rooms for protective clothing, places where the crew could meet for training sessions, and often shops for fund-raising. Many of the new ones, sensitively designed to fit in with their locations in areas of outstanding natural beauty, have won design awards yet remain wholly functional. There is scope for a whole book on lifeboat houses – a limited readership, to be sure – but the range, from Victorian chapel through functional corrugated shed to architect design statement, is fascinating.

CHAPTER FIVE

All at Sea

However stirring and dramatic, the gold medal rescues, harsh, extreme and dangerous, do not represent ordinary lifeboating. While many lifeboat crews experience intense discomfort and all will be called upon to use skill and initiative, most rescues represent little risk to the crews as their boats, equipment and training are all geared to doing the job safely and efficiently. But no crew member knows what they may have to face and when, and that is the point. It is not an option, when the wind howls around the harbour on a dark winter's night, to ignore the call to go out, quite literally, into the unknown. For if you fail to join your comrades, even as a volunteer, you're out of the crew.

The other point that every gold medal rescue makes, as powerfully now as in the days before helicopters, radios and high technology, is that lifeboats will always be needed in extreme situations. There was, in both the Penlee and Lerwick rescues, a clear belief that powerful ocean-going tugs and rescue helicopters could cope. The lifeboats were put on standby, but it was hoped that they would not need to be sent into raging storms. At Penlee, the lifeboat managed to rescue seafarers where a helicopter could not, though in the end all perished. At Lerwick, the wonderful combination of helicopter and lifeboat working together saved a whole ship's crew, with the terrible loss of a heroic helicopter winchman.

So while most rescues – on average quite short, in moderate conditions – are unremarkable, the need remains for every crew member to be trained and ready and every boat to be built and equipped for the most extreme conditions, challenges that most will never face. As usual in real life, the best stories often come from seemingly ordinary events.

ANOTHER LITTLE SITUATION DEALT WITH

Charlie Bowry of Sheerness was a great raconteur and fond of tales that showed how no two rescues are ever the same and that solid seamanship must be complemented by imagination and initiative. Take his account of the rescue, in

Charlie Bowry of Sheerness with his son, Charles. *(Terry Norman)*

the lifeboat *Gertrude*, of a man in a cabin cruiser that had run aground on mud flats:

> We saw red flares go up underneath Eastchurch Cliffs. A 46ft cabin cruiser was in the surf and the wind was north-easterly. There was no time for anything fancy. I got *Gertrude*'s stern up to wind, right up into the sea, and I charged her in. Hit the dirt; she travels a bit; then she comes up all standing because her aft end's aground although her bow is still afloat. Now that's handy because, although her bows may be wishy-washing around, you never get a swing-round, broach-to situation with the stern aground, as the bow, being still afloat, always blows down wind.
>
> The tide was coming in and the sea started to wash in our open-backed wheelhouse. Now as the sea was coming up it was riding us up as well so I drove *Gertrude* and drove her and drove her and we landed up 200ft from the cruiser. All stopped. Washed right through. All you could see was the top of the wheelhouse and the mast. The rest was under the 'oggin because I had driven all the rise out of her.
>
> A helicopter, he's arrived now and he's doing his sort of fluttering bit up there; he told the coastguard he thought I had sunk, because he couldn't see a

lot of me, do you know what I mean? We put a couple of gun lines in but the fellow on the cruiser couldn't get them. Now, I am drawing 4ft 9ins and I'm in 4ft 9ins of water and the breakers are rolling through. So we are washing round the deck and I'm beginning to run out of ideas.

Now, I come across this big lad of mine, Malcolm. I says to him, 'How tall are you Malcolm?' He says, 'I'm 6ft 3in, aren't I?' 'Well', I says, 'there's only 4ft 9ins of water there, cock. Off you go!' Well, Malcolm blows up his life jacket and veers into the cruiser. Climbs aboard. 'Morning Harry,' he says, because we know the bloke quite well. 'Have you off here in a minute, mate.' Turns up a towline. I just back off, dragging Harry off with us and we went home, picking up another yacht on the way because his rudder had fallen off as well. And that's another little situation dealt with.

SAVING BIRDS

Another of Charlie's favourite tales was when a cabin cruiser broke down in the Medway: 'We came alongside him and there's no sign of life, just the boat bobbing up and down. So I put one of the lads on her, he opens up the hatch and there's this bloke with a bird and all she's got on is this little pair of red socks. "Shall I stay on to look after the tow?" asks my lad. So I says, "No, you leave 'em to it," and we towed them back.'

Best of all was Charlie's tale of the Radio Caroline rescue. It contrasts starkly with the RNLI's official account, which starts, 'On the evening of March 19th 1980, the radio ship *Mi Amigo* was reported to be dragging anchor in the vicinity of NW Long Sand Beacon. Sheerness lifeboat under the command of coxswain Charles Bowry slipped her moorings and in an easterly strong gale, force 9, headed down the Thames estuary against the flood tide.'

Charlie remembered:

Got under way, six o'clock in the evening. Force 9 north-easterly. Head into it. No water, really from the start. We were sticking to the fairways because, in the Thames estuary, even in the fairways you can be in something like 17m and it comes up to 7 between fairways and then goes back to 17 or so in another fairway. And the motion of the sea across the shallow patches is bad news because it's fluffing it up there.

Driving spray and heavy seas forced the lifeboat to reduce speed and visibility was almost nil.

Sheerness lifeboat. *(John Mercer)*

I managed to hold the revs on the lifeboat until the Red Sand Tower and then she was coming out and burying herself up to the wheelhouse windows and there was a lot of vibration in the boat. I fetched her back to 2,000 revs and that wasn't too bad. We couldn't see anything at all. Nothing out of the wheelhouse windows. Nothing on the radar. So I stuck two lookouts, one on each side, just inside the safety lines and got them to identify the characteristics of the buoys they could see and give them to me in degrees off the bow. And I found my position that way.

It was decided that the lifeboat should stand by until *Mi Amigo* refloated on the rising tide. Two hours later, the ship did refloat but could not start her pumps and she was rolling and pitching violently, shipping heavy seas.

Mi Amigo gave a shout that she had come afloat. Well, she was only a little ship. I don't suppose she was drawing much more than about 8ft of water at most because we had a rise and fall of 12–15ft on the echo sounder. I run up on the neon sounder and then, because I like to see the shape of the bottom coming up and know exactly when I am going to dust the boat on, I switch over to the paper sounder and I can watch the bottom coming up to meet me and I can see how far I have got to travel back to get afloat again.

It was no time to wishy-washy about. The name of the game was to get alongside. You have got hold of the wheel and, after a while, as she's coming off the top of a sea and starting to jump down, you can feel your old hands tightening up, waiting for the crunch. When it doesn't happen you think, 'Well, that can't be bad. We got away with that.' And you are off again.

By now the wind had risen to storm force 10. Coxswain Bowry brought the lifeboat towards the casualty through a number of peaking, confused seas. A number of approaches had to be made before all four survivors were safely taken off.

They had three big tyres on the starboard side as fendering. We did a little bit of parleying about. Whether he should bring off his belongings. So I said, 'I will now show you why we shouldn't take your gear off.' They watched from the wheelhouse window. One minute we were down below looking at his rudder, his prop and about 15ft along his skeg; the next minute my lads, who are now up on the bow, are looking down at him. So he said, 'I see what you mean.' Then he said to me, 'Can I bring a bird on board?' I said, 'Have you got a woman on there?' He said, 'No, it's a canary.' I was speechless.

Three of the men had come out to the gunwale. One man was clinging to it and two others were just inside the bulwarks hanging onto his legs. Of course you wonder what's going to happen to the last man off, because there will be nobody to hold on to him but you think, 'I'll come to that later'.

Well, we took one man off, did all the business and went in for the next. One man is crouching up on top of the bulwark, holding on to the stanchions with the other man behind him holding on to him. We grab him off. Then the fourth man comes running along the deck with this canary in the cage and throws himself on board. This canary, I could see it in the light of the searchlight, he's pressed up against the side of the cage and there's a gale of wind blowing though his feathers. We put the man and the canary down in the cabin. Then we took the last man off, backed off and I took the nearest direct line to Black Deep. And I'm winding her up and there are these two great big seas following me. 'Hurry, Chas, get us out of here,' goes the crew.

Soon after the lifeboat had pulled away, *Mi Amigo* sank. Charles Bowry was awarded a silver medal for gallantry for the rescue, but wondered if it came from the right organisation.

Once we'd got clear of the banks, I opened the door to look down to the cabin to talk to this bloke who was responsible for the ship. And they were all down there, smoking away, and the cabin was black with smoke. And this old canary is on the table wheezing and coughing and his eyes are popping. I said, 'That's going to have a cardiac arrest if you don't get it out of here.' Never mind a lifeboat medal, I reckon I should have one from the RSPCA!

SPEAKING OUT

Telling tales is one thing but giving public speeches is another. Most coxswains are far more scared of appearing on a stage than facing a howling storm. Perhaps the wittiest way of dealing with this was shown by Griff Griffiths of Salcombe. A wonderful, weather-beaten, ruddy cheeked, straw-haired fisherman, Griff had taken his crew through a capsize and survived. His slow Devon drawl was known by lifeboat people throughout the country. He was invited to speak at a lifeboat dinner in Wales. His speech was short and to the point: 'I know why you've invited me to speak – so you can take the mickey out of my accent. Well you can't!' And he sat down. It went down a storm.

Derek Scott of the Mumbles (an ironic place-name given his eloquence) was such a good public speaker that he was on the books of a commercial agency. His tales brought home the reality of lifeboating to hundreds of people and, through his friendship with dramatist and scriptwriter, Alun Richards, a novel, *Ennal's Point*, was turned into the first ever RNLI television drama series in 1982. There was also drama off screen as a stand-off developed between two proud institutions, the RNLI and the BBC. The television crew needed to use a real lifeboat station for the series. The strait-laced RNLI, suspicious of these arty types, demanded the right to vet the script, to protect its reputation. The BBC was outraged. Artistic freedom was at stake. Stalemate ensued.

Luckily, Alun Richards not only wrote realistically about people, he also knew how they ticked. His aim with the series, which is also the aim of this book, was in his words, 'To leave the impression of very ordinary men who became extraordinary because of the very nature of their task, saving life in any weather.' He persuaded the BBC that he should discuss his scripts with the RNLI. He convinced the RNLI that their public relations officer and Derek Scott should 'advise' him. The result was a jolly meeting in a Mumbles pub, when the whole matter was dealt with over a few pints. Both institutions saved face and an acclaimed series, starring Philip Madoc, was made. In today's world of corporate lawyers, it would probably not be possible.

Another award-wining television man, Paul Berriff, was working on a lifeboat series at about the same time. His was one of the early 'reality TV' or 'fly on the wall' series. He first made one programme about a winter with the Bridlington lifeboat and later a six-part documentary at Humber lifeboat station. Given Humber's history, it was disappointing that in a full six months of winter filming, with Berriff living in a caravan at Spurn Head, there were no dramatic rescues. He was on the spot, however, when the oil rig *Piper Alpha* blew up in the North Sea off Aberdeen a few years later, and it was Berriff's footage of the horrendous inferno that was broadcast around the world.

Berriff had his own views on how to tell the public about the reality of lifeboating, drawn from hours at sea with crews: 'You shouldn't tell them it's heroic, you should tell them what it's really like. Ten hours at sea, soaked through, so cold that you pee inside your oilskins, searching, searching and finding nothing, coming back with no cheering crowds, just a dull, dank feeling, then washing down the boat, rehousing, refuelling, and being ready to drop everything and do it all again. That's what it's about.'

It's not a popular message for today's public, fed by 24-hour news, creating five-minute heroes. The lifeboatmen's experience is of the sheer slog of prolonged searches, with hope fading as they go on, that is intensified by the terrible disappointment if a body is found, and of the lingering uncertainty if there is none.

LOSING LIVES

Failing to save a life is something that weighs heavily on lifeboatmen. According to Robin Castle of Sheerness, 'It does affect the crew if you carry out a search and regrettably you can't find anyone. The other effect on the crew is the result of a period of very high stress and physical and mental exertion. The reaction comes after you have got back.'

Derek Sargent, former Weymouth coxswain, agrees: 'Fortunately it does not happen too often but we have, sadly, picked up one or two bodies, more so in the sailing fraternity, who have gone out in a new boat. Perhaps anglers. We have been searching all night and possibly about eleven o'clock in the morning you see a life jacket with a body in it. Yes, it makes your fingers tingle a bit. You think of the families.'

The families of lifeboat crews also need to be considered. Many coxswains have said it is much more difficult for those left on shore. At sea, there's plenty going on, plenty to do. At home, there's worry. Most lifeboat families get used to it. Margaret Clark, from Lerwick, admits to worrying when husband Hewitt and son Neil were out in bad weather, but adds, 'I always had great faith in their ability and used to think that if it was any of my family who were in need of the

Robin Castle of Sheerness. *(Margaret Murray)*

lifeboat, I would be glad to know that they were there. Usually when Hewitt went out on a call, particularly if it was in the middle of the night and if the weather was bad, then I would get up and listen on the radio because you couldn't sleep anyway and it's always so much easier if you know what's going on.'

Margaret remembers one of Hewitt's very first rescues, just a few months after they were married, when he was the lifeboat mechanic. The lifeboat was called out to Fair Isle to escort some Norwegian boats that were in difficulty in storm force winds and driving snow. With a friend, whose husband was also on the crew, Margaret watched as the lifeboat went out past Bressay Light: 'I honestly wondered if they would ever return.'

Information can help. On the *Green Lily* rescue, Margaret listened to the drama unfold on the radio: 'I was not so much worried as very anxious for Hewitt, knowing that he would be so disappointed if he could not do the job he set out to do, which was to save life. I know it sounds silly but you almost felt that you were there in the situation with them sometimes. After they had completed the rescue and had gone back out to search for the helicopter winchman, I think that was the only occasion that I ever heard him sounding worried when he actually said on the radio that he was returning with his crew as this was a dangerous situation.'

HURRICANE

The night of a famous hurricane in the south-east of England took its toll on families and lifeboat crews alike. Television weatherman Michael Fish had soothed a viewer's worries about a storm as the forecasts had not picked it up.

There are times when natural forces overwhelm the land, sweep away people and destroy buildings. The dreadful tsunami of 2004 caused enormous devastation; hurricanes regularly batter the Caribbean and the southern coastal states of the USA. In deep oceans, waves of over 100ft high have been recorded and it is estimated that they have sunk over 200 supertankers and container ships in the last two decades.

The British Isles, by comparison, see so little of such extreme conditions that best-selling American author and confirmed anglophile Bill Bryson has mused on why we spend so much time discussing the weather. But the hurricane of October 1987 brought devastation on a scale rarely seen on the domestic landscape. It also showed that, in very severe conditions, the systems we rely on can fail completely and the emergency services have to improvise.

There were dozens of lifeboat launches in the area affected by the storm as it swept up from the West Country. Technically, the wind reached force 16–17, gusting to over 100 knots. This is well beyond the original wind scale devised in 1805 by Admiral Beaufort, who stopped at force 12. The highest point now is 17, marking wind speeds of 109 to 118 knots. It is rare indeed around the coasts of Britain and Ireland. Kent had no reason to anticipate it that October evening, as at 8 p.m. it was a beautiful night with barely a breath of wind.

The hurricane arrived in the early morning. For the Dover and Sheerness lifeboat stations, the danger started as soon as they were alerted. 'Called out' is not the appropriate expression as a power failure in Dover meant that the bleepers didn't work and maroons had to be used. In Sheerness, the normal bleeper routine, allowing the coxswain to select his crew, failed and a general alert was issued. The men had to abandon their cars at the entrance to the dock road and run a bizarre obstacle course, over fallen trees, past overturned lorries, cars and trailers, for a mile before they reached the lifeboat berth. It was no better in Dover, where one crew member was just about to get into his car when his chimney was blown down onto it.

Complete power failures in both ports meant the crews had to don their gear by torchlight and board the boats, ranging up and down on their moorings, in darkness. Vital shore systems were also devastated by the storm. The coastguard radar scanner at Dungeness stopped turning due to the ferocity of the wind so coastguards were relying on what they were told over the radio by ships at sea and the Folkestone pilots. However, the wide viewing window at the Folkestone pilot station was in danger of being blown in, so the pilots could only glance at their radar for short spells in between taking shelter. Dover port control evacuated their control tower; they too were operating blind, relying on pilot and ship information.

Dover's was a short, sharp rescue. Seas inside the harbour were 20ft high; outside, they were 60ft. The lifeboat was on standby to launch in case the ship *Hengist* got into trouble. They were told she had gone aground, but not to launch as it would be suicide to try and get out of the harbour's western entrance. Then a second ship, *Sumnia*, a 300ft bulk cargo vessel, started dragging her anchors and hit the breakwater. She was ranging 30ft up and down the breakwater and rolling 80 degrees, in imminent danger of capsize. The lifeboat, tossed like a cork, got within 20ft of the ship and spotted two of her crew on deck, but they were swept away by a huge wave. Spray and spume made it almost impossible to see, but the eagle-eyed crew spotted one man in the water and Roy Couzens managed to drive straight to him. The lifeboat crew hauled him in and soon saw his companion. With huge skill, Couzens reached the second man in one go and he too was hauled in. *Sumnia*'s bow broke off as the lifeboat searched for more survivors, dropping off a 60ft sea, almost capsizing. Then, in the midst of a slick of diesel oil and debris, lifeboatman Michael Abbott spotted a life jacket. As they grabbed it, they saw there was a man inside, unconscious. The official record says that Robert Bruce 'restored his breathing'. If you have in mind the use of mouth-to-mouth resuscitation, think again. On a wildly bucking deck, you need one hand to hang on and one to keep the man on board. A large lifeboatman's wellie, applied with vigour, made the man vomit up blood and oil and start breathing. The Dover men kept searching, but Couzens had to ask Abbott to take over the helm as he felt unwell. It later transpired he had suffered a heart attack. Ambulances could not reach the harbour because of blocked roads, and Roy was driven to hospital by Ken Miles of the lifeboat committee. The lifeboat had rescued three men. A harbour launch found one other. Two of *Sumnia*'s crew died.

Rescues of this severity leave their mark on crews. In Dover, seamen had died in front of the lifeboat which had been unable to save them. The crew were badly shaken but, after less than five minutes alongside to drop survivors, put out a second time. 'There was a sort of driving force, no one even questioned that we might go out again,' said Roy Couzens. When they got back, a regular crew member who met the boat said the crew appeared to be in a state of shock. Roy, in hospital after his heart attack, was troubled by the death of one of *Sumnia*'s crew. By amazing coincidence, rescuer and rescued ended up on the same hospital ward: 'Three beds down from me was the third survivor we picked up. I could not wait to speak to him. In my own mind I wanted to know whether, if I had gone out there twenty minutes earlier, we might actually have got everybody. He reassured me, actually.'

By contrast, Sheerness went to help a small fishing boat that was in danger of being pounded to pieces on a sandbank. The two people were rescued but to reach them the lifeboat had to go right up onto the bank and became stranded for ten hours, while the storm died away.

Humour helps the crews to bounce back. The Dover crew came to London to receive medals for the rescue. On their way to the Royal Festival Hall in a coach, they passed the London Fire Brigade's Lambeth pier, where a fireman on the brigade's catamaran was testing the hoses, squirting an impressive stream of water across the River Thames towards the Houses of Parliament. From the Embankment, the hose was obscured, leaving just the fireman and the water jet in view. Recalling a current television advert, one of the crew piped up, 'I bet he drinks Carling Black Label!'

EXPLOSIVE EXPLOITS

The bleeper problems faced by the crews in the hurricane are rare; electronics both on and off the boats have transformed many aspects of rescue work. Navigation and communication are easier and more reliable than ever before. To a limited extent, technology also helps to make up the gap between the day-to-day local knowledge of the fishermen crews of old and the need for modern landlubber crews to acquire this knowledge.

Bleepers have increased the reliability of call-outs, allowing some crews to opt for working on rotas. The traditional call-out was done by firing maroons – in effect, large fireworks. The maroon was placed in a mortar box or a firing tube and would, if all went well, send two charges high into the sky to explode with a bright flash followed by a loud bang. Nobody in the community could miss them, and the crew, together with the supporters to either help launch the boat or just witness the spectacle, would rush to the boathouse, adrenalin surging through them.

However, any explosive can go wrong. Not so many years ago, in the north-west of England, there was a misfire and one of the charges dropped back to earth, unexploded. A local farmer claimed it had landed in his field and demanded compensation because the field was now too dangerous to harvest. The quick-witted lifeboat inspector organised a search of the field, with no result.

The old-style mortar box maroon. *(Irish Times)*

Dismissing the crew's protests, he told them to look again. He walked ahead of them and surreptitiously dropped a spent maroon, and was suitably surprised and delighted when it was found. The field was harvested safely.

Other maroon misfires were more serious. In Torbay, one lodged in a roof space and exploded, blowing down several feet of cast-iron guttering, which hit a parked van but mercifully no people. In north Devon, a maroon arched back into the boathouse, ricocheting off the walls and injuring the crew. So although low, the risk was real and maroons are now largely gone, the remaining ones being fired from new custom-designed launchers.

They could, though, have benefits beyond alerting the crew, even helping to save lives by letting survivors know that help was coming. In 1983 the Penzance–Isles of Scilly helicopter was making a routine flight, hampered only by dense sea fog at low levels. As the aircraft approached the Scillies around midday, and descended into the dense fog bank, the pilot made a fatal miscalculation, dropping short of the land and straight into the sea. Both the pilot and co-pilot managed to escape through the front of the machine while all but four of their passengers trapped inside were drowned. However, two women and two children got out and among those was Mrs Langley Evans, chairman of the St Mary's Lifeboat Guild. The two children were on their own; their parents did not escape. Terrified, cold and helpless the children and Mrs Langley Evans struggled to stay afloat. Then the lifeboat maroons exploded, loud and confident. 'Don't worry now, loves,' said Mrs Langley Evans, 'Matt's coming to get us.' True to her word, Coxswain Matt Lethbridge was soon at the crash site to pick up the shocked survivors.

Even with his extensive local knowledge, finding the helicopter was not easy. At first, radar sightings suggested that the helicopter was afloat but, having checked two of the radar plots and found they were large becalmed yachts, the dreadful realisation came that the helicopter had probably sunk.

Lethbridge stared intently into the radar screen, spotting what he could only describe as a 'shimmer' a mile and a half ahead. Then the lookouts on the foredeck reported that they could smell paraffin. Lethbridge left his command position on the radar to go back to the upper steering position. Now the crew could hear shouting. Lethbridge reduced speed and two boat-lengths ahead people were seen in the water. With enormous care the coxswain brought his powerful lifeboat around to stop it alongside the young boy and girl, who were pulled in. The inflatable boat was launched to pick up the two women, then the helicopter pilots. They told the lifeboat men that there were probably no more survivors.

A Sea King helicopter was soon on scene along with local fishing boats, and, after they had landed the survivors, the lifeboatmen returned to lead an intensive search with the local boats and the Penlee lifeboat. For the next five hours they scoured the whole area from the crash site to the Bishops Rock Lighthouse. Nothing was found.

Matt Lethbridge comes from a lifeboat family, with his father, also Matt, and grandfather serving as coxswains. He has two daughters, neither of whom joined the crew. A small wiry man with a big grin, Matt rarely left the Scillies but had to go to Poole with his crew to pick up a new lifeboat. On the passage home, they stopped overnight in Weymouth. At that time the chairman of the lifeboat station was also the chairman of the local brewery, Devenish. Whenever a visiting lifeboat crew put into the harbour, they were invited to the board-room for a drink. Matt is a strict teetotaller

Matt Lethbridge of the Isles of Scilly.

– a rare though not unique attribute in lifeboat crews. Turning first to Matt, the chairman asked what he would like to drink. 'Bitter lemon please, sir,' said Matt. Unimpressed, the chairman told the coxswain that he was never going to be accused of being unable to organise a piss-up in his own brewery. Without hesitation, Matt replied, 'Okay, I'll have a double bitter lemon then.'

The year after the helicopter rescue, Matt Lethbridge was coaxed off the island to join a discussion on lifeboat and helicopter cooperation. While the results were used in an article, it was actually a ruse to trick him into appearing on *This is Your Life*. Towards the end of the programme, the two children saved from the helicopter came on and simply said, 'Thank you.' There was not a dry eye in the studio.

SICK OF IT ALL?

There's a way of telling how tired, cold and even frightened a lifeboat crew has become. They stop talking.

David Cox of Wells said after his epic eleven-hour service in a blizzard, 'It is the first time I have known my crew to be very quiet. I think the extreme cold was getting everyone that day. It was rough, we know, but it is the intense cold that gets you. You are standing there, taking everything that comes.'

Cold at sea is a killer. Even Henry Blogg lost a lifeboatman to exposure, now known more scientifically as hypothermia. And a Moelfre lifeboatman died from extreme cold on a seventeen-hour rescue in 1927 that left Coxswain William Roberts temporarily blind. It seems incredible that, half a century later, the Wells lifeboatmen came perilously close to death from prolonged exposure to a biting gale in the North Sea.

On the same day, the Humber crew had a similar experience: 'It's a sure sign that the weather is getting really bad; the quietness,' said Brian Bevan. 'Everybody can be talking and chatting away, probably for the first twenty minutes, half an hour, and then conversations gradually dwindle away.'

Robin Castle, in command of the Sheerness lifeboat on the night of the hurricane, said the same: 'I knew it was going to be a bit bad, but I've never heard the crew so quiet. They never said a word, nothing at all.'

As well as silence, there is sickness. Fishermen, who are at sea virtually every day, become used to its motions. Today's crews, with shore-based jobs, spend days or even weeks ashore between call-outs and so, if it is rough, sickness often overtakes them. The acid test is how they cope. John Petit of Guernsey said, 'Most of our crew are not usually seasick. Just on a very bad service under abnormal conditions they may become a little sick. But once they have brought it up they are fine again. They get on with their job. It hasn't put them out of business.'

As for Brian Bevan's Humber crew: 'We had a couple of lads who suffer from seasickness from time to time but they can still do the job. It's one of those things. If you have got a crew of people who are at sea all week, then seasickness never bothers them. But any crew that might be weeks ashore at a time and then get chucked in on bad days, they'll suffer from seasickness because they are not at sea long enough or regularly enough really to get over it.'

Seasickness can become dangerous, as the Dunbar crew found on an arduous nineteen-hour struggle to recover the stricken vessel *Coromandel* after it became stranded 25 miles east of Eyemouth. It was so rough that one lifeboatman became severely dehydrated through seasickness and had to be airlifted to hospital. The lifeboat ended up towing the *Coromandel* 70 miles to safety at Leith.

SEAMANSHIP

The Oxford Dictionary defines seamanship simply as 'skill in managing a ship or boat'. In the midst of stirring tales of danger and gallantry, the sheer skill and resourcefulness of lifeboat crews can be lost. Professional fishermen and merchant navy captains comment on it; yachtsmen may experience it at first hand. For a lifeboat coxswain or helm, it is an essential ingredient in every successful rescue.

Seamanship is elusive because the sea presents so many variables. The surface of the water alone is moving in three dimensions, with the tides running underneath and winds above. In addition, there are three basic motions for boats under way – rolling, pitching and yawing. So placing two vessels of different sizes, shapes and weights on top of the sea gives an almost infinite combination of movements. Seamanship, in the context of a rescue, is an instinctive combination of analysis and experience in time-hardened crews.

A discussion about seamanship among lifeboatmen will focus on facts, not dangers.

Dave Clemence of Ilfracombe had only a quarter of a mile to go from his station to reach a yacht dragging its anchor and heading for dangerous rocks. What he did not know was that the skipper had died and the other man on the yacht had never been on a boat before. Dave recalled, 'His anchor was jammed in the rocks so we asked the chap on deck to let go the cable but he didn't know what to do. He couldn't start the engine, couldn't tie a knot or anything. We managed to pull him clear of the rocks but his anchor cable jammed so that he was pulling us onto the rocks. We got him off, though, and made a bridle which enabled us to come round towards the pier again, otherwise we wouldn't have been able to tow him. Then his cable became jammed on some buoys so we swung round and pulled him clear again.'

Clemence was matter of fact about the rescue, 'He was going to jump over, you see', and the consequences. Would the man have made it to the shore? 'Well I expect so, but he would have been drowned, there's no doubt about it.'

Only at the end of the discussion did he mention the weather: 'A sort of north-west gale, 7 to 8. Very big swell, very big sea with 15–20ft waves.'

FISHERMEN

Every rescue is different. Fishermen are easier to rescue, in that they should know how to respond, but they are more likely to be in serious trouble before they call for help. Off Wick, Donald McKay had to reach a salmon coble that had fouled her propeller on fishing nets and then had been driven onto rocks. He had to use all his skills and ingenuity for the rescue. 'It was gusting 6 to 8 and that was one of the reasons she got into trouble; the weather was too bad. These salmon cobles are fitted with a hatch that can be lifted so that anything round the propeller can be cleared. This could not be done. She'd driven over the top of the shoals and when we arrived there was no way we could get to her,

Torbay lifeboat stands by a sinking fishing boat. *(Torbay Crew)*

the sea was just breaking solid over the boat. The waves were 8–10ft and the water was very sallow. We tried to let the breeches buoy drag down on a line before the wind.'

It didn't work, as the swell and broken water swept the buoy away from the coble. The lifeboat was only 70yds away, but too far to throw a rope.

We tried to approach again, with quite a bit of difficulty because of the nets. There were also lobster creels, there was everything you could get in the way and also a number of shoals. At one point we grounded and it was just a case of going full astern. We decided then to get head into wind and used our line-throwing gun to fire a line towards her; we managed to manoeuvre so that the crew could get a grip on the line. We made fast a nylon rope, which they made fast to their bow. When we started to make way, they let go of the leader that was attached to the salmon nets. This saved their lives, I reckon, because if they'd gone any further in, then no way would they have been alive.

Hartlepool's Trent class lifeboat. *(Tom Collins)*

Amble lifeboat crew. *(Geoff Smyth)*

Baltimore lifeboat rescues the crew of a freighter moments before she sinks.

Peterhead lifeboat in a tricky rescue close to rocks. *(Revd Michael Gaunt)*

Tobermory lifeboat stands by a stranded ship. *(Phil Wren)*

Two lifeboats and a tug stand by as a coastguard helicopter lifts a man off ship. *(J. Mathieson)*

Thurso lifeboat rescues a yacht in rough seas off Scapa Flow. *(Frank Bradford)*

All the lifeboat stations in England, Wales, Scotland and Ireland sent a representative to the opening of RNLI College in Poole in 2004, where they met the Queen, the Duke of Edinburgh and the Duke of Kent.

Eastbourne's Mersey class lifeboat. *(Rick Tomlinson)*

Opposite: Happisburgh inshore lifeboat puts to sea.

The Atlantic inshore lifeboat has an ingenious airbag system for self-righting.

Porthcawl's Atlantic helmed by Aileen Pritchard. *(Andrew Lloyd)*

Kinghorn's volunteer lifeboat crew. From left on both photographs they are: Scott McIlravie (computer engineer), Colin Stoker (KwikFit brake specialist), Evelyn Stoker (road traffic surveyor), Judith Frame (housewife and mother), Mhairi Hay (college lecturer in chemistry), Liz Davidson (pensions manager), Keith Hay (police constable), Rob Moore (improvements manager), Mike McErlane (jetty operator), Norman Souter (mature student) and Paul Wibberley (marine pilot).

Dunbar's inshore lifeboat; note the inflatable keel, which helps performance. *(Rob McDougall)*

Newquay's two inshore lifeboats, an Atlantic and a D class, both involved in the rescue of a child from the rocks. *(Chrissie Laming, Newquay Voice Newspapers)*

The Dutch lifeboat service has adopted rigid inflatables for the whole fleet and operates the largest in the world of these types of boat. *(KNRM)*

The mighty Arun, at Donaghadee – one of the most successful lifeboats ever designed. *(Rick Tomlinson)*

The crew of a French fishing boat, sinking off the Isles of Scilly, are rescued by the St Mary's lifeboat. (Steve Farrall)

Montrose inshore lifeboat crew in enthusiastic mood as they pass an Arbroath fishing boat. (Alan Richardson)

Calshot, on the Solent, is surrounded by yachts and helps out with a tow rope. *(Eddie Mays)*

Only one gold medal rescue has ever been photographed: the *Green Lily* rescue by Lerwick lifeboat. Pictured here (from the rescue helicopter) are the lifeboat and tug standing by before the rescue.

People aboard *Green Lily* – just visible on deck – are rescued by the lifeboat.

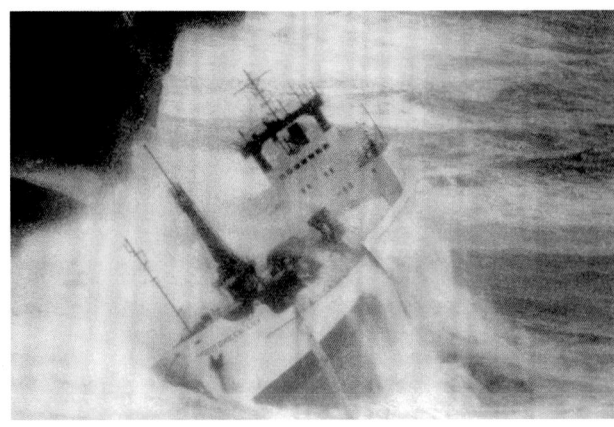

Green Lily aground, being pounded by the storm.

The Tamar class lifeboat relies on a robust, watertight superstructure for her self-righting properties.

The Tamar at speed. *(Derek King)*

The very latest lifeboat design, codenamed FCB2, designed to launch from a carriage and powered by waterjets.

Beach lifeguard services are part of the RNLI's expansion to save more lives at sea. *(Deborah Johnson)*

The RNLI River Thames rescue service is inaugurated as the new lifeboats speed under Tower Bridge. *(Derek King)*

Many fishermen will try and avoid calling the lifeboat rather than face the embarrassment of being towed into port. When Alan Tarby was second coxswain of the Padstow lifeboat, he was out fishing when his steering gear failed: 'I went six miles with no steering but I didn't want a tow from the lifeboat.'

Joe Martin of Hastings also dealt with a lot of fishermen: 'If you've got experienced fishermen that are in trouble you've got somebody handy at the other end of the tow rope.'

Joe had to tow a Lowestoft trawler much larger than his 37ft Oakley lifeboat, in a force 8 gale: 'The difficulty with this rescue was it was quite a hair-raising one, we were towing a bigger vessel to leeward. The reason it's very dangerous is because the heavier vessel can be picked up by a sea and she will run forward on top of you. So we were running at low speed and every time she caught up with us on a sea, we had to put on power to keep ahead of her.'

It's difficult enough controlling a large vessel under tow in open sea where there is plenty of space to manoeuvre but Martin then faced the challenge of bringing the trawler into harbour: 'We had to get across the bar and no way could we go straight into the harbour because she would have been lifted up on a sea and come on top of us. So we dropped to leeward and then came back to windward to keep her behind us. That means crossing the bar a little bit on the broad side.'

A harbour bar is where the sea is shallower at the harbour entrance, usually due to a sand bar built up when a river meets the sea, slows down and deposits some of the silt it carries. This means that waves crossing the bar gather power, and going broadside on, that is, putting your boat parallel with the breaking waves, is an invitation to immediate capsize. Joe Martin had no choice. 'In my opinion it was the only way.' Both the lifeboat and the trawler made it safely, in spite of the high risk.

Often, lifeboat crew have to transfer to the casualty vessel to help survivors or sort out a tow. According to Martin, 'This is where it is most dangerous for lifeboatmen. I have one man, a great fellow, who I call my jumper. If you have a situation where it's impossible to stay alongside, he jumps and assists them out of the vessel. This is a much better system, if you can do it, because he is actually throwing them on board and in some weather conditions I would forget the yacht and start considering lives and getting them back home.'

It's a difficult decision to abandon a vessel and coxswains will usually try and save them where it is possible. Occasionally lifeboat crews have been put in great danger by arrogant yachtsmen who stubbornly refuse to abandon, but Charlie Bowry at Sheerness claimed he never had this problem. When asked why, he explained: 'I goes alongside and tell them to come off. If they don't, I go in again and bump them a bit. I don't have to bump them again – they come off.' It may not be in the rule book, but that's seamanship!

MAN OVERBOARD!

It's a cry nobody at sea wants to hear. It's a cry nobody on a lifeboat ever expects to hear. But it happens and it shows why the RNLI spends so much on its top-of-the-range life jackets, for if you are swept off the deck of a lifeboat, it's going to be in bad weather. Protective clothing and life jackets cost the RNLI a pretty penny, but in the worst conditions, every expensive feature of them is worth-while, for they can save a crew member's life.

Going overboard seems to be rather a habit in north-east England, judging by what happened to Coxswain Billy Carter of Teesmouth in the 1960s (he was soon spotted due to the light on his life jacket), second coxswain John Trotter of Scarborough in 1991(he was nearly crushed against a merchant ship) and Robbie Maiden at Hartlepool in a force 10 in February 1983.

Robbie had been going back into the wheelhouse, unclipping his lifeline to do so, when he was swept overboard as a huge wave capsized the lifeboat twice. Robbie kept calm and thought about survival. He needed to keep control, so he pushed his legs down to stop being turned over, inflated his life jacket, activated his light and tightened the securing straps. RNLI clothing is fitted with Velcro straps, so Robbie tightened them to stop cold water rushing round his body and pulled the jacket hood over his head and face against the spray and sleet.

On a desperate search, the lifeboat came within yards of him but could not see him. Fortunately, a helicopter that had been standing by for the rescue had landed nearby and was scrambled immediately. In the dark, a simple strip of reflective tape, cost about £3, shone out in the searchlight's strong beam. Within seconds, and after thirty-five minutes in the chill North Sea, Robbie was in the helicopter strop with an RAF air crewman. Robbie told him, 'If you weren't so ugly I could kiss you.'

Most vulnerable of all are the crews of inshore lifeboats (ILBs), where lifelines are impractical and where the crew are always inches from the sea. Perhaps the greatest potential danger is the performance of the boats themselves, for the crews need to be constantly reminded that the ILBs are not for all weathers – yet still they push them beyond their safe limits. If the boats capsize, they can usually be righted, but if a crew member goes overboard, getting them back can be very tricky.

Amos Bewick (right) and the Borth crew. *(Ron Davies)*

Like Robbie Maiden's companions, the Aberdovey Atlantic crew must have feared the worst when helmsman Phil Nicol was swept overboard in a force 7 while the boat was on exercise on 10 December 2000. His crew immediately set to finding him but could not haul him back into the boat and he was caught in an eddy caused by the strong ebb tide, the flow of floodwater out to sea from the River Dovey and the south-westerly waves. Nicol was swept into shallows that the Atlantic could not reach and lost his helmet.

By chance, the D class lifeboat from neighbouring Borth had just finished an exercise. She was returning to station as the weather was so poor. The crew heard the radio messages between the Aberdovey boat and the coastguard and diverted to head for Aberdovey. She was there in twenty minutes and started a search for Nicol, who by now was floating low in the water. The D class should really not have been at sea; it was, in RNLI parlance, at the very limits of its capability. Arguably, it was beyond them. Helmsman Amos Bewick described how, on the passage to Aberdovey, they met such huge swells in the onshore wind that they had to climb slowly up the waves, so as not to hit them like ramps, which would leave the boat in mid-air and vulnerable to capsize. Nonetheless, Amos did find himself clawing up big seas which then dropped away, 'leaving you, your crew and boat in mid-air, causing you to land standing on the transom, which does cause you to think a bit!'

The Aberdovey crew had been doing their best to keep Phil in view but waves were breaking all around and they only had a rough idea of the area he was in. The Borth lifeboat went in, searching, thought they spotted him and diverted, but it was a false alarm. Going back to the original search line, they saw him almost immediately over to port.

Amos knew that, with Phil in breaking seas of over 6ft for more than half an hour, he would be battered, weak and hypothermic – he had to be reached straight away. There might be no second chance. Crew member Alex Shepherd grabbed him and pulled him onto the sponson, and Martyn Davies also quickly took hold, the two fit young men struggling to pull Nicol into the lifeboat.

Just as he was safely in the boat, a large wave, foaming and breaking, swamped the boat, turning it straight into the breaking seas. As Amos struggled with his single outboard engine to regain control, Martyn and Alex threw themselves onto the port sponson to stop the boat being flipped over. Amos still had to get his comrade to safety. 'Once Phil was in the boat, we turned towards Aberdovey and raced out of the surf. On the way in, it was good to be able to tell his crew that he was safe.' In fact, Phil was far from safe. As the hypothermia began to kick in he slipped in and out of consciousness and by the time they reached the slipway he was unconscious. His own crew started to work on him and within ten minutes an ambulance arrived and the paramedics took over. When his drysuit was cut off it was found that his body temperature had dropped to a dangerously low 25 degrees. He was whisked by helicopter to hospital in Aberystwyth where he stayed for three days and made a full recovery.

Phil made a very different journey in the inshore lifeboat on Easter Saturday three months later – along the village streets to his wedding. The boat was ready to launch if needed and was never more than 150m from the boathouse. Phil, on the other hand, was under firm instructions from his bride to keep his bleeper muted and to stay 'off service' all day.

Lifeboat man Michael Weeks was washed off a boat that Appledore lifeboat was towing to safety. It was a dark, rough December evening in 1994 when the lifeboat found a motorboat which had steering failure off Hartland Point. Michael Weeks jumped aboard to secure the towline. After a three-hour tow, the lifeboat was nearing Appledore but the coxswain wanted to wait for the tide to flood, giving calmer conditions to cross the bar at the harbour mouth.

Turning back out to sea, the lifeboat hit three heavy seas in succession. For the sturdy steel Tyne there was no problem, but the motorboat, with no steering, rode one wave, dived into the trough and rolled over on her beam-ends. Michael Weeks slipped on diesel that had spilled on the deck and grabbed the flimsy guard rail, which broke and threw him into the sea. Luckily, one of

Appledore lifeboat working with a helicopter. *(Nigel Millard)*

the crew on the lifeboat spotted him going overboard, but it was only when they reeled the motorboat in on the towrope and took off the three survivors that they realised it was Weeks in the water. By now the lifeboat was near the surf and the motorboat was swamped so the coxswain cut the tow, called for the inshore lifeboat and desperately started to search for the missing lifeboatman. Even though parachute flares were used to light up the scene, they could not find Weeks, and one of the survivors was slipping into unconsciousness due to hypothermia. Quickly they landed him and resumed the search but Weeks was still invisible from the lifeboat and they asked the coastguard to scramble a helicopter from nearby RAF Chivenor. Within minutes, the Wessex helicopter was in a search pattern above the surf and as the aircraft turned, through the night vision equipment they picked up the infra-red glow from Weeks, 200yds from the shore. They swept in, scooped him up and, after a chilling thirty-five minutes in the ice-cold winter sea (exactly the same time Robbie Maiden was in the water before a helicopter rescued him), Michael Weeks was whisked to the intensive care unit of Barnstaple hospital where he made a full recovery.

ALWAYS ON CALL

Lifeboat crews are constantly on call. Some operate rotas, but whatever system they use there must be a crew available, day and night, every day of the year.

The Harwich crew once shocked the yachtsmen they were called out to rescue. The crew had appeared in the town carnival dressed as greenflies because there had been a plague of them in Harwich that year. Sure enough, the lifeboat was called out and they left the parade; the people they rescued must have thought they had had too much sun when a lifeboat full of greenflies came to save them.

In Aberdeen, the crew were called out from the annual lifeboat ball. The yacht crew they towed in later said, 'We knew the RNLI provided a good service but this was ridiculous.' The crew still had their dinner jackets on under their oilskins.

Another 'shout' at Aberdeen happened when a head office official from London was visiting. It was a reasonably calm day and the lifeboat had to take medical assistance to a trawler. Within minutes of the maroons being fired, the boat was under way, the official on board. The coxswain, proud of the speed of the launch, asked the official to be sure to tell them back in London of Aberdeen's efficiency. A moment later, he turned the lifeboat back towards the harbour. 'What's wrong?' asked the surprised official. 'We've forgotten the bloody doctor,' said the flustered coxswain.

PLAYING GAMES

Sheringham lifeboatman Brian Pegg and his colleague Graham Walker from Wells were in the trials team when the Mersey lifeboat was developed. Working from the Isle of Wight, they took the prototype boat on sea trials and returned to a local café. Brian had some pre-decimal coins in his pocket and made to pay with them. The woman behind the counter was astonished but Brian, his broad Norfolk accent exaggerated just a little, explained that these were still the currency in Norfolk. As the woman looked unconvinced, he turned to Graham, who, straight-faced, confirmed the story, which they maintained for a good few minutes before paying up properly and leaving.

Brian, a member of the Salvation Army, was one of the RNLI's strict teetotallers, though he was always happy to stand his round in the pub. One Sunday before Christmas, when he knew many lifeboat stations would be exercising or making radio checks, he assembled the Salvation Army Band in the Sheringham boathouse. Using the maritime radio channels (a practice which might now be frowned upon) they broadcast a short concert of Christmas carols to their lifeboat colleagues and other seafarers up and down the east coast.

Brian had a tip to determine how long a person had served in one of the old lifeboats. 'Count his teeth,' he advised. 'They get shaken out over the years. That's why I've got a full set of false ones – thirty years in the crew!'

The best lifeboat humour has no respect for position. A much-respected staff coxswain, Tom Beattie from Arbroath, was known by crews around the coast as a very fine seaman with a quick and dry wit. One winter, the Post Office tele-communications stand at the Earls Court Boat Show was featuring the ease with which ship-to-shore links could be made and demonstrating this by calling up ships at sea and broadcasting the resulting conversations all over the boat show. Tom was taking a lifeboat on passage up the east coast of Scotland and was linked to the boat show. A top official was hauled off the RNLI stand to talk to him.

'Earls Court Boat Show, this is lifeboat 878, Tom Beattie speaking, over.'

'Lifeboat 878, RNLI at Earls Court here. Sorry but I don't know the lifeboats by number, only name. Which boat are you on? Over.'

Short pause.

'Earls Court, lifeboat 878. Ach, the ignorance of the English!'

A radio featured in another escapade, this time in the south-west. The crew had been called out on a rain-lashed Saturday night, only to find out, four hours later, that it was a hoax call made by a local auxiliary coastguard. As the crew set out down the harbour, a dazed yachtsman climbed up to the quay and remonstrated with lifeboat secretary Bill Budgett. His yacht was tucked under the quay, yards from the mortar box which had launched the maroons, and, waking with a start from the explosions, he had banged his head on a bulkhead. He was pacified when he heard it was a lifeboat call and, that problem resolved, Bill settled down in the boathouse and tried to tune in the radio to the distress channel. The faint signal from the lifeboat finally faded as she rounded Start Point, and by now the second coxswain's wife had turned up and was looking for a socket to plug the kettle in to make tea. 'Oh, use the radio socket,' said Bill, 'You'll get better reception on the kettle.'

SEA BABIES

The Oban lifeboat can claim an unusual extra occupation – midwife. Three times in the last ten years babies have been born as the lifeboat took expectant mothers from Mull to the mainland. In August 1997 Hazel Banner was born as the boat came into harbour after the half hour crossing; in September 2001 Kerrie MacGillivray was born at sea in a storm; in October 2005 Rachel Holliday had a baby girl halfway across the sound. The lifeboat is the only one in the fleet adapted to carry an incubator if one is needed. Even though the births are anticipated, the crew find themselves involved emotionally. Coxswain Ronnie MacKillop said after the 2005 birth, 'I have to say that we all found it very moving. There was an air of urgency at first, but the baby came very quickly and five minutes later everybody was so happy. A couple of my lads were quite close to tears. We had picked up a midwife on our way to the call and after she cut the umbilical cord she handed the baby to one of the lads. He was quite emotional. I hang around all these rufty-tufty lifeboatmen all the time, but I saw a different side to them all this morning.'

CHAPTER SIX

Pomp and Circumstance

It takes inspiration to be creative and courage to make change. In both cases, with big ideas, the line between genius and eccentricity is a very fine one. So when Sir William Hillary, a bankrupt, bigamist and baronet, who had moved to the Isle of Man to escape his creditors, started writing to the Admiralty in London in the early nineteenth century, his plans for a national lifeboat service were rejected. Although Hillary had been created a baronet for raising, at his own expense, a company of soldiers from the Essex population to fight a feared war with Napoleon, his grand ideas were not matched with business acumen. His money came from his wife's family's sugar plantations in the West Indies, and his regiment drained away the cash, leaving him with a title but bankrupt. Once safely in the Isle of Man he joined the crew of the Douglas lifeboat, one of thirty or so placed around the UK by Lloyds of London, the insurers. Hillary soon saw that this ad hoc arrangement was seriously flawed. Lloyds were principally interested in saving merchant ships and their cargos, so huge stretches of coast had no lifeboats and any rescues were carried out by fishermen in their own boats. The price of failure was high for the families of the fishermen or lifeboatmen who died on rescues; there was absolutely no compensation for the loss of a breadwinner, leaving widows and children completely destitute. Hillary was motivated as much by this human cruelty to rescuers and their families as he was by the need to protect all seafarers, not just those in charge of valuable cargos.

The gentlemen of the Admiralty were unimpressed by any of his arguments, humanitarian, financial or logical. Even though Hillary was highly eloquent in his letters, the Admiralty refused to get involved. If they had, then there would never have been a voluntary lifeboat service but simply an extension of the Royal Navy or the Coastguard service. It is a supreme irony that the RNLI now has more boats than the Navy has ships, a fact noticed by Rear Admiral Wilfred Graham when he became Director of the RNLI in 1979. Another admiral, Falkland war hero Sandy Woodward, eyed the RNLI lifeboats with envy in his capacity as head of naval planning, saying that in the event of a European

Sir William Hillary, founder of the RNLI.

conflict he would use them for naval purposes, to be told firmly that the Geneva Convention makes specific provision to preserve the neutrality of rescue vessels which can display the red cross for protection. The two Dutch lifeboat services used this during the Second World War. They faced pressure from the occupying German forces to use their lifeboats for military purposes, but both fleets were painted white with large red crosses and kept up their humanitarian work. Two lifeboats escaped to England loaded down with Jewish families and resistance fighters facing execution.

William Hillary had the same dogged determination as these later admirals and was not going to let the Admiralty stop a good idea. He lobbied influential MPs, including anti-slavery campaigner William Wilberforce, and wrote a stirring 'Appeal to the British Nation on the Humanity and Policy of Forming a National Institution for the Preservation of Lives and Property from Shipwreck'.

In it he proposed 'the formation of one great Institution which would in itself embrace every possible means for the preservation of life from the hazards of shipwreck'. Its objects would be:

First; the preservation of human life from shipwreck . . . always the first great and permanent object of the Institution

Secondly; assistance to vessels in distress

Thirdly; preservation of vessels and property, after people have been rescued

Fourthly; the prevention of plunder

Fifthly; succour and support of those rescued – food, clothing, medical aid, shelter, getting home

Sixthly; rewards to rescuers, provision for widows and families.

This was not Hillary's only grand scheme, for he proposed a seaman's hospital on the banks of the Thames, a tower of refuge for Douglas Harbour (which was built) and various inventions, some of which were far ahead of their time.

His vision for the lifeboat service was remarkable not least because his fundamental principles remain firmly in place almost two centuries later.

By gathering the great and good of the day (another tradition maintained by the RNLI) Hillary achieved his goal of a lifeboat service for all of Britain and Ireland, though he was never invited to become a member of its Committee of Management. The early days saw a flurry of activity with money pouring in and new lifeboat stations being set up, but the impetus soon faded and the first boats provided were often left unmaintained. By the late 1840s the lifeboat service was in poor shape. There was no appeal for funds from 1841 to 1850 and many boats were by then so decrepit that their crews, nearly all of them fishermen, preferred

The tubular lifeboat at Rhyl had a similar shape to a modern Atlantic inshore lifeboat.

(Geoff Smith)

to use their own boats for rescues. Then a disaster in 1849, when twenty men were lost from the South Shields lifeboat, rekindled public interest.

In its long history, the RNLI has had a succession of different leaders: admirals and aristocrats, barristers and brigadiers; and while some have left a mark by steering a new course, many are now sadly forgotten. Two men in the 1850s saved the RNLI from oblivion: one is remembered while the achievements of the other are largely ignored. The first was an aristocrat, the Duke of Northumberland, who was appointed President and famously launched a competition for new lifeboat designs. The second was the secretary of the Institution, Richard Lewis, a barrister who set about rebuilding the RNLI with a quiet determination, aided by a new chief inspector of lifeboats, John Ross Ward.

The Duke's competition was a roaring success with 280 entries, ranging from the pedantic to the barking mad, as one might expect from Victorian inventors. Among the more whimsical entries were a wicker frame covered in canvas that could be rolled along the beach and opened at the launch site and a strange contraption whose hull incorporated two hydrogen-filled cylinders. One design was even to be 'propelled by a fish tail'.

Such inventions kept on being sent in to the RNLI and were published, with elaborate etchings, in such newspapers as the *Illustrated London News*. Inventions can bring out the worst in their originators. Captain George Manby, who devised a highly successful rocket-firing apparatus for getting a line across to ships wrecked close to shore, long maintained that the idea for the lifeboat service was his, not Hillary's. Manby had written a pamphlet on life-saving, also sent to William Wilberforce, as early as 1813. He had carefully surveyed long stretches of coast and recommended precise locations for mortars to fire lines to stranded ships.

Similarly, the Duke's design competition caused divisions, the winning design of James Beeching being judged in need of further work, which was given to a member of the judging committee, James Peake.

A design that seemed quite outrageous at the time was for a 40ft tubular lifeboat, submitted by father and son, Henry and Henry Thomas Richardson. It could be considered the forebear of today's inflatables in that it had two air-filled tubes for the hull. The Richardsons were even more outrageous than their boat, *Challenger*, which they took up and down the north-west coast and on a voyage from Liverpool to London, playing practical jokes on the way and recording their escapades in a book.

They encountered fog off Lytham, appearing suddenly to find 'a great many people on the shore, evidently alarmed at our novel and sudden appearance. We hailed them in French and fired our brass swivel gun. . . . The effect was prodigious. All fled like frightened sheep, shouting that a French lugger had landed. . . . These occurrences gave us the idea of procuring masks, which appendages on our voyage around the coast of Wales, caused much terror. . . . We procured a set of masks of differing degrees of ferocity and ugliness – a boar's head with tremendous tusks, a nose a foot long with a French red cap, a devil's mask, a crocodile's head and others. . . . Pilots and all fled from us.'

The Richardsons had certainly crossed the line from genius into eccentricity!

But while they were terrifying coastal villages, Lewis was concentrating on raising money, building boats and putting in proper organisation. As the last thirty years had shown, local stations could sustain themselves for a while, but after a few years deterioration set in. Central direction and support was, and still is, needed, though the balance between local initiative and central diktat is one which must be handled with sensitivity. Many naval and army officers, imbued with a command and control mentality, have received a polite welcome from lifeboat crews over the years, who immediately revert to local practices as soon as the officials and inspectors leave.

Lewis had a deep respect for the local communities of which the lifeboat stations were an integral part, but proper standards were needed to keep crews and boats safe. The relevance of Hillary, Northumberland and Lewis is that they set in place structures and traditions that have lasted. Hillary realised he needed the support of influential people to get his ideas into practice. Once he had gathered them, he soon got royal patronage for his new organisation and the royal family has been involved ever since. Northumberland encouraged innovation and Lewis put in structures and standards, still in place today. And all challenged the status quo.

So in our story of the last fifty years, such names as Richard Oakley, who designed a safe self-righting lifeboat; Gerrard Dutton, who championed the first fast offshore lifeboat; Wilfred Graham, who halted the building of slow traditional boats; David Stogdon and Desmond Hoare, who pioneered inshore boats; and Brian Miles, who dealt with two major disasters and never forgot the families, might take their place alongside the dukes and admirals of the nineteenth century.

ROYAL SUPPORT

Ritual and tradition are important in larger service organisations. The army, navy, police and the coastguard all have their own cultures backed by the stricture of uniforms. Lifeboatmen have been bedecked over the ages in red woolly bobble hats, scratchy blue Guernseys with RNLI in deep-red letters

Len Patten presents the RNLI official colour to the Queen Mother.

across the chest and a range of oilskins, sou'westers and life jackets. At most stations there is a reluctance to adopt any uniform other than perhaps a crew jumper with the name of the station and perhaps a picture of the lifeboat.

The lack of a uniform is accompanied by a lack of formality and disregard for military-style regimentation. This can cause merriment when lifeboat crews get involved in ceremonial events, which usually pass smoothly but often feature a good deal of improvisation behind the scenes. When the Queen reviewed the fleet at Spithead as part of her silver jubilee celebrations, a hand-picked crew was to line the side of a lifeboat as she passed. Peaked caps were issued, making the crew feel uneasy from the start. The procedure was to 'cheer ship' – take off their caps and wave them in a circle. It was obviously important that all the caps rotated in the same direction – clockwise – but in rehearsal one man just couldn't do it; every time his cap went the wrong way. Alan Tate, the staff officer in charge, tried and tried again to get him to change but the more flustered the man became, the more stubborn his arm became. The man offered to stand down but Alan told him just to forget about it and not worry – it would be all right on the night. It was. When the worried coxswain doffed his cap, inside was a large white circle of card with a bright red arrow pointing clockwise.

Caps have caused other problems, as crews feel uncomfortable in them. They are meant to be carried under the arm when crews go up to receive medals but they can be forgotten. Len Patten, then the Newhaven coxswain, was waiting at the bottom of the steps of the Royal Festival Hall stage to present the RNLI's newly made official colour to the Queen Mother. The magnificent flag was handmade from silk, with thousands of silk thread stitches making up the RNLI letters, anchor and crown painstakingly sewn by members of the Royal College of Needlework. Len was waiting, cap on, with the flag erect in its holder. In front of him, a coxswain was about to step up for his medal when he realised he had left his cap on his seat in the auditorium. There was a quick consultation and he borrowed Len's cap and came off the other side of the stage with his medal; the cap was then hurriedly smuggled up the aisle, out into the foyer, backstage and out of a side stage door to be re-united with Len and his flag just in time for the presentation. It was indeed a memorable meeting, as the Queen Mother's speech had been drafted by a member of the PR staff in a launderette in Tooting, London.

Other traditions run deeper and have been celebrated in the same way for many years, particularly the naming of lifeboats.

Every boat has a naming ceremony and, while the RNLI has a formula which is used by all stations, the results vary enormously. The climax of the naming is the breaking of a bottle of champagne over the bow of the boat. The tradition of appeasing the gods of the sea and seeking their blessing on new vessels goes back into almost all cultures. The Greeks would call on Poseidon for protection and the Romans on Neptune, both drinking wine and pouring water onto the ship. Early Jews and Christians would seek protection by blessing their ships with water.

Holy water was used until medieval times, but by the seventeenth century the tradition was to take a sip of wine from a standing cup, a large vessel made from precious metal, then pour the rest on the deck of the ship and throw the cup overboard. It would usually be retrieved and kept by the finder. As more ships were built, this practice became too expensive and a bottle was substituted and broken over the ship's bow. The old ineffectual method of swinging the bottle at the boat (it usually bounced and swung back unbroken) has not been used for years. Lifeboat inspectors have put as much energy and ingenuity into their bottle-breaking as into any piece of the boat's life-saving equipment. One trick was to score the bottle with a glass cutter to weaken it and ensure a clean break. This was a high-risk technique, as the bottle might explode before the due time on a hot sunny day. Some inspectors wrapped the bottles in muslin to avoid glass shards hitting the crew or the crowd. And wise coxswains would always station a crew member on the bow with a hammer to break the bottle if it stayed intact.

Over to the technical department at headquarters: with all the seriousness applied to designing anchors and rope cutters, skilled draughtsmen and naval

A typical naming ceremony. *(Derek King)*

architects spent months dreaming up the perfect bottle breaker. Prototypes were built, modifications made and then the result put into practice: a cradle with an electrically released hook holding the bottle. When the mechanism operated, the bottle crashed onto the edge of a piece of angle iron. Its only flaw was that eager or clumsy fingers ashore could, if the control switch was badly positioned, cause a premature launch of the bottle. So a split pin was added, to be removed a couple of minutes before the ceremony. And, of course, a standard operating procedure was written for the equipment!

Ceremonies range from the moving to the comical and many are a mixture of the two. Take the *Fishermen's Friend*. Because this Mersey class lifeboat was the gift of Lofthouse of Fleetwood, manufacturers of the world-famous Fishermen's Friend cough sweets, the naming was organised in Fleetwood docks. Part of the ceremony is a non-denominational dedication of the lifeboat, so there is usually a short reading from the Bible. The coxswain and crew objected to the chosen passage, which had a reference to 'reeling and staggering like a drunken man', which they felt would be taken as a personal reference. An alternative passage was printed in the programme. The guests were assembled, the boat polished and sparkling, and it fell to David Jones, the regional fund-raiser, to ask the stragglers to take their seats. Reaching for what he thought was the microphone switch, he sent the champagne crashing across the bows and the boat was immediately nicknamed the 'Oh, bloody hell!', David's exasperated expression. The ever resourceful crew quickly commandeered the ship's brandy, re-rigged the bottle breaker and the ceremony proceeded with no further hitch. The gods of the sea ended up with a brandy and champagne cocktail that day.

The variety of donors adds another dimension to the ceremonies. At Filey, where the Keep Fit Association had given the boat, fifty middle-aged ladies had a workout on the sands before the naming, and a grumpy Yorkshireman complained to the police that he couldn't walk his dog along the promenade, as he did every day, because the chairs were in the way.

The *Sun* newspaper had fun when a Scottish laird, in full traditional dress and sitting on the platform with knees wide apart, caught the eye of Princess Diana. The photo, with Diana's lovely smile and the bearded aristocrat gazing ahead in blissful ignorance of what was on display, made the front page.

All the senior members of the royal family have met lifeboat crews and visited stations, led by the current president, the Duke of Kent. He took over the role on the death of his mother, Princess Marina. His sister, Princess Alexandra, is also a great lifeboat supporter and her easy charm and genuine interest has been appreciated at many lifeboat stations. When she visited Penarth to name the new inshore lifeboat, she was determined to meet as many people as possible. A young girl from the choir told the Princess that her mother had met her some years ago. 'Is she here today?' asked Princess Alexandra. The girl nodded and was despatched to fetch her mother who arrived, flustered and in her jeans as she was working behind the scenes. The Princess, quite unconcerned, chatted away until the police became anxious that the schedule was slipping. An official was asked to hurry the Princess along and was told, 'When I was seventeen I realised I could either do what other people told me or do what I wanted. I chose the latter, so I think I'll just finish talking to everybody.' And she didn't leave until, half an hour behind schedule, she had spoken to everybody in the room. On a visit to Portpatrick in 1989 she had done just the same, diving away from officials to speak to the women in the kitchen as they brewed the tea.

The Duke of Edinburgh is also famous for his independence. In 1982 he presented the RNLI with a Design Council award for the Arun lifeboat. The ceremony was followed by a visit to an Arun at Tower Pier in London, and the Duke was invited to inspect the boat. He went below into the survivors' compartment and, out of the gaze of the media, immediately asked, 'Where's the chunder bucket?'

The Duke of Kent, President of the RNLI. *(Derek King)*

Other private royal moments deserve mention. The Duchess of Kent, before she largely withdrew from public life, was a frequent official visitor to lifeboat stations. After the Penlee lifeboat disaster she made a completely private visit to Mousehole to meet the widows and families. For each of the bereaved wives and mothers, she had a simple silver cross, handed over personally and with no publicity.

Her husband, the Duke of Kent, is a very active RNLI President. Most of his engagements are tightly timed and strictly choreographed but occasionally there is a little time for relaxation. On a tour of west coast stations in Scotland, he was whisked in the company of a series of Lords Lieutenant to Islay, Campbeltown, Portpatrick and Stranraer. There was an overnight stay in Portpatrick where lifeboat people from all around the district came for a meal. The time for the Duke to retire came and went after the host produced a very pleasant bottle of

Princess Alexandra addresses the RNLI annual meeting.

the local malt. The Duke, having enjoyed a comforting dram, went upstairs but his equerry, a young Guards officer, remained to sample the hospitality. On leaving the hotel the next morning the Duke was presented with a bottle of malt as a keepsake, which the rather green equerry had to clutch as the royal party went to sea on the lifeboat.

Every year, lifeboat people are invited to attend the Queen's garden party at Buckingham Palace. They assemble first in a hotel in Victoria and walk a few hundred yards to the Palace. All except one coxswain, who took a taxi, 'Because it's the only time in my life I'll get in a cab and say, "Take me to Buckingham Palace"!'

AWARDS

The great gathering of the RNLI is the annual presentation of awards, held in London. It strikes fear into the hearts of most lifeboat crew members who have to process across a brightly lit stage in front of two thousand people to have a medal pinned to their chest, often by a member of the royal family. So relaxation after the event is understandable. For Mike Scales and the Guernsey crew the relaxation went on long into the night and at dawn it seemed a good idea to go and feed the ducks in St James's Park. All the hotel's breakfast rolls were scooped up and any ducks foolish enough to be asleep were coaxed into the water by large lifeboatmen's boots. The merry scene suddenly took a dramatic turn when bubbles were seen coming up from the lake and a quick head count showed a man missing. 'Christ, he's fallen in!' was the cry until the missing lifeboatman, perched on a bough overhanging the water and dropping breadcrumbs in, burst out laughing.

At another awards ceremony, the metropolitan attitude of an intransigent barman was challenged by the seafaring knowledge of a lifeboat coxswain. The barman wanted to go home early and called last orders at 10 p.m. Maurice Hutchens from Sennen Cove was in the bar, as was Ben Usher, the Withernsea inshore boat helmsman and a policeman by profession. 'You can't shut the bar at ten. That's illegal, isn't it, Ben?' said Maurice. However, the barman was unimpressed and started to pull down the shutters with a hook on a pole. 'Well bless me, there's a boat hook. Now I think we should take charge of that,' said Maurice. He commandeered the pole and the bar stayed open until the wee small hours.

Not all get-togethers are so jolly. In 1982 the whole Guernsey crew were to receive medals after the *Bonita* rescue, along with Brian Bevan and others. Three

Maurice Hutchens of Sennen (centre) meets the Icelandic trawler skipper he saved, with the President of Iceland, Vigdis Finnbogadóttir (left). *(Keystone Press Agency)*

women from Penlee were also to be presented with the posthumous medals for their husbands and sons on the crew. Slowly, everybody gathered in the bar, lifeboatmen in one corner and the Penlee women in the other. Bevan saw the embarrassment and sought advice. 'What can I say to them?' he asked an official. 'Just go across and say hello, that's all you need to do,' was the reply and the ice was broken, though the mood remained muted.

The next day Mary Richards, Caroline Blewett and Janet Madron displayed enormous dignity and courage as they received the medals from Princess Alice, one of the Queen's cousins.

FOG ON THE TYNE

Another ceremony is a press day. Every new lifeboat design is proudly shown off to the press, who are taken to sea as the boat is put through its paces. Late spring is a favourite time, with good light for photographers and usually calm weather. In 1982, the press boarded the train from London to Portsmouth in bright sunshine and travelled through the verdant countryside to see the new slipway lifeboat, the Tyne, on her debut launch. What they and their minders from the RNLI press office did not know, until they were within a few hundred yards of Portsmouth Harbour, was that there was a thick sea fog blanketing the English Channel. A small cruise boat had been hired, complete with the Portsmouth harbour pilots required by law. On board with them, from the RNLI, were two admirals, two commanders and a naval engineer. Navigation to Selsey, just around the corner, should have been no problem with the assembled experience.

The fog, though, had played havoc with the plans. Lifeboat inspector Roy Portchmouth, who was to show off the new boat, started the day stranded in Southampton, unable to get across the Solent to the Isle of Wight to pick up the boat. Then the Selsey lifeboat crew, who were to help with the launch of the new boat from their slipway, were called out on two rescues, to an angling boat and a yacht, both of which had run aground in the dense fog.

Undaunted, the press boat edged carefully out of Portsmouth. Expert eyes scanned the sea and the chart, though none of the assembled mariners felt the need to mark a plotted course. Nearing the channel that leads to Selsey, the press boat passed a moored angling boat. About five minutes later, there was another angling boat, with fishermen whose bobble hats and anoraks were remarkably similar to those of the first – because it was the same boat. The press boat, with its pilots, admirals and commanders had done what Winnie the Pooh did on his hunt in the Hundred Acre Wood – gone round in a circle.

The bemused skipper of the angling boat simply pointed in the direction of the channel to Selsey and eventually the lifeboat station loomed out of the fog.

After a wait, and just as the coffee and sandwiches were running low, the new lifeboat arrived and was hauled up. The fog was beginning to thin but was still very patchy. A communications strategy was agreed with the press photographers. As they looked west down the Solent, they could see the next clear patch arriving. 'Launch!' they shouted to the RNLI press officer. 'Launch!' the press officer shouted up to the bridge. 'Launch!' they shouted into their radio. 'What?' shouted the man in the Selsey boathouse and the fog closed in again. The second time, it worked. The press had to be ferried ashore in the inshore lifeboat and taken by coach, organised at the last minute by the ever-resourceful station secretary, to get back for their deadlines. Another fine plan was rescued by initiative and improvisation, the staple fare of all lifeboat stations.

ALL PRESENT AND CORRECT

One of the most impressive lifeboat gatherings ever was in 2004 when the Queen officially opened the new lifeboat college in Poole. Every single lifeboat station sent at least one crew member and they were gathered in an immaculately organised series of ranks – over 200 thick lifeboat jumpers causing their wearers to wilt as the sun beat down and the Queen's programme was delayed. In the audience were the head of the International Maritime Organisation, Admiral Thimio Mitropoulos, and the heads of several European lifeboat services – Zip Wiebenga from the Netherlands, Rolf Westerstrom from Sweden, Udo Fox from Germany and Einar Johnsson representing Iceland. RNLI chairman, Admiral Sir Jock Slater, having already shown the Queen, Duke of Edinburgh and Duke of Kent the sea survival pool in the college, brought them out onto a podium for a short and simple ceremony. Then the Queen and the two Dukes, having met RNLI gold medallists, were asked to stand in the middle of the 200 assembled lifeboat crew. The photographer had only two chances to get it right – one for black and white and one for colour. He got both, perfectly recording an absolutely unique event, unlikely ever to be repeated, the only time that all lifeboat stations have been linked in one place at once. The photograph represents the whole RNLI endeavour around the coasts of Britain and Ireland with its diversity of crew members from all walks of life. It was a warm and friendly day, the sort of occasion that the RNLI organises so well, months of careful planning turning into a flawless royal visit of under an hour, leaving timeless memories.

So for all the pomp and circumstance, the spirit of the lifeboat service is unchanged. It was admirably captured at a grand dinner held to celebrate the RNLI's centenary in 1924. One of the speakers was the young Winston Churchill. His oratorical power was already well developed, as the conclusion of his speech showed:

Great waves may thunder on the shore, winds may drive and beat with their utmost fury, the boat goes out, thrusts its way ahead to the wreck, it is twisted and turned by convulsions of the sea, it is swamped with water, it is driven back, again and again it returns, it pursues and perseveres on its mission of rescue, of salvation, to those who are in peril, it drives on with a courage which is stronger than the storm, it drives on with a mercy which does not quail in the presence of death, it drives on as a proof, a symbol, a testimony, that man is created in the image of God and that valour and virtue have not perished in the British race.

CHAPTER SEVEN

Finding the Funds

Charity fund-raising is built around a few basic elements: donations, social gatherings (usually involving food and drink), entertainment, sponsored events and selling goods. The variations on these themes are endless as is the imagination used to persuade a generous public to give millions of pounds each year to charity. Of the 180,000 or so charities in England and Wales (Scotland and Northern Ireland do not have a Charity Commission to provide figures) only a minority actively raise funds, as many are very small charities endowed decades ago and rely on land or investments to generate their income.

The Victorians were great philanthropists and set up thousands of charities. Their benevolence tended to be paternalistic, the wealthy benefactors deciding how the deserving poor should be helped. Nowadays these attitudes are strongly challenged by most of the larger charities, though there are many smaller ones comfortably carrying on in those Victorian traditions. A Victorian lifeboat tragedy can be linked to the start of widespread public fund-raising, setting a pattern that remains to this day.

On the night of 9 December 1886, the German barque *Mexico* was bound from Liverpool to Guayaquil in Ecuador with a crew of twelve. In the middle of the day she was being driven towards the Lancashire coast by a west-north-westerly gale and through the sleet and hail, Captain Burmester could see the low sandy shoreline. He ordered two anchors to be dropped but they dragged and the ship drifted on so he ordered the fore and main masts to be cut down. Eventually, in the mid-afternoon, the anchors held and *Mexico*, now off Southport, seemed safe. However, by 9 p.m. she was drifting again, into the breakers, and the captain ordered distress signals to be fired and told the crew to lash themselves to the rigging. Within minutes, *Mexico* hit a sandbank.

Southport lifeboat crew rushed to the boathouse where Coxswain Charles Hodge picked three extra men because of the severe weather. The lifeboat and carriage were hauled along the beach to get upwind of the *Mexico* so they could sail down onto the wreck. As they approached, Hodge dropped his anchor, intending to veer down, but his lifeboat was overwhelmed by a huge wave,

Fund-raising should be fun. *(Simon Culiford)*

capsized and was swept towards the shore. Of sixteen men who set out, only two survived, trapped inside the upturned hull.

Meanwhile a lighthouse keeper at St Annes had seen the distress signals and the St Annes lifeboat was rowed off the beach at 10.25 p.m., setting the sails 500yds offshore. Then she capsized. All thirteen lifeboatmen drowned.

Further up the coast, *Mexico*'s signals had been spotted at Lytham. Even though the wreck was 7 miles away, and south of the Ribble estuary, Coxswain Thomas Clarkson decided to launch. His lifeboat differed from those at Southport and St Annes in one vital, life-saving respect. Four water ballast tanks, set into the hull, improved the trim and stability, making the boat heavier and lower in the water.

As she approached the *Mexico*, a powerful breaking wave caught her and threw her onto her side, breaking three oars. The water ballast kept the boat safe, she came upright and the crew dropped the anchor and veered down to save the whole crew of the *Mexico*, though two were badly injured. Last down the rope was Captain Burmester who calmly told Coxswain Clarkson, 'You have a very good boat.' The rescue was completed around 12.30 a.m. and the Lytham boat sailed home safely.

By a particularly cruel twist of fate, the *Mexico*'s crew had already been rescued when the Southport boat reached the barque at around 1.30 a.m. Communications were so rudimentary that none of the lifeboats knew the others were out.

The only telephone in St Annes was in the home of a Manchester businessman, Charles Macara, who was also a member of the lifeboat committee, and through the night telegrams were sent up and down the coast, but there was no news of survivors. The next morning Lytham and Blackpool lifeboats set out to look for the Southport and St Annes men.

Twenty-seven men had died, twelve had been saved. There were sixteen widows and fifty orphans in the two towns and a disaster fund of £50,000 was raised.

At the RNLI, questions were asked about boat design and soon water ballast tanks, saviours of the Lytham men and their boat, were fitted to all boats of that design. But the business instincts of Charles Macara caused him to ask different, more penetrating questions and the more he looked into the RNLI's finances, the greater was his determination to change them.

Victorian philanthropy of a few wealthy landowners and gentlemen from the City had sustained the RNLI since its foundation. It had no mass support and no way of engendering it. Macara arranged for lifeboats to be paraded through the streets, collecting money in bags on long poles. The first procession, in 1891, saw the St Annes and Southport lifeboats hauled through central Manchester with thousands of onlookers. This was almost certainly the first large-scale charity street collection and a great spectacle for its time. As well as the lifeboats on carriages, there were three bands and groups from the fire brigade and ambulance corps. Money was thrown from upstairs windows and from the tops of trams into collecting carts and the lifeboatmen had collecting bags on poles. More than £600 was donated, mostly in coppers. The lifeboats were later launched into a lake in a local park and a rescue was staged using rocket apparatus in front of a crowd of 30,000 people.

Following the success of these street collections, in 1915 small paper flags were introduced to be sold, the start of flag days.

Macara's wife joined in the effort and set up a network of ladies' committees to help with the collections. Lifeboat Saturday spread throughout the land, as did the groups of Ladies' Auxiliaries, forerunners of local volunteer fund-raising committees. Macara, a strong personality in the RNLI's history, had his iron grip on the Lifeboat Saturday movement eased as the campaign went nationwide and he fell out with the RNLI. For the next five years rumours and complaints were made, leading to an article in a monthly magazine making allegations of mismanagement which were investigated by a parliamentary select committee. The committee regretted that Macara 'should have allowed personal ill-feeling to so influence his conduct as he did in regard to this matter'. They put down a marker about fund-raising expenses, a contentious issue to this day, when they noted, 'Street demonstrations are necessarily a costly means of collecting money and great care should be taken to prevent their expense from becoming excessive.' However, they were satisfied that the RNLI had the matter in hand and was not, as alleged, hiding legacy income by the way it presented its accounts. Most allegations were 'absolutely unfounded' or 'completely disproved', and, to the charge that the boats were so badly maintained that the RNLI ought to be prosecuted for manslaughter, the committee replied that this was wholly unfounded and preposterous.

One can surmise that, like William Hillary before him and others to follow, Macara was a man who could do things only one way – his way – and that it was this determination that created popular fund-raising for the lifeboats and for charities in general.

Once the idea of raising money from the many not the few took hold, there was no stopping it. Street collections were followed by dinners, concerts and balls, all organised by local committees.

WHERE THERE'S A WILL

The breadth of fund-raising today is much greater but the principles are the same. The RNLI has almost two thousand voluntary fund-raising committees, making it one of the biggest community fund-raising organisations in both Britain and Ireland. They devise a huge range of activities, from the traditional and still very popular events, such as coffee mornings and dinners, to the more unusual sponsored head-shaving or adventurous overseas challenges.

A century ago, the RNLI was one of very few charities with active public fund-raising. There are now hundreds, and the RNLI is untypical, and potentially vulnerable, in one aspect of its income: legacies, which now account for almost two-thirds of its income.

Since its early days, legacies have been a vital source of funds. It is instructive to note that the RNLI's first legacy, £1,000 from John Henry Hecker of Finsbury Square in London, in 1825, was followed by only seven more by 1852. Then came the Duke of Northumberland and Richard Lewis, who rejuvenated the lifeboat stations, and Macara, who brought lifeboats onto the streets and into the lives of ordinary people throughout the land. By 1900, sixty-two legacies worth a total £31,500 were received in one year.

The largest ever received was from Roy Barker of Jersey. He was a Lincolnshire-based agricultural businessman who had retired to the Channel Islands. He was also a keen yachtsman and often went down to St Helier harbour when lifeboats called in on passage. Having looked over an Arun, he ordered a scaled-down version for himself from the lifeboat builders William Osborne of Littlehampton. Living in a small island community, he wished his financial affairs to remain private, so only three RNLI officials knew that he intended to leave around £6.5 million to buy new lifeboats. That figure was almost slashed to the cost of one boat when Mr Barker took offence at the treatment he received from the RNLI – and the officials in charge only found out after his death.

Only three people in the RNLI knew about Roy Barker's intentions and he swore them to secrecy. They kept in touch with Mr Barker discreetly so that his

Roy Barker III, the third lifeboat provided from one will. *(Nicholas Leach)*

secret was never known during his lifetime. However, their discretion went wrong, nearly causing a major change in the will and they never knew that he felt badly snubbed by their behaviour.

It happened when Jersey received a new lifeboat and there was the usual naming ceremony. The three officials thought they should invite Mr Barker but could not put him with the other VIPs without explaining to local people who he was and why he was getting special treatment. He was therefore allocated a seat towards the back of the crowd, impersonal and ordinary. And he did not like it. He subsequently started discussions with his advisers about substantially reducing the RNLI share of his will, but luckily for the lifeboat service he never got round to it and in the end his original wishes remained, and Alderney's next lifeboat was named *Roy Barker I*. The second Roy Barker boat went to Wick, the northernmost mainland station, and the third to Howth in Ireland.

Another donor who liked the idea of living on through his name on the side of a lifeboat was Kenneth Thelwall. He ran an oil business and lived in the attractive East Yorkshire village of Walkington in a large though relatively modest house on the edge of the village. Unmarried, he had no close family. His one outward sign of wealth was his personalised number plate, KT 1. In that lay a clue to a decision of enormous consequence.

Thelwall's lawyer was Christopher Hobson of the Beverley firm Rollits. Like most professionals, he numbered other local solicitors and accountants among his acquaintances. He had recently spoken to the Hull accountant acting for a Mr Sanderson who lived in a rest home overlooked by the Humber Bridge and had donated a lifeboat, *Enid of Yorkshire*, to serve in the relief fleet. The RNLI had organised for it to be named in Bridlington, giving Mr Sanderson enormous pleasure.

When Kenneth Thelwall called 'young Mr Hobson' (Christopher's father had also been a partner in the firm) to discuss his will, he asked for ideas. After some small personal bequests, he wanted to leave everything to charity. That was as far as he had got. Hobson named several local good causes. None took Thelwall's fancy. Then Hobson recounted the tale of the *Enid of Yorkshire*.

'Will they put my name on a boat?' asked Thelwall. Hobson nodded. 'That's it then, leave them the lot.'

And he did, some £3 million, including the house, the adjoining plot and another piece of land at the crossroads on the village boundary. The last gift turned into something of a liability. Charities must take professional advice before they sell land or property. A plot on the edge of a desirable village has planning potential but that is all it is, potential. For years the plot, occupied by gorse bushes and rabbits, has been waiting for the planners to give the green light for development, which would significantly increase its value. Nevertheless, Kenneth Thelwall provided a new lifeboat for Humber, a second for the relief fleet and an extension for the RNLI Headquarters built in 1990.

Other legacies have caused bigger headaches. Seven charities were named in the will of an elderly English lady who lived her last years in France. On her death a jewellery box disappeared from her house, together with a young man who had shared it. The contents were unknown. Worse than that, the French authorities wanted to tax the estate at punitive rates. French inheritance tax increases with the remoteness of familial relationship to the deceased, so charities, with no family links, are hit with the highest rate. Much of the money was in England, and the executors were only prepared to release it if the charities would indemnify them. However, the charities' own assets could be seized, or, in theory at least, their people arrested whenever they visited France if the tax was refused. Two of the charities agreed to pay the tax; two refused; the others kept looking to their lawyers. At the time of writing, over ten years after the death, the case remains unresolved.

Most legacies are modest, a few hundred or a few thousand pounds. Although leaving money to charity in a will is very straightforward, some of the bequests have been far from simple. There have been gifts of a pig farm, a night club, a caravan park and a house in Tenerife, which was quickly occupied by Dutch squatters. It took some years to have them evicted and the RNLI's urbane lawyer, visiting the island on holiday and making a visit incognito, was chased away by a snarling dog. A smallholding of very old South African shares was vigorously pursued by the executor of a multi-million pound will – and yielded £13!

A direct descendant of Sir William Hillary, Dr Cecil Preston Hillary, was an active fund-raiser in Nottingham. He retired to Hastings where he kept up his lifeboat work and he and his wife left in their wills a medal awarded to Hillary's son, a portrait of Sir William and a substantial bequest on the specific provision that the RNLI should only benefit if it was still an independent organisation.

Plymouth artist Sybil Glover left a whole collection of paintings and some fine antique furniture. Doris Mann, another active lifeboat fund-raiser, gave the RNLI two houses in her lifetime and bequeathed seventeen more in two Bedfordshire villages.

Other people with obvious reasons for leaving large bequests were Mary Doig, daughter of trawler skipper John Doig; Lieutenant-Commander Hugh Macquarrie Stone, whose father was a North Sea ferry captain, and renowned yachtswoman Susan Hiscock.

There is even a story, said to be true, that £10,000 was received from a will because of somebody seeing a flag day collector standing all day in the rain and admiring their dedication to the lifeboat cause.

One story that is certainly true is that of a wealthy Midlands man, Frank Clifford of Stourbridge. One of Frank Clifford's close friends was a member of the Stourbridge branch of the RNLI who had organised a talk by Harry Jones, former coxswain of the Hoylake lifeboat. A long-serving and distinguished lifeboatman, with a bronze bravery medal, Harry is nonetheless a modest man and told stories of his rescues in straightforward language. Frank Clifford was so impressed that he decided to change his will. When he died he left the RNLI £300,000 to help provide the Newquay lifeboat, *Frank and Lena Clifford*. Harry and Margaret Jones were among the crowd at the naming ceremony and had to be prised out, somewhat reluctantly, to meet the VIPs present.

Another man who held lifeboat crews in high regard was Frank Atkinson, who built up a successful engineering business in Nottingham and retired to the south coast. He was a no-nonsense man who bought the Atlantic 21 for Lymington and used to take the crew out for dinner each year, telling them they could bring their wives or girlfriends – but not both!

The proudest possession of this wealthy and generous man was the Lymington lifeboat sweater presented to him by the crew. From time to time, Frank would arrive at RNLI headquarters in Poole, unannounced, and ask if anything was needed. As long as he was given a straight answer, and one he liked, a cheque would be in the post.

RECLUSIVE DONORS

Perhaps the most private of all lifeboat benefactors was Sir David Robinson. He started his business life with a bicycle shop and went on to found Radio Rentals. Sadly, in later life, his wife became seriously ill and Sir David devoted his time to her. Although she could not communicate, he spent every day with her. She died a few days after him in January 1987.

Sir David was a great philanthropist. He used his considerable fortune to found a Cambridge college, provide a new hospital wing and, when he heard of the Penlee lifeboat disaster in 1981, he gave the money for a replacement lifeboat. The new lifeboat was named *Mabel Alice* in honour of his wife, but he was not at the ceremony as he hated publicity.

Sir David gave another lifeboat in his lifetime. His colleague, introduced as plain Mr Evans, rang Brian Miles and asked where new boats were needed and if the payments could be made in stages. Miles was in a quandary. Was this a test of trust or business acumen? If he said no, then the implication was that he did not trust Sir David. If he said yes, a shrewd businessman might say he was taking too great a risk by, in effect, extending credit. Miles didn't have to ponder long, as he used sound instinct to reach an answer. Sir David had given a boat and asked to give another. There really was no doubt – he should be trusted. The money arrived exactly as promised and the lifeboat went to Buckie.

Sir David left money for two more boats in his will. One was named in his memory and was stationed at the Lizard, the station next to Penlee, where *Mabel Alice* still served. His daughter performed the Lizard lifeboat naming and was moved to feel that it had brought her close to her father, whom she had not seen for some years.

Sir David also asked for help from the RNLI to preserve his privacy after death. Because of his wealth and his reclusiveness, the media wanted to tell the story of the end of this enigmatic figure, who had not even appeared publicly when the Queen opened Robinson College. Sir David had already spoken to Brian Miles about his plans to be buried at sea. The press raced down to Cornwall, expecting him to be taken out on the Penlee lifeboat, and the RNLI did nothing to disabuse them. Meanwhile, Sir David's coffin was on the

Gorleston lifeboat, the nearest to his Newmarket home as he wanted minimum expense and fuss, for a committal miles offshore by lifeboat inspector Dick Perks.

For some curious reason, parrots seem to figure in a number of lifeboat legacy tales. As well as dealing with Sir David Robinson's requests, Brian Miles used to visit an elderly lady donor in Kent. When the lady left the room to make tea, he was still being talked to by a parrot, which went on to outlive its owner. Another parrot had the same good fortune, and his owner, Victoria Brown, not only left enough money to buy a lifeboat for Harwich, but also set a sum aside to care for her parrot. The executor of the will brought photographs to the lifeboat naming ceremony to show that the bird was being properly looked after.

Few people are lucky enough to see the results of their generosity in buying a lifeboat, and for Miss Heather 'Mickie' Allen, naming a lifeboat after her great-grandfather James Burrough not only brought her enormous pleasure but also gave her what she described as her family. Burrough was the founder of the famous Beefeater Gin company whose first distillery was set up on the banks of the River Thames at Chelsea.

As a direct descendant, Mickie Allen had inherited a substantial share of the company and decided she would like to honour her great-grandfather by donating a lifeboat to Devon, his home county. Brian Miles had just been appointed Deputy Director of the RNLI and was summoned to an office in the City of London to meet the no-nonsense Miss Allen, who quizzed him in detail about the finances and plans of the lifeboat service before she made the offer to donate a lifeboat – for Devon. Miles had done his homework and knew that all the Devon stations were up to date and no new boats were planned for the county. This was the first time he had dealt with a wealthy donor, so he plucked up his courage and offered a Cornish station instead. 'That's fine,' said Mickie, and the deal was done.

When the *James Burrough* went to Padstow, Mickie gradually got to know the crew and their families, eventually moving from Surrey to Cornwall to become more involved with the station. In the Padstow lifeboat community, Micky had found a new family and a worthwhile outlet for her energies. Although she was essentially a private person, she did agree to a television programme about her gift as it would help her beloved RNLI.

Two people watching the programme, Eric and Jean Cass, were impressed by the way Padstow had taken Mickie's gift as a personal matter, rather than anonymous beneficence, and decided they would like to do the same. They needed to know that they, too, could follow the fortunes of their boat if they bought one and, after discussions, were introduced to the Dungeness lifeboat station.

Sponsored runners in Padstow, where Mickie Allen gave the lifeboat. *(Simon Culiford)*

Dungeness is a desolate place, a shingle corner of Kent known for its lifeboat, power station and the late actor Derek Jarman's beach garden. There is a story about the building of the nuclear power station, which, if not true, certainly deserves to be. Apparently civil engineers spent many months studying the beach, the erosion of gravel and the strength of the underlying ground, for putting a nuclear core close to the sea demands careful calculation. As they marked out the site, an old fisherman told them they were too close to the water – shingle would be washed away by the sea, exposing the reactor. Naturally, the engineers ignored this unqualified local and, equally unsurprisingly, he turned out to be right. With every tide, shingle from the front of the power station was washed a couple of miles along the coast onto private land. The landowner then sold the gravel back to the power company, who trucked it back to the beach, only for the next tide to wash it away again.

Along the beach are small wooden houses, the homes of fishermen for generations. Dungeness is famous for its lifeboat families, the Oillers and the Tarts, and for the women who used to launch and recover the lifeboat as their men went out as crew.

Eric and Jean Cass took to the place and the people. One of their passions was ocean cruising on luxury liners and Eric persuaded his favourite cruise company to divert one of its ships away from its normal tropical climes to make a diversion to visit the D-Day beaches and then call into Dover Harbour. The Dungeness lifeboat *Pride and Spirit*, which was dwarfed by the huge liner, was on display, and the mainly American wealthy passengers received a talk on the RNLI.

Unfortunately most of them were late back to the ship after a tour of Kent, taking in Canterbury cathedral, so the lifeboat crew outnumbered the paying guests in both numbers and drinks consumption.

Other self-made men had equally straightforward attitudes. Tony Guy, of Guy Motors, which made armoured cars during the war, was president of the Wolverhampton branch of the RNLI in the 1970s when an art exhibition was mounted in the local gallery. Celebrity guests included footballer Derek Dougan, then with Wolves football club, Georgina Keen of the Committee of Management, the mayor and other dignitaries. Tony Guy provided a generous buffet and drinks and led the way by pouring himself a large whisky. A timid official, trying to get the protocol right, asked whether Mrs Keen might be served. 'Look lad,' said Tony, 'I paid for the bloody things. I think I'm first.'

At first glance it might seem curious that some of the best fund-raising is done furthest from the sea. Birmingham, Wolverhampton and Coventry have outstanding records of generosity, all providing several lifeboats with special appeals. The committees attract sailors and there are great links with Welsh lifeboat stations as West Midlands people often holiday there. In Dudley the committee chairman was Karl Falk, who served in German U-boats in the war and was tireless in his lifeboat collections, often reminding the audience at RNLI AGMs that he would be out around the Dudley pubs on Boxing Day – and asking if the paid staff could match that.

BUYING A BOAT

The earliest lifeboats were funded by insurers Lloyds or by the local gentry. The more widespread tradition of giving a lifeboat, often with a name, was described in the lifeboat magazine of 1870 with its rather quaint language: 'Fourteen years since, a movement commenced of an altogether novel character in lifeboat work, and which is without precedent in this or any other country. At that period a benevolent lady presented the National Lifeboat Institution with the cost of a new lifeboat, to be stationed at a part of the coast where one was needed. Another lifeboat soon followed from a gentleman. A third was presented by a yacht club; and a fourth was given by a lady as a thank offering after a providential preservation from drowning.'

The article went on to note gifts to commemorate deceased relatives, two sisters remembering a third with the lifeboat *The Sisters' Memorial*. Then inland towns, Ipswich being the first, bought boats, the citizens 'feeling a desire that their own communities should be represented on the coast as performing their share of the national duty of affording protection to shipwrecked persons'.

Then came mutual benefit societies, the civil service, universities, yacht clubs, even commercial travellers. This was the genesis of the major capital appeal, still an important part of any large charity's income. For the RNLI, this means the huge effort needed to raise over £1 million for a new lifeboat. Committees are formed, plans made and enormous effort expended, over a period of up to two years, to raise the funds – unless, as happened in Lincolnshire, things go wrong. A new lifeboat was needed for Skegness and a major appeal was prepared. Months of planning led to an appeal launch in a blaze of publicity and the committee was about to go into action when John Geest, of the famous banana company, offered to buy the boat outright!

The committee were thrilled and disappointed at the same time. All their plans had suddenly become redundant, yet they had achieved their target at a stroke. Mr Geest did not even want his name on the boat. He asked that the crew be consulted and they chose a bit of Lincolnshire folklore and named the boat *Lincolnshire Poacher*.

From Whitehall and White City

Two completely different organisations have bought seventy-one lifeboats between them. The Civil Service Lifeboat Fund, founded in 1866, later became the rather unwieldy Civil Service, Post Office and British Telecommunications Fund (CISPOTEL) and is now simply known as the Lifeboat Fund. It is the biggest ever single supporter of the RNLI. Its fund-raising task became more difficult in the 1980s and '90s as the civil service shrank and parts were privatised, but it is still going strong, raising money in an annual appeal to serving and retired civil servants, British Telecom and Post Office workers. The latest lifeboat, the forty-sixth bought by the fund in 2005, is an inshore boat for the relief fleet, named *Guardian Angel*.

The second organisation is BBC's *Blue Peter*, which has raised money for lifeboats since 1966 when viewers were asked to send in paperback books. The aim was to raise enough for three of the inflatable lifeboats the RNLI had just introduced. The response was so great that the RNLI's warehouses at

Konnie Huq names a *Blue Peter* lifeboat. *(Derek King)*

Borehamwood were overwhelmed, and the trade association representing second-hand book sellers complained that the RNLI had cornered the market. Four inshore boats were bought and stationed at Littlehampton, Beaumaris, North Berwick and St Agnes. *Blue Peter* editor Biddy Baxter followed the fortunes of the boats and their crews, and when they needed to be replaced launched another appeal. As the result of the 1985 appeal, 800,000 packets of buttons and postcards arrived and two new *Blue Peter* stations were added, at Cleethorpes and Portaferry. Over a million parcels of coins, medals and collectables were sent in 1993. Everything was delivered free by the Royal Mail, which dedicated extra vans to cope with the overwhelming response, a particularly impressive gesture, as they were also coping with the Christmas post. So much was raised by this appeal that an offshore boat *Blue Peter VII* was bought for Fishguard. At the naming ceremony *Blue Peter*'s Lewis Bronze eloquently described the boat as 'a gift from a community of the air to a community of the sea'.

Littlehampton has had four boats named *Blue Peter I* and the total number of *Blue Peter* lifeboats reached twenty-five when a new *Blue Peter IV*, the latest D class, was named at the 2005 London Boat Show by television presenter Konnie Huq. The record of the *Blue Peter* lifeboats is impressive; as Konnie named the new boat, the *Blue Peter* fleet had clocked up 4,300 launches, saving over 1,000 lives – all paid for by books, coins, medals and bring and buy sales.

GIVING TODAY

One of the biggest fund-raising innovations, though not the most lucrative, has been in trading. It is one of the most labour intensive ways of making money. The effort required to administer a £1 million legacy is, of course, greater than that for £1,000 but to raise £1 million from selling goods is a much greater task.

In the 1960s, the RNLI offered a statuette of a lifeboatman as a car mascot, painted pencils, a souvenir booklet and tea towels – and that was about it.

Now there are two prize-winning mail order catalogues each year, shops in all reasonably accessible lifeboat houses and in some high streets. It's a specialist skill to organise such an endeavour and, even when turning over £3 million or so a decade ago, it managed to lose money. Poor stock control, lack of immediate sales information and poor cash flow were the root causes, all of them known to bring down businesses as they nearly did for RNLI (Sales) Ltd.

Staff and trustees alike were nervous of the possible reaction of the dedicated teams of volunteers running stalls and lifeboat shops across the country when they were told that they would have to change their methods. It was an unnecessary reaction, as the volunteers, once the situation was fully explained, quickly grasped the importance of change and embraced it, showing that while volunteers must be respected they should never be patronised.

Fund-raising is now an industry with its own professional body, qualifications and career structure. Increasingly, paid fund-raisers flit like butterflies from charity to charity, alighting long enough to make changes and leaving before the consequences catch up with them. The RNLI has been largely protected from this phenomenon, not least because of its rather conservative approach. From the annual reports it can be seen that the regional fund-raisers were drawn from the ranks of retired colonels and commanders, or spinsters with army or navy connections, many with service pensions. This was the traditional recruiting ground for charities of the 1950s and '60s, looking to pay modest wages in return for a relaxed run-up to retirement, working on gentle fund-raising in the shires. Even today, some charities remain stuck in this time warp, although fund-raising has moved on and has its own language of 'high level donors' discovered by 'segmentation' of databases; 'lifetime values' are calculated to refine advertising and direct mail campaigns. Hard-headed statisticians and emotive copywriters use finely researched techniques (always add a PS to your direct mail letter, ask for money as soon as possible in the text); it may seem cynical but in the crowded charity market it works.

In simpler days, the fund-raising message still had to go out to the public. Long before celebrity endorsement had become a mini-industry in itself, the RNLI ran an advert in the national papers. It showed a pair of yellow wellingtons, with the headline '£6 buys him a pair of boots'. Quite spontaneously, Spike Milligan sent in a letter and a cheque, 'Dear RNLI, I can't see your boys going out to sea any longer without boots. Herewith £6 – please buy a pair of boots. Love Spike.'

A LONG HAUL

The eccentricity of Milligan is reflected in some of the sponsored events that are staged to raise money. Peter Thompson, the former Whitby coxswain, was voted national Volunteer Fund-raiser of the Year in 2005 for his work in the Whitby lifeboat museum. He retired as coxswain in 1993 and continued to work for the RNLI as the honorary curator of the museum, which had been founded by his father in 1957. Peter launched an appeal to raise £30,000 to buy launching equipment for the station and ended up with over £100,000; hence his award.

Peter Thompson, with megaphone, directs the sponsored lifeboat haul.

A few years earlier, he had been approached to join a scheme to re-enact the overland launch of the Whitby lifeboat, which was dragged through deep snow across the North Yorkshire Moors to Robin Hood's Bay for a rescue in 1881. An old rowing lifeboat, *Queen Victoria*, had been lovingly restored by Martin Woodward, coxswain of the Bembridge lifeboat. She was built in 1887, served as the Bembridge lifeboat until 1907 and, amazingly, eighty years later, when she was a century old, was still in one piece, albeit being used as a houseboat and stuck in the mud of Bembridge harbour. Martin saved her, stored her and set about finding the money to rebuild her. It was a labour of love but, with the persistence typical of a lifeboat coxswain, he carried on until, ten years and £10,000 later, *Queen Victoria* took to the water again, all shipshape, in 1998.

She was taken up to Whitby for the re-enactment and dray horses hauled her up out of the town on a carriage. Then teams of people took over, with a useful pub stop half way. Robin Hood's Bay nestles in a coastal cleft; red-tiled houses are scattered down the cliffs with a narrow road winding in between. At the top of the village, the teams rested before the final descent. A vintage road tractor was on hand to stop the boat plunging down the hill. Hundreds of sightseers had gathered to witness the spectacle. Then the police stepped in. It was, they said, too dangerous. They could not accept responsibility. The launch would have to be scrapped. Luckily, the search and rescue world, when it works well, is one of cooperation and controlled risk-taking. Local auxiliary coastguards were out in force and told the police they would control the crowds and keep the road clear. They knew, and Peter Thompson knew, that risks remained. They also knew that the crowds would never forgive them if they turned back so close to the end of their mission. Slowly, the boat was edged down the steep lane, held safely on a hawser attached to the huge tractor. At the bottom she was dragged off the carriage to be hauled by teams of volunteers across skids and through the village. Then a non-human problem threatened to halt the endeavour. The road has two sharp right-angled bends and the boat got stuck on the first, firmly wedged between walls on each side. She couldn't go forwards, she couldn't go back. In came the auxiliary coastguard. Sheer determination, backed by solid muscle, eased the boat free, missing flower-bedecked gardens and café windows by inches, their anxious owners pleased with the influx of tourists but worried about collateral damage.

After an hour's struggle, the boat reached the sea, was launched and rowed back round to Whitby.

The Duke of Edinburgh views the collection of historic lifeboats at Chatham.

HERITAGE

The RNLI's rich heritage is now protected, as a special trust was set up as a subsidiary charity of the RNLI in 2004 specifically to look after museums and archives, though sadly it was formed too late to save many wonderful photographs and historic items that have now disappeared. There are museums all over the country with lifeboat artefacts or even whole lifeboats in them and there is a magnificent collection of lifeboats at the Historic Dockyard in Chatham. This unique collection, the only one in the world to trace a nation's lifeboat service with real boats, originated in Bristol where lifeboat fund-raiser Peter Elliott procured a dockside warehouse and started scouring the country for old lifeboats to display. Sadly, there was never enough money to make the museum work in Bristol and the collection was transferred to Chatham. It won one of the very first grants from the National Heritage Memorial Fund, a lottery grant-making body. There are now seventeen lifeboats on display, including a lovely little harbour boat from Poolbeg, the *Helen Blake*, complete with sails, and the mighty Arun *Edward Bridges*, the boat in which Keith Bower won his gold medal.

FUTURE FUNDS

The future of fund-raising will be in diversity, as there is no sign of public support for charities diminishing, but the nature of the support is changing. People are increasingly reluctant to join committees, particularly shunning such offices as chair, secretary and treasurer. So individual subscriptions, lotteries, sales and legacies are all ways of helping charities that involve little effort and even less time.

Even though the RNLI is one of the biggest charities, or indeed perhaps because it now costs so much, there is a barely hidden unease about its dependence on fund-raising and legacies.

The RNLI is unlike most other charities in that its needs are finite. This has worked to both its advantage and disadvantage at different times. Building new lifeboats has always been an expensive business, but the length of their working life is flexible, so if money is short existing boats can be kept in the fleet a little longer. However, new designs bring flurries of building, causing peaks and troughs of capital spending and destabilising the finances.

Planning ahead was not a strong feature of the early 1970s, when the combination of high inflation, industrial unrest, and a fall in the stock market hit both funds and fund-raising. Management consultants had advised that the place to run a lifeboat service was by the sea, so the lease on the imposing but ramshackle London headquarters was sold. In the middle of the sale, the property market slumped and the plans for a new headquarters in Poole were scaled back. On top of the financial turmoil, work on the new Arun and Thames lifeboats was forging ahead. Then came the realisation that there was no money to pay for the ambitious boat-building programme. At one point, daily calculations were made on which bills could be paid. Chairman Ralph Swann started warning supporters of dire financial difficulties and the possibility of needing to go to the government for help. Swann wrote to Michael Heseltine, who was then the minister for aerospace and shipping, setting out the position and suggesting that the government might give help in kind. He then met the minister and, as the forecast deficit for the year was £1.3 million, the RNLI committee minutes recorded that the Institution was 'now in sight of the point where financial assistance might have to be sought and because of this the minister was being kept informed'. Reserves were down to three months of expenditure, eaten away by inflation, but by September fund-raising income from branches and legacies surged ahead to give a surplus of £70,000 for the year. The immediate crisis was over but the unpleasant memory lingered on for many years.

Then two things happened. The RNLI celebrated its 150th anniversary in a blaze of publicity, energising fund-raising across the land. As a lifeboat magazine put it, 'Balls up and down the country gave enormous pleasure during the anniversary year.'

In parallel, a charming and determined vice-admiral, Peter Compston, took charge of the newly created fund-raising committee. In contrast to his chairman's gloomy warnings, Compston's tactic was to inspire the volunteers. His message was clear: we are in trouble, but you can get us out of it. They did.

The anniversary, Compston's energy and a flow of legacies, perhaps inspired by the recent tragedies of Longhope and Fraserburgh, reversed the situation.

The RNLI had actually received government money in an earlier financial crisis. In the late 1800s a government grant was taken for a few years. With it came a degree of control, which was resented and made it difficult to mount public appeals. The grant was stopped as soon as the RNLI regained financial stability. The spectre of government intervention had re-emerged in 1970 after the Fraserburgh disaster. This time it was not lack of money but the bizarre idea that lifeboat disasters could be avoided if the government was in charge. When the money became short, there was serious talk of a large gift from the government to mark the 150th anniversary, though this was declined and a large silver platter was presented instead.

The private doubts about sustaining such a vital rescue service on voluntary donations remains in some minds. A heavy dependency on legacies, so difficult to predict and plan upon, is worrying. Any amount of modelling of patterns of personal wealth, calculations on increasing life expectancy and estimates of the cost of care in old age cannot provide a list of who will die when and whether they will leave money to charity.

House prices, investment values and tax regimes, all equally unpredictable, add yet more variables to the matrix. So wise business heads in charities look with scepticism – and considerable concern – on plans that claim to be able to predict legacy income.

The RNLI's response has been to redouble its fund-raising efforts, even in times of relative prosperity, in order to diversify and reduce the legacy dependence. It has tended to follow the Institution's traditional careful line, rarely trail-blazing, waiting for the rough edges to be knocked off new ideas by other charities in challenge events, national 'fun' days (though the annual Soles for Souls' Day, launched in 2005, when people are encouraged to wear trainers to work and school, has to be admired for ingenuity) but the vigour in reaching out beyond traditional supporters to widen the appeal is a well-considered strategy to secure the future of the organisation. It may also help to shake off the RNLI's rather fusty image among other charities and to draw more financial support from a younger age group which would match more closely the ages of the crews.

CHAPTER EIGHT

Overseas Adventures

Many new lifeboat services have emerged around the world in the last fifty years, thanks in no small measure to a slow but steady increase in international work by the RNLI.

The British and Irish lifeboat service was the first in the world, followed within a matter of months by the Dutch. Although there are no proven links between the founding of the RNLI in March 1824 and the two Dutch services in November of the same year, both countries were seafaring nations at the height of their powers and both already had local life-saving groups in place. People in Holland may have heard about the RNLI but the catalyst for action was the capsize of a local fishing boat at Huisduinen, near Den Helder. The boat had put out on a rescue and all but one of her crew drowned. As a result, five influential Amsterdam citizens decided to set up a proper sea rescue service. In Rotterdam, a similar group decided to do the same. While it may now seem strange to have separate organisations for a relatively short coastline, the lifeboat services were based on pilotage districts, one run from each city, which was a logical link. So the NZHRM, in the north, was founded on 11 November 1824 and the ZHMRS in the south nine days later. They finally amalgamated in 1991.

Originally the ZHMRS was intended to cover the coast of Belgium (which was at that time united with the Netherlands) but the Belgians declined. They now run their lifeboat service as part of pilotage services in Zeebrugge and Oostende. The Zeebrugge boat was one of the first to reach the ferry *Herald of Free Enterprise*, which capsized just outside Zeebrugge harbour on 8 October 1987. The Dutch have remained great innovators, taking over the larger rigid inflatable project from the RNLI and turning their whole fleet into rigid inflatables, large and small. As other countries set up sea rescue services, different models were used, some copying the voluntary principles of the British, Irish and Dutch and others, such as the Americans, going for a government system.

Dialogues between nations started to develop and they were formalised when the RNLI called an International Lifeboat Conference in 1924 in London as part

Dutch lifeboat. *(KNRM)*

of its centenary celebrations. Nine services were represented and lifeboat designs and equipment were discussed. Count Yoshi of Japan proposed that, in order to improve the saving of life at sea, an international association be formed, like the Red Cross, with all lifeboat services as members. He optimistically predicted that 'if this conference declares its opinion that all maritime countries should have a lifesaving association and sends that declaration to the countries concerned, I think the people of those countries would at once organise such an institution'. So the lifeboat organisations of Great Britain and Ireland, Holland, the USA, Denmark, Norway, Sweden, France, Spain and Japan took it upon themselves to set up an international organisation through the League of Nations in Geneva to urge all maritime nations to set up lifeboat services.

Although that grand ambition has not been realised, cooperation has led to much better protection for seafarers around the world. International Lifeboat Conferences have been held every four years, except during the Second World War, and the organisation linking the services, the International Lifeboat Federation (ILF), has observer status at the United Nations body for the sea, the International Maritime Organisation (IMO) and won the IMO International Maritime Prize in 1998, the first time the prize had ever been awarded to an organisation rather than an individual.

Dutch (left) and Swedish lifeboat at an international conference.

GLOBAL RESCUE

Sea rescue is not the sole territory of lifeboat services. Every vessel at sea has a duty, under maritime law and tradition, to help another in distress. Across vast tracts of deep ocean that cover 70 per cent of the planet's surface, ships and ocean-going yachts are on their own, far beyond the reach of land-based rescue services. However, the open wilderness of the sea is now covered by a global search and rescue plan, devised by the IMO. Rear-Admiral Thimio Mitropoulos, now the IMO's secretary general, drove the plan forward in the 1990s, convening meetings across the world. His task was formidable. The 362 million square kilometres of ocean were divided up into search and rescue (SAR) areas. In each area, the countries concerned have defined SAR regions for which they take responsibility. Politics had to be pushed aside, as some neighbouring states were in dispute over coastal boundaries, fishing rights and exclusion zones. Time and again Mitropoulos had to explain patiently that the Global SAR Plan was humanitarian, not territorial, and eventually it started to come together. It was a major achievement meaning that a distress signal broadcast anywhere in the world, using the global maritime distress signalling system (GMDSS), should be picked up by a satellite, relayed with the casualty's position to a ground station and the information passed to a rescue centre in the relevant country. They would then alert rescue services and all ships in the area and try to find the nearest one to take on the rescue. Using GMDSS, rescues can be organised from thousands of miles away. It works! Ask round-the-world yachtsman Tony Bullimore, rescued by the Australian Navy after spending five days trapped in the hull of his capsized yacht in the Southern Ocean.

Or ask Falmouth coastguard, which takes on this work in the UK. They have been responsible for the rescue of a yacht 200 miles east of the Maldives, involving the Maldives Coastguard, Indian Coastguard, the Rescue Coordination centre in Canberra and a passing tanker; another yacht 300 miles west of the Cape Verde islands, whose crew were picked up by a tanker; and a cargo vessel sinking off the coast of Somalia whose five crew were saved by US Navy helicopters.

In its early years a major drawback of the system was the number of false alarms from automatic rescue beacons. The idea is that if a boat or ship sinks quickly, with no time for the crew to make a rescue call, the beacon will release automatically and send out a distress signal. Unfortunately, human failings have meant that rescue positions from these beacons have been traced to the middle of Dartmoor (never explained) and the centre of Coventry (the beacon was in a bag on top of a wardrobe in a yachtsman's house).

The IMO system is impressive and important, giving hope to seafarers who would otherwise literally have disappeared off the face of the earth. However, the greatest density of shipping, fishing boats and yachts is in coastal zones where there are also the greatest hazards. Rocks, cliffs, sandbanks, tides and currents, shallower water and the need to approach the shore to enter harbours make maritime accidents much more likely close to the shore.

Spectacular disasters do happen in the deep ocean, with huge ships disappearing without trace. The incredible power of the sea can literally tear steel hulls apart, imposing incredible strains on ships designed to sail right around the globe. 'Rogue' waves, once regarded as a myth, are now recognised by oceanographers to be a reality, but they are rare and, though ships are still lost far out at sea, coastal rescue remains vital.

RESCUE IN AMERICA

Just as there is no monopoly on life-saving systems, so there is no 'right way' of organising a rescue service. Across the world, most developed countries have a dedicated sea rescue service, with shore-based coordination centres directing the activities of specialist rescue boats and aircraft. The mighty United States Coast Guard (USCG) is the biggest state-run sea rescue service, though that is only one part of its duties, which range from security to safety inspections and buoyage to smuggling. The USCG has uniformed officers in a rank and career structure and is wholly funded by the government. It also has an auxiliary of volunteers who may put their own boats forward for rescue or patrol duties, and there is a boat safety inspection scheme that the RNLI studied when setting up its own sea safety programme. The USCG, with its broad range of duties, can be called up in wartime to support the US Navy.

The diversity of the USCG's activities is shown by a tale of a rescue outside US territorial waters. A speedboat had been spotted, wallowing and in obvious trouble. A coastguard boat found her and offered a tow. The crew vigorously waved them away, refused to take a line and kept shouting that they did not want help. Eventually the coastguard decided to take control and towed the boat back to the safety of the nearest port. It didn't take them long to find that the boat was packed with drugs and the crew were marched off to be charged with smuggling. They were never convicted. Their imaginative lawyer pointed out that they were found outside territorial limits where, as conscientious citizens, they had been trying to sink this boat with its illegal and evil cargo! He failed to explain how they would have survived at sea, having sunk their boat, but they walked free from court.

Another feature of the USCG is its sporadic boat design. The 44ft surf boat, developed in the 1960s, was the best small rescue boat in the world at the time. The hull shape, speed and use of aluminium for the hull were revolutionary. Over a hundred were built.

They served for around thirty years but in that period there was little development. So for the next boat, the 47-footer, the designers had to start from scratch. Other, less well-resourced services, such as the Europeans, build a handful of boats every year and have a constant process of evolution and testing of designs and equipment. In the 1980s the most advanced boats were in Germany and Norway; in the 1990s probably in Sweden, Holland, the UK and Ireland.

Many other countries, such as China, Russia and Japan, have state systems. Others have hybrids, stitching together different patchworks of voluntary and state activity.

VOLUNTARY SERVICES

The UK, Ireland and Channel Islands have a complex system, the voluntary RNLI being the common factor. HM Coastguard operates in England, Scotland, Wales, Northern Ireland and the Isle of Man to coordinate rescues and to run, under contract to commercial operators, some rescue helicopters. Other SAR helicopters are provided by the Navy and RAF. In the Republic of Ireland, the coastguard service is run by the Irish Maritime Emergency Service. In the Channel Islands the harbour masters of Jersey and Guernsey coordinate rescues, often in conjunction with coastguards on mainland Britain, and there is a voluntary-run small aircraft for SAR. It's not a neat model but it works and it demonstrates how developing countries can set up rescue services by using existing facilities.

In Kenya, for example, the assistant harbour master of Mombasa developed a plan involving the harbour office (with its communication capacity), the police (with their boats) and the armed forces (with boats and helicopters).

Most European and Scandinavian countries have voluntary services. France relies on volunteer crews but its funding is complex, relying in roughly equal parts on charitable giving, local government and central government grants. They also provide seasonal lifeguards on many holiday beaches and this service was carefully studied by the RNLI before it started beach lifeguard work.

The French divide their boats into different classes; *canot tout temps* is an all-weather boat and *première*, *deuxième* and *troisième* class have less capabilities. Some boats, particularly in Normandy and Brittany with their enormous tidal ranges, are locked in tidal marinas; others are always available. The French service is run by retired admirals who always seem to be selected as much for their charm as their undoubted seafaring knowledge. Several stations are twinned across the English Channel, so it is best not to need rescuing off Dunkerque, Boulogne or Calais if there is a naming ceremony in Dover or Ramsgate, as the French lifeboat crew, barrel-chested and jolly, will be in England, probably with their boat, for the party. Although many of them will have excellent English, it always seems that those without do better as the evening goes on!

Parties and lifeboat crews go together, so when many nations meet at international lifeboat gatherings, the parties can be very long. At the International Lifeboat Conference in Bournemouth in 1999, the Norwegian cruising lifeboat was a popular first port of call as they had 'found' some large lobsters; coincidentally, the Norwegians carried full diving gear. The Finns were the furthest travelled, having sailed their ex-German rescue cruiser over 2,000 miles to the UK. At previous conferences the most popular vessel was the Polish salvage tug – big, battered and workmanlike with a small crew galley and a plentiful supply of vodka.

Germany's lifeboats are also run by charity. The Deutsche Gesellschaft Zur Rettung Schiffbruchiger (DGZRS) pioneered large cruising lifeboats with full-time paid crews living on board. The boats carry a *tochterboot* – literally a 'daughter boat' – in the stern, ingeniously launched from a short ramp once small stern doors are opened. The concept of a small boat to go into the shallows, get alongside people in the water and other tasks where size and manoeuvrability are important was the inspiration to put inflatables on RNLI

Norwegian lifeboat.

boats. The latest RNLI slipway boat, the Tamar, mimics the German style of launching a small boat from the stern.

Germany's large rescue cruisers are fantastic craft, the biggest purpose-built SAR vessels. Widely admired for their design, equipment and facilities, the largest even have a small helicopter landing pad. They were regarded as almost invulnerable until a terrible tragedy in January 1995 when the rescue cruiser *Alfried Krupp* capsized and two men drowned. On the night of New Year's Day, two Dutch lifeboats had been called out to help cargo ships in a storm in the North Sea and one of the Dutch lifeboatmen was swept overboard. A search started and the Borkum lifeboat *Alfried Krupp*, joined other ships and helicopters looking for the Dutchman. After 2½ hours, he was spotted and recovered by a helicopter, so the searchers turned for home. As *Alfried Krupp* got closer to the shore, she was suddenly hit by a series of huge seas, thrown off course and capsized. She righted immediately but Theo Fischer was missing. The lifeboat's engines had stopped and the boat was wallowing badly, and Bernhard Gruber, injured in the capsize, was swept overboard and drowned. A German rescue helicopter managed, with great difficulty, to winch up the two surviving crew members and the disabled lifeboat was towed back to port. It was a huge shock, not only for the German lifeboat service, but also for their friends in other European lifeboat services who had always seen the huge rescue cruisers as some of the finest and safest rescue boats in the world.

The German lifeboat service also runs the rescue coordination centre, in Bremen, and is the only large voluntary service to take on this important role.

The unification of East and West Germany in 1990 posed some interesting challenges for the two separate lifeboat services. Both the Germanys ran a lifeboat service, voluntary in the west, state controlled in the east. It was agreed that they should merge. Conscious of the difficulties of reaching all East German stations by road, former DGZRS director Captain Uwe Klein took to the water and visited all the stations in a rescue cruiser. What he found was quite a surprise. At one station in the Baltic, near the border, the Stasi (secret police) confiscated the boat's propeller to prevent the lifeboat crew escaping from the country. At another station, Klein was quizzed on the chain of command: 'Who will give me permission to launch?' asked the coxswain. 'Nobody,' answered Klein, 'you have that authority.' 'But who gives me that authority,' asked the bewildered coxswain, used to the iron grip of the state. 'I just have done,' said Klein.

The Norwegians, too, have large cruising boats with stern-launched daughter boats and they were the first to use fibreglass hulls. These had early problems, from which others learned, though interestingly the Germans and Americans have resisted changing to the modern composite materials, such as FRC, used widely elsewhere.

The interchange of ideas and experiences is conducted mainly by the regular meetings of the ILF. Concrete examples of the benefits of international cooperation are scattered throughout this book. The Bretons in France pioneered the use of inflatables, which the RNLI adopted; the Americans revolutionised rescue with their 44ft steel surf boat and willingly shared their technology; larger rescue cruisers of Germany and Norway work well for them but failed for the RNLI when they tried to copy them; ex-RNLI lifeboats have been sold to Australia, New Zealand, Chile, Uruguay, Iceland, China, Canada and South Africa.

The last of these, South Africa, has had its own innovative streak, copied by others. It is one of the few African states to have a dedicated sea rescue service and is modelled on the RNLI with volunteer crews and charitable funding. South African lifeboat crews are so well regarded for their local knowledge that at Knysna, a beautiful town on a lagoon with a perilous entrance between two towering cliffs, the South African Navy uses the lifeboat crew to guide them in.

The National Sea Rescue Institute (NSRI) has always been a great innovator, mainly with beach and surf boats. One design provided safety buoyancy by packing ping-pong balls, enclosed in nets, into compartments in the hull. The NSRI was also the first to use jet skis for rescue, a practice adopted much later by the RNLI for its beach rescue service. For its larger boats, the NSRI has used

South African lifeboat, formerly an RNLI Brede. *(Derek King/Winston Churchill Memorial Trust)*

tuna fishing boats with various adaptations. The Knysna boat had a stern box added to hold three enormous outboards, giving a speed in the calm of the lagoon of 40 knots. The basic design was unchanged and was vulnerable as the well deck could fill with tons of sea water and the cabin had a simple, non-watertight door. In the 1990s, the NSRI started buying Bredes from the RNLI, a great improvement on the tuna boats but still vulnerable given the huge distances between most of their stations.

Australia also has vast stretches of coast to cover and has no unified service. Voluntary services are strong, the largest being the Australian Volunteer Coast Guard and the Royal Volunteer Coastal Patrol. Repeated attempts have been made to bring the organisations closer together but differences in outlook, mission and issues, such as the use of uniforms, have kept them separate to date.

The New Zealand Volunteer Coastguard is more unified, though there are still strongly independent stations that defend their own identities.

The voluntary ethos extends to South America. Chile has a voluntary lifeboat service in Valparaiso, the main naval port. Crew members pay a subscription to

New Zealand lifeboat, formerly an RNLI Waveney. *(Chris Wood, PO Waiheki Station, NZ)*

belong and can sleep in dormitories which are an integral part of the lifeboat station. Above them is an exclusive restaurant with fantastic views across the harbour, whose profits help to pay for running the lifeboat. When the Chileans decided to replace their ex-RNLI Barnett lifeboat with an Arun, they travelled to Poole to inspect the boat and insisted on joining the passage to Liverpool, from where she was to be shipped to Chile. The staff coxswain in charge was prepared to take two as crew, so this was conveyed to the delegation of four plus translator, in their hotel. The next morning all five turned up on the quayside five minutes before sailing and tossed their bags aboard. There was no time to negotiate, so they set out bravely, until a westerly force 9 around Portland Bill persuaded three to leave the boat at Falmouth and hire a car to get to Liverpool. The stocky sea captain, one of the Valparaiso coxswains, and lifeboat president Camillo Cabrera, stuck out the rough passage with no problems and gained valuable experience of the boat in storm conditions.

Across the Andes, Uruguay deserves special mention as the South American country that has been at the forefront of encouraging the development of lifeboat services. They have to rely on used lifeboats from other nations, having had British and German boats. Unfortunately, their German rescue cruiser, a gift arranged by the ambassador in Montevideo, eventually proved too expensive to maintain, which was a great loss as the mechanic turned out excellent *empanadas* (a small meat pastry snack) before the boat was replaced by an ex-RNLI Waveney with no galley. Dynamic businessmen Guillermo Perez Lavignini and Denis Georgeoglou, as successive leaders of the voluntary Asociacion Honoraria De Salvamentos Maritimos Y Fluviales (ADES), have not only developed the Uruguayan lifeboat service by opening new stations with RNLI Waveneys, but also hosted two conferences, one international and one regional, to promote the exchange of ideas between nations. The first was a gamble for the nations of the ILF, nervous about the capacity of a tiny group, with an annual budget smaller than the cost of a new lifeboat, to organise such a venture. They need not have worried as the

The crew of the Valparaiso lifeboat, Chile.

17th International Lifeboat Conference in Montevideo in 1995 was one of the friendliest and best organised and led to the aim of alternating the conference, wherever possible, between the northern and southern hemispheres.

When the RNLI sells its lifeboats to other countries, after twenty to twenty-five years' service, they are robust but, from the RNLI's perspective, have been overtaken by new designs. If they are going long distances, they are shipped as deck cargo on container ships. Thus they have travelled to New Zealand, Australia, Uruguay, Chile and the Falkland Islands. Iceland has bought several ex-RNLI lifeboats and they have usually been sailed across. The first one to be taken as deck cargo was the Arun *Richard Evans*, which broke free in a storm and was washed overboard from the container ship. Days later, she was found on a rocky Icelandic shore. The only remains were a solid Caterpillar engine and a few scraps of the hull.

FLOOD RELIEF

A quite different aspect of work overseas has developed in the last thirty years. In 1970 terrible floods hit Bangladesh, killing people and animals, wrecking low lying villages and cutting off thousands of people, leaving them without food, clean water or medicines. The British Red Cross asked the RNLI for help. In the first-ever mission of its type, twenty inflatable boats were airlifted to Dacca, accompanied by David Stogdon and Mike Brinton from the inshore lifeboat centre in Cowes. They were later joined by two Littlehampton lifeboatmen. Assessing relief needs was very difficult; in some areas, villages were deserted as inhabitants had already moved inland to food distribution points, while in others whole villages had been swept away, the bodies of men, women and children, cows and goats piled together close to the shore. Not surprisingly, the relief effort was initially chaotic and took a frustrating four days to get under way. The boats left Stansted airport on 21 November but it was not until 2 December that they could start delivering food and blankets. Once started, they worked for a solid week. In the meantime, the RNLI team had been training local people to use the boats and by the time useful supplies arrived they were efficiently distributed, along with doctors who were able to carry out mass inoculation programmes. The doctors worked on into the night, once causing alarm when they were mistaken for pirates as they returned, noisily, in a local boat.

Floods struck Bangladesh again in 1988 and again the Red Cross asked if the RNLI could help. The response was slower this time, as the team was kept waiting for a plane to transport the boats to Bangladesh and although they did not arrive until 12 days after the original alert, vast areas of the country were still under water. The RNLI group, Dick Perks and Mike Brinton, were at work within hours, with the task of showing a group of twenty-two Bangladeshi Red Crescent staff and volunteers how to use ten inflatable boats. During the next eight days there was training in boat handling, engine maintenance and repair, and three expeditions were mounted to distribute relief supplies to isolated communities around Dacca, up to 25 miles away. While much was learned, some vital points, such as how quickly two boats come together when both are travelling at 20 knots, and who should turn which way, had been missed, so there was a hastily convened session on the Rule of the Road.

Dick Perks commented that he was frequently asked by the team if he and Mike thought they were getting better, 'and depending on the degree of the latest near disaster – be it a near miss or the sound of a gear box nearing disintegration – the answer was framed accordingly'.

Nevertheless the task was completed and the boats were split into two groups and based up-country to ferry food and medicines to isolated communities which, even all those days later, had been out of contact with the outside world since the beginning of the floods.

One of the Bangladeshi volunteers, an eighteen-year-old student named Alok, afterwards wrote to Mike Brinton:

Dear Mr Michael,

Take my regards and love. How are you? Hope you are well. When you were in Bangladesh we passed a very pleasant time, specially I. You came to help the distress people of our country. It was really a noble job, we will ever remember you.

Your country gave us some speedboats and you gave us training that is a great help for the flood-affected peoples.

Do you have a desire to come to our country again? If you come you are always welcome to my house.

Yours cordially,
Alok.

The second Bangladeshi intervention was effective, but frustratingly long-winded. In an effort to weave the RNLI's capacity to respond into international relief plans, Mike Brinton and a colleague went to the headquarters of the British Red Cross in London. They were told by the young desk officer for the region that, in spite of the two successful missions, this type of aid in emergencies was no longer considered appropriate and that locals should be trained and equipped for the floods. Given that the floods would probably destroy locally held equipment, this London-based theory sounded a little impractical but the RNLI's offer to set aside inflatables and train selected volunteers as an emergency team was rebuffed.

The RNLI decided to take matters into its own hands, however, and set up a rapid response unit. After Bangladesh came Mozambique and a series of domestic floods where the RNLI's boats and crews excelled themselves. The RNLI wanted to be fully prepared. Equipment was one issue: for example, water-cooled engines in hot countries can overheat. Skills were another, the sea behaves differently to inland waters and driving an inflatable in flood waters is a specialist skill. There can be extra perils in flooded towns, and RNLI inshore lifeboats have been used in many domestic floods inland. A smallish Welsh coxswain wading through flooded streets alongside an inshore lifeboat nearly disappeared down a sewer whose manhole covers had been blown out and was only saved by his bulky life jacket. Live electric cables in water are another hazard to be avoided.

Whatever the dangers, the inflatables prove invaluable in floods. They can be deflated, transported and re-inflated on site. They are agile, tough and have a shallow draft. The crews in the new Rapid Response Unit (RRU) are all inshore lifeboat people with extra training. Captain Hugh Fogarty, a large-framed and big-hearted RNLI staff officer, lists the talents he looks for: 'Each team must

RNLI response team help in Guyana floods.

have an HGV driver, a crane rigger, a linguist, a first aider, paramedic or doctor, a forklift driver and someone with previous experience in disaster relief. They must also have a main communicator, who is good with radio and a Mr or Ms Fixit – a logistician, who is good at organising, has an orderly mind, knows where everything is stowed and where everything else can be begged or borrowed from. The rest bring their skills as lifeboatmen and women and generally all-round good eggs.'

The RRU is now formally linked to the UK's Department for International Development which can call on it at 24 hours notice and which pays for deployment. The RNLI provides infrastructure and training and RRU members have to declare where they are when on short-term standby and keep up to date with jabs.

In February 2005 the whole system swung into action for the first time to send four groups to Guyana in South America to help with floods there.

It might not be quite what Count Yoshi had in mind in 1924, but it is humanitarian work on a worldwide scale. The ILF is now planning to become a separate registered charity by 2007, still run from RNLI headquarters and with some of its resources provided by the RNLI but with plans to raise funds externally to expand its work.

CHAPTER NINE

Why Do They Do It?

The most frequently asked question about lifeboat crews is 'Why do they do it?' It is also the most difficult to get them to answer.

Most will simply say, 'Somebody has to.' Others have family links or personal stories. But perhaps it is the wrong question to ask, because it assumes that lifeboating is always dangerous and a chore. In fact, driving a modern powerful lifeboat is quite thrilling and most rescues are workmanlike and rewarding rather than perilous. Being part of a team, with shared strengths, social life and a standing in the community, adds to the motivation. Some lifeboat crews are legendary drinkers, others strict teetotallers, but all share a wicked sense of humour and irreverence which often helps them through difficult times.

The lifeboat service has been described as the finest club in the country. Lifeboat people can turn up at any one of over 200 locations, the lifeboat stations, and receive a warm and immediate welcome. The camaraderie that binds together crews, committee volunteers and supporting staff provides strength in good times and bad. There's tradition, duty, honour but most of all humanity at the heart of every lifeboat station community.

It was vividly illustrated when fisherman Finton Sinnott died after the Kilmore Quay lifeboat capsized twice on Christmas Eve 1977. Most newsrooms had already closed down for Christmas, so there was no media attention, and hence no public outpouring of generosity. But the lifeboat grapevine worked so swiftly that, all around the coasts of Britain and Ireland, the crews organised collections among themselves, providing an immediate fund for Sinnott's young widow and children.

So why do they do it?

WE SANG ALL THE WAY HOME

Derek Scott explained his motivation in a BBC radio appeal. He had joined the Mumbles lifeboat crew after a disaster when the whole crew, under Coxswain William Gammon, had been killed trying to rescue the crew of the ship *Santampa*.

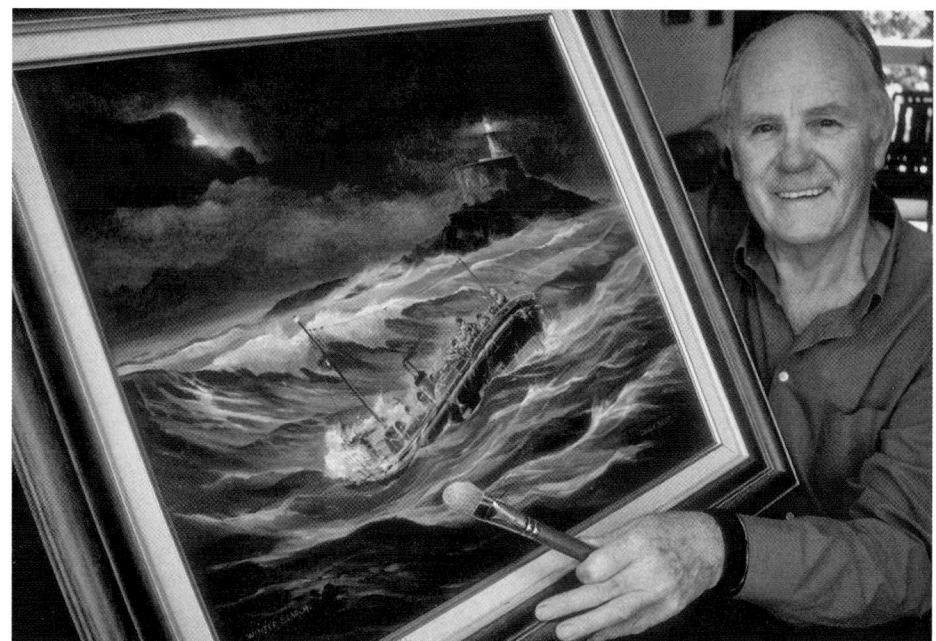

Derek Scott of the Mumbles.

Many years later, Derek and his crew had to go to exactly the same spot, where a sand dredger was aground on a spur of rock. When they got there it was as black as pitch and the crew had all been washed away from the dredger on a raft. They picked them up at once. That, reported Derek, was easy. But the raft had broken away from the ship, leaving the skipper on board. Now they had to go back for him, running over rocks this time, with the dredger on its side and surf breaking over it: 'We saw the skipper hanging on to the wing of the bridge, dressed in everything he owned with an overcoat, suitcase and carrying the ship's papers. We had to put the bow of the lifeboat actually on the deck, but when the skipper jumped, the ship rolled and he almost went into the water. One of the lads grabbed him and all his gear. This is what we had come to do and we sang all the way home.'

Not all Derek's rescues were as dramatic. As he told 2,500 people at the RNLI's 150th anniversary annual meeting, the discomfort and tedium can be broken by light-hearted moments: 'I remember one beautiful occasion when I was asked by the coastguard repeatedly, "What is your position?" We were being thrown around really badly at the time. He said it again and before I had a chance to answer him the mechanic looked up and said, "I don't know what his position is but ours is bloody desperate."'

For all the humour, the crews must be able to trust each other absolutely. It is a very strange thing, almost unnatural, to volunteer to be ordered into danger. In the thick of a rescue, there is little time for consultation, and if the coxswain or helm says jump, the crew must do it. So trust is, quite literally, vital – lives depend upon it.

In his radio speech, Derek Scott explained:

I have always said that a coxswain is only as good as his crew. When you are setting off in the blackness of the night into a gale force 9, into God knows what, the feeling of unity between a lifeboat crew is inexplicable and no matter how frightened you feel, you know that the crew of the ship who are waiting for you are a great deal more frightened than that. Then, maybe after hours of battling through heavy seas and being beaten to death, you arrive and you are wet and cold and thinking, 'What am I doing here?' and then you see the casualty, which can be a terrifying situation with life hanging by a thread, but this is the moment we have all been prepared for. From the time that lady sold her flag or arranged her coffee morning to raise funds that was when this rescue started, not when the maroons were fired. If you could share with me and see the look on a survivor's face at the moment of rescue and share that marvellous feeling with the lifeboatmen when they are coming home in the boat and the job has been done, then you would all know that this last 150 years has been more than worthwhile.

FAMILY AFFAIRS

The idea of a guiding hand may help some crews. Back in 1881, Ramsgate coxswain Charles Fish rescued eleven people from the sailing ship *Indian Chief*. It was a spectacular rescue and eclipsed many other equally brave rescues of the period because the *Daily Telegraph* printed a first-hand account from Fish. After describing the rescue, he said, 'From the hour of leaving Ramsgate harbour to the moment when we sighted the wreck's mast, there was only one thought in all of us and that was that the Almighty would give us the strength and direct us how to save the lives of the poor fellows to whose assistance we had been sent.'

However, invoking the Almighty can also cause bitter resentment. When the St Ives lifeboat capsized in 1939, seven men were killed. Only one of the crew, William Freeman, survived. Another man, John Stevens, had gone down to the boathouse to help with the launch, but did not join the boat. Neither man was a regular lifeboatman though both were fishermen. Stevens later claimed that

St Ives lifeboat disaster, 1939.

voices, 'my angels' told him not to go. The two men, who passed each other on the street almost every day, never spoke again for over three decades.

Then a television crew came along, anxious to explore the story further. The coxswain at the time, Tommy Cocking, had lost his father in the 1939 capsize. He was only too well aware of feelings still present in the town and of the silence between Freeman and Stevens. The story of the voices, suggesting divine intervention for one man only, when the rest of the crew were just as God-fearing, was unacceptable and should be left alone. There would be no cooperation with the TV people.

Television producer Barry Cockcroft had handled tricky situations before, making famous the Yorkshire Dales woman Hanna Hauxwell, and certainly did not want to ruin his standing in St Ives, the community where he took his holidays. He promised to report facts, not rumours. But he wanted Freeman and Stevens to meet.

Three generations of Thomas Cockings. *(Peter Hadfield) Below:* the youngest Thomas Cocking is third from the left. Eric Ward is on the right next to Princess Anne. *(St Ives Times & Echo)*

The scene was as simple as a traditional western film set. Stevens sat down on the quay as Freeman walked slowly down the street. A simple greeting was exchanged. After more than thirty years, the ghost of a lifeboat disaster was finally laid to rest.

Cockcroft also used his documentary to explore the dynamics between the St Ives coxswain and his son, also called Tommy. Young Tommy complained that his father was harder on him than the rest of the crew, a charge accepted by the coxswain who knew that neither the crew nor his son would allow any favouritism. Indeed, Tommy junior did not succeed his father immediately but travelled as mechanic with Eric Ward as coxswain when they went to collect their new Mersey lifeboat from Poole. During the week's training, the crew decided to take advantage of Poole's nightlife. The Splashdown flume rides were Monday's treat, followed by a Grab a Granny disco on Tuesday. A rather subdued crew complained on Wednesday morning, 'Them Grannies were all younger that us,' and reverted to Splashdown for the evening thrills.

Meanwhile, having served his long apprenticeship, Tommy eventually did go on to take the helm of the St Ives boat, becoming the third Thomas Cocking to hold the position.

Family connections are still a feature of crews, though the traditions of several generations serving at one station are weakening as people move away from coastal communities to find work inland.

Gary Barlow, helm at Cleethorpes, followed his father into the crew and speaks for many when he describes why he spends so much time on call, training and checking equipment. 'If you didn't love it, you wouldn't do it,' he said. 'But we've got a great crew, we socialise together, our families socialise together and it's a great team spirit.' And to father and son we can now add a mother and daughter dynasty. In 2005, Aileen Pritchard became the first woman to win a bravery medal in a lifeboat. Aileen's husband and daughter are also in the crew, and for her, being in the lifeboat brings its own reward: 'It's a great feeling, when you've successfully helped someone without anyone getting hurt . . . you're on a high when you get home.'

Aileen was catapulted to fame in 2005 when she became the first woman in 121 years to win an RNLI bravery medal. She joined a roll of honour only twenty long, including Grace Darling, with Aileen the only one a member of a lifeboat crew.

Porthcawl is one of the stations set up in Victorian times with a rowing lifeboat. It closed and then re-opened in 1965 with an inshore lifeboat. Its companion station with an all-weather boat is the Mumbles and both worked together on a tricky rescue on the morning on 24 August 2004, which earned

Aileen her bronze medal. The fishing boat *Gower Pride* had engine failure and was close to the Nash Sands, a treacherous spot where a number of fishermen have died over the years. The force 8 south-westerly gale was pushing her closer to the sands and as rough seas tossed the boat, the crew member broke his arm. Skipper Gordon Woosnam radioed Swansea coastguard for help and within ten minutes Porthcawl Atlantic 75 lifeboat *Giles* (named after the famous cartoonist) was on her way with Aileen at the helm. She had decided to take extra help, so had three crew with her, Stephen Knipe, Simon Emms and Mark Burtonwood. Waves were breaking over the pier and the Atlantic had to take a course around the sands through steep, confused seas and swells of 3m to get to *Gower Pride*. Aileen realised they were operating at their limits and asked for back-up from the Mumbles.

Meanwhile Stephen, on the radio, had to ask Gordon Woosnam to speak slowly and clearly so they could establish his position. The arrival of the lifeboat, said Woosnam, '. . . was the most pleasing thing I have seen in my whole life . . . it was like winning the national lottery'.

However, for the lifeboat crew, problems lay ahead. Aileen brought the lifeboat close enough to pass a rope to the fishing boat and slowly she was pulled away from the bank. Then the towline snapped, leaving *Gower Pride* at the mercy of the wind, sea and tide, being pushed back towards the sands. It was, as Aileen said later, 'not a nice place to be . . . quite dangerous', but she went in again, this time nudging up against the fishing boat so that Simon Evans could leap across with the towline, radio and first-aid kit. Just then, a huge breaking sea hit *Gower Pride*, hurling her against the lifeboat and dislodging a dan buoy which fell onto Mark. Luckily he was not injured and the lifeboat pulled clear and gingerly took up the tow again. Battling through the surf breaking across the shallows, the Atlantic 75 lifted right out of the water as the heavy fishing boat held her back.

An hour after the first tow started, Mumbles lifeboat was on scene to help and Simon Emms, still on *Gower Pride*, had to crawl forward to take a rope from the bigger offshore boat. *Gower Pride* was rolling heavily, the deck was slippery and there were few handholds. Twice the Mumbles crew tried to throw a rope but it was too difficult to catch and coxswain Martin Double had to bring his boat within arm's length to pass the rope to Simon. He recalls, 'It was quite a sight, seeing Simon climbing all over the boat. The *Gower Pride* was in danger of going right over and our own rails were under water at times. You have to time it just right.'

Mumbles lifeboat took over the tow, the injured man was taken to an ambulance and *Gower Pride* was berthed safely in Porthcawl harbour before the

Aileen Richards of Aberdovey. *(Andrew Lloyd)*

Mumbles men started a rough trip home. 'We took a beating, but we're used to that,' was Martin Double's comment.

And Aileen? 'It was one of the best services I have done personally, but anybody on the boat that day could have done the job. I was pleased we got to the boat before they got onto the bank and glad no lives were lost. We just worked so well together and the lifeboat is a brilliant piece of kit.'

Fishing skipper Gordon Woosnam was blunt and clear: 'They were very brave that day. If it was not for Aileen and her crew, I would not be here.'

TRAINING

Training is a major part of any crew member's life and most is carried out at the lifeboat station. In the old days it was a question of bringing knowledge from a seafaring life onto the lifeboat and learning from the old hands. Nowadays the crews are not seafarers but there is still a lot to be learned from experienced crew. There is a task book to be filled in after training in the boathouse, in special caravans converted for radar, radio and first-aid classes, on exercise in the lifeboat and by attending courses at the RNLI training college in Poole. It is also important that new members fit into the crew. 'It's about making sure personalities gel with the people already there,' says Coxswain Ronnie

MacKillop of Oban. Alan Tarby of Padstow agrees: 'Like a football team you can all be good individually but you need to perform well together. That's what so much of the training is about.'

Rod James was helmsman at Hayling Island and had a typical modern crew: 'We don't have any professional seamen. We've got one crew member who has an RYA [Royal Yachting Association] certificate and there is a sailing instructor, but other than that we have no sailing tradition. Maybe that's an advantage, we don't have to retrain anyone from a fishing tradition or anything like that. They all come new to the game. So it's not a problem.'

However, getting a raw recruit used to the quick pace of an inshore lifeboat takes time: 'We find that when we get a new crew member it is impossible to train them in preparation for the first half dozen calls. It seems to be something to do with adrenalin or the excitement when they first go out. Everything is happening very rapidly and they tend to get an overload of information. They try to take everything in and as a result they become very clumsy and not very helpful. We use a new crew member as a sort of extra body, it's a learning situation.'

Rookies have to earn their place on a crew. Mark Barker, a motor mechanics lecturer at Hartlepool had known some of the crew for a few years and was persuaded to join: 'You are wary at first because you are the new kid on the block. It's like when you get a new girlfriend and have to meet her parents for the first time, and of course it is fine. The way everyone was so friendly made a big impact on me.' As a college lecturer, Mark is in a good position to assess the training, which was a lot better than he expected.

Rhyl's first female crew member, Jess Myatt, came into the crew in a different way – she had been talking to a friend whose grandfather had been on the crew – but found a similar welcome: 'I've only lived by the sea for a couple of years – I lived inland before that and knew nothing about boats or the sea. The rest of the crew are like brothers to me. They look after me.'

Jess couldn't drive, so when her pager went off in the middle of a lecture at college, she got a bus to the lifeboat station, arriving in time to help recover the lifeboat. Like Mark, Jess was impressed with the training. 'If you went out on the boat without the training, you'd be stuck and would not be able to help anybody. I've done the first aid and boat handling training. The capsize exercise was especially memorable; as the boat went over I swallowed water but I can laugh about it now. I've been on quite a few rescues already. There was one the other day where a drunk man ended up in the sea. He was hypothermic. I had to get the first-aid kit out and set up the oxygen. He was very scared but relieved that someone had come to save him.'

Joe Martin (in cap) presents the Hastings crew to the Queen Mother. *(Evening Argus, Brighton)*

JUST THE LOOK ON THEIR FACES . . .

Another eloquent description of a lifeboatman's motivation came from Joe Martin at Hastings. Joe's father had been in the lifeboat crew for forty years. As a child, Joe watched shire horses pulling the lifeboat into the sea: 'I remember sparks rising in the dark as their great hooves pounded and pounded, trying to get a grip on the shingle.' Joining the crew was natural for Joe, following in his father's footsteps, and his rationale was very clear: 'It's the exhilaration. Most of us are fishermen and patience is in our blood. One day you'll be battling with fog for twenty-two hours, looking for a casualty, and just as you're frozen stiff and giving up hope, you spot them. Just the look on their faces when they realise they are not going to die – that's enough.'

Joe was a kind man; he showed hundreds of children around his lifeboat station and gave talks around the country to Women's Institutes, Rotary clubs and the like. He retired from the RNLI a distinguished man, decorated for gallantry, but his personal life went sadly and badly wrong and, some years later, his many lifeboat friends were shocked when he took his own life. Lifeboat heroes can be as frail and vulnerable as anybody else and many of Joe's RNLI colleagues felt guilty that they had not spotted the signs. So the myth of the invulnerable character, so strong as to need no support, must be challenged.

SAYING THANK YOU

For most volunteers, their passion is doing the job. Perhaps the volunteer groups that are most like lifeboat crews are mountain and cave rescue teams – people who deliver a front-line rescue service, respect their surroundings, join because they want to help and value their independence. Governments have tried to encourage volunteering with centrally organised initiatives that often miss the fundamental point of why people put themselves forward. A 2005 House of Commons committee report on rescue services came out with the worthy statement that 'the UK's search and rescue effort relies heavily on volunteers and voluntary organisations. Unless further support is given to volunteering, we fear more employed staff will be required in the future, at greater cost to the taxpayer.'

It is therefore particularly ironic that the RNLI is forced to pay millions of pounds in VAT, even though specific concessions have been made over the years. It was interesting that, some eighteen months after Patricia Hewit (then in the Treasury) had received a delegation from the Charities VAT Reform Group, the day after five lifeboats had spent all night in the Irish Sea searching for a fishing boat, another helpful VAT relaxation was made for rescue services.

However, what volunteers really want is not more encouragement but less interference. They need equipment, not pay, public appreciation, not red tape. They don't want administrators, regulations and paperwork, yet there are scores of tangible examples of these getting in the way of what used to be a process of straightforward volunteering. And if the government encouragement comes in the form of grants, the form filling and assessment against imposed targets that accompanies them often means that voluntary organisations either cannot cope or have to employ people to do the administration. Unless there is a fundamental rethink, small voluntary search and rescue groups will continue to struggle to raise funds in order to keep away from government, whose support is given so inappropriately. In this regard, the RNLI is fortunate in being large and well established, able to fend for itself. Smaller organisations, such as mountain and cave rescue, are not so lucky.

Many rescue services share the challenge of a role which is changing from that of rescuers to nannies. As a Lakeland mountain rescue leader, Stuart Hulse, said in an article in *The Times*, 'You used to take pride in being prepared and having the equipment to confront the elements. Self-reliance was the name of the game. Nowadays people don't think twice about calling us out for the slightest thing. They don't take responsibility for themselves because they think they have the ultimate safety blanket in their coat pocket – their mobile.'

For walkers, read yachtsmen, power boaters or divers and there are immediate parallels. Sweeping generalisations are dangerous, as both mountain rescue teams and lifeboat crews have many genuine call-outs, but there is a danger of having to deal with those who are not really in trouble. 'If people hear stories about people using us frivolously as a fell taxi service, it makes them less likely to put money in the collection tins,' says Hulse. The same applies to the lifeboat service, and it is sometimes difficult to decide what constitutes a rescue and what is a get-you-home service. There are also times when the lifeboat is simply being exploited, to save people time and money by towing them home when there is no danger. On a sunny early September Sunday off Poole, a diver's RIB broke down, near to the beach. The outboard had failed, but the eight divers on board could easily have swum the 50m or so to the beach or paddled their boat ashore. Instead, the RNLI beach lifeguards turned up in their much smaller boat and towed, with some difficulty, the RIB to a buoy, where it was secured until the inshore lifeboat turned up and towed it to Poole harbour. It was a simple, well-executed job, no life was in danger and the volunteer crew probably enjoyed the outing. It is only to be hoped that the divers made a good donation to the RNLI, as the public's support is already under threat from the suspicion that some calls are for people who could or should help themselves.

COMPETENT CREW

However, contrary to popular myth (among landlubbers) not all yachtsmen are rich and reckless. While some stretch the patience of the rescue services almost to breaking point, others are competent, experienced, well equipped and are hit by bad luck.

The crew of the yawl *Pas Seul*, a well-found vessel with a steel hull, might have thought little of a force 6 wind until they suffered engine failure off the Essex coast. The yawl then lost its steering and ran onto a sandbank. The crew wisely deployed two anchors, but these were not enough to avoid *Pas Seul* being driven further onto the shoals, taking a fierce pounding in the breaking surf.

By now, with the weather forecast to worsen, help was needed and Walton and Frinton lifeboat came out. John Weld, a member of *Pas Seul*'s crew, later wrote:

> I should like to place on record our admiration of the skill and courage of Coxswain Bobby Kemp and his crew in effecting the tow. The conditions, although perhaps not extreme, were very difficult, the seas being confused by wind over tide in shallow water, yet the quality of seamanship and boat handling were superb. After the rescue and a rough, time-consuming tow, it

The yacht *Wild Goose* sinks after efforts by Irish crews to save her. *(Kelly Allan)*

was dawn the following morning before they safely manoeuvred us into a marina berth and arranged for the boat to be pumped out. Instead of rushing off home, they invited us aboard and gave us hot drinks to warm us up, patience and kindness beyond that which was necessary.

While letters of thanks do not exactly flood into lifeboat stations, those that are written show gratitude for the professionalism and also the humanity of the crews.

When David King of Cheltenham set out in his 29ft yacht from Salcombe for the Channel Islands, conditions were fine until his propeller became fouled and the wind dropped. It was a sunny day, the sea was calm but the tide was pushing him dangerously into the busy Channel shipping lanes. He needed help and was towed, in a quite straightforward rescue, into Braye Harbour by Alderney lifeboat. However, Mr King recalled, 'The courtesy and consideration of the lifeboat crew did not end there. They contacted an amateur diving group operating in the harbour and within thirty minutes of mooring up, our propeller had been cleared of a large quantity of fishing net and line. The divers, who had interrupted their holiday activities to help us, refused to accept any payment.'

Steve Masterman from London was similarly impressed by the Rolls-Royce service from the Swanage crew. In a race from Poole to Weymouth, he ended up on the rocks near St Alban's Head 'as a result of the skipper's absentmindedness', and the yacht was towed back to Swanage. Not only that but he was also given a lift to the bus station in what he described as a sympathetic and generous gesture. Swanage already had a reputation for the politeness of its radio operator, Dave Corben. Talking to a casualty, Dave always seemed to give just a little more than the bald facts needed, always reassuring and calm. Quizzed about this, the coxswain of the time, dentist Chris Haw, said it was easy to explain: 'Dave's an estate agent, you see, and he's always on the look-out for a sale!'

Even large yachts can hit problems. In the 1980s the 85ft yacht *Drum*, with pop star Simon Le Bon on board, was competing in the Fastnet Race when she lost her keel off Cornwall and capsized. All the twenty-two crew managed to scramble onto the upturned hull. Falmouth lifeboat, with an inflatable, and a helicopter from Culdrose were soon there. Yachting writer Malcolm McKeag was one of *Drum*'s crew and wrote a light-hearted account for the *Lifeboat Journal*:

Funny, isn't it, how little things bother you when all you should be worrying about is avoiding death by drowning? Most of us had been in a boat but not many had had a ride in a helicopter. Now that the danger was past, this looked like too good an opportunity to pass up, so the poor lifeboatman was having a hard time getting takers. 'Come on then, I can take two more this run.' Only Irv was behind me, with Woody and Phil in front – we were the last four and the chopper could take two, the lifeboat two. Looked like I wasn't going to get my ride in a chopper after all. 'You going in the chopper, Woody?' said Irv.

'Blow that,' said Woody. 'Dry ship, those darned things. Doesn't the RNLI still carry brandy? I'm a survivor you know. I'm entitled.'

I looked round for Irv, but it was too late. He was already sliding down the hull into the waiting dinghy . . .

Twenty years later, Simon Le Bon was re-united with Vivian Pentecost, who was the Falmouth lifeboat coxswain who led the rescue. The original *Drum* crew was brought back together by the Duran Duran singer to have another go at the Fastnet Race in 2005. The race passed without incident and *Drum* raised a tidy sum and generated a lot of publicity for the RNLI.

SELF-HELP

If there is any lingering doubt about the competence of some yachtsmen, and their ability to help themselves and others, an incident off Suffolk should dispel it. A 19ft yacht, *Wombat*, on passage from Holland to Orford, got into difficulties in the night. Her rigging was damaged in rising winds which increased during the morning to gale force, so the crew made temporary repairs, but she was uncertain of her position. A companion yacht had to leave *Wombat* and go on ahead when her own navigation lights failed, to avoid collision. However, another yacht, *Mako*, kept company with *Wombat*, helping her with navigation. *Mako*'s crew had an exhausting and difficult time, as they had to circle around *Wombat* to make enough speed to counter the very rough seas. Constant gibing and tacking took their toll on the crew and they worried that they might also damage their boat. Aldeburgh lifeboat was called, took the three crew off *Wombat* and towed her to Orford Quay, a relatively straightforward six-hour rescue in a force 8 gale. For *Mako*'s crew, the relief was immense.

The owner wrote to Coxswain Billy Burrell:

This letter is merely to express my admiration to you and your crew, making difficult conditions look like a Sunday walk. I would like to stress that the very presence of the lifeboat gave a tremendous amount of reassurance to all who saw her, inspiring confidence even in those not needing help. By mid-morning *Wombat* was in trouble. Her makeshift repairs were beginning to fail for the second time. However, the courage of the girl on board her astounded *Mako*'s crew. She was under water, feet above her back, lying on the cabin roof, constantly swept by green water as she worked on the foredeck changing foresails and yet she went back again several times to crawl over the cabin to complete the work as best she could.

When you and your crew of brave gentlemen arrived, the relief with which *Mako*'s crew were able to shed the responsibility was enormous. Suddenly we could look to ourselves, put up the sail we needed to control the boat and start trying to avoid the breakers.

Mako, a well-found boat with a competent crew, had been escorting *Wombat* for hours, in very difficult conditions, and now went on her way safely. The skipper bought a new RNLI Shoreline flag 'as the old one got rather shredded in that wind', and sent a generous cheque, with the message, 'I cannot thank you enough for being around and I am very aware that whereas the seas built up gradually for us, you are always suddenly thrown into the middle of it.'

Not all survivors are grateful to be rescued. In the 1970s the Skegness lifeboat towed a boat in and the crew hauled it up the beach to safety. The owner, using legal aid, sued them for damaging his boat. Not long afterwards the Padstow lifeboat was called out to a sinking fishing boat. The skipper had been taken off by helicopter but coastguards were worried that the boat was a hazard to shipping, so the Padstow crew towed it in. They were surprised that a well-maintained boat should start sinking on a calm day and soon discovered why. Somebody had sawn through the pipes – it looked like a case of scuttling to claim insurance. The crew put in a salvage claim, which is their legal right, though frowned on by the RNLI. In this case, the lifeboatmen wanted the facts to be established, but the insurers prevaricated, leaving the fisherman to have a field day in the media, claiming the lifeboatmen were trying to ruin him. It later emerged that he had done the same thing two years earlier, off Plymouth.

Some rescues do not have a straightforward outcome and have a harrowing effect on the crews. In the case of Albert Sutherland and the Fraserburgh lifeboat crew, the simple rescue of a boy stretched their emotions almost to breaking point for several days. The day was ordinary enough – not rough, nothing untoward at all. The lifeboat crew were in the station, chatting, and a group of lads was playing close to the edge of the harbour. Suddenly, one tumbled into the water. The backwash as the sea hit the harbour wall held him

Albert Sutherland of Fraserburgh. *(Sue Denny)*

close in and tossed him to and fro like a limp doll. The rugged 47ft steel lifeboat, designed for the worst storms, was there in minutes, but it was a blunt rescue instrument in those confused waves where absolute precision was needed to reach the boy. As the seconds ticked away and Albert desperately fought to get his boat near the boy, without crushing him against the stone wall, the boy drifted into unconsciousness. Lifeboatman Graham Campbell jumped into the sea, grabbed the boy's jacket and the rest of the crew pulled him on board. He and Tommy Summers immediately started mouth-to-mouth resuscitation and chest compressions, but the boy was not breathing and had no pulse. Within moments, he was landed on the pier where the paramedics from the ambulance crew took over, getting the faintest flicker of a pulse. In hospital, he was put on life support and for the next week he fought for his life. Bulletins from the hospital prepared his family and the lifeboat crew for the worst. It looked as though all their efforts had been too late. He was not likely to pull through.

A letter on the wall of the lifeboat station, delivered by the boy himself, shows that he did. It is so touching that it is almost impossible to read aloud without a tear coming to your eye. Try it.

To Albert and the crew of the Fraserburgh lifeboat *City of Edinburgh*.
I, Edward McDonald, age thirteen years, would like to thank you all very much for saving my life on Saturday 2 October 1993. What you have done will be remembered in my heart always.

E. McDonald.

COPING WITH LOSS

An even worse emotional trial is to search for your own friends, knowing they are probably already dead.

Coxswain Trevor England and his crew faced this when they had to search for hours after two local fishing boats were lost on consecutive Sundays, with five fishermen drowned, three of whom were on the lifeboat crew. One of the boats capsized on Padstow bar, while the other, loaded up with gear, was overwhelmed by the weather outside it. Alan Tarby was second coxswain at the time. 'We all know what happened, but nobody will say,' was all Alan would give away. The lifeboat couldn't even put out on exercise for a few days, in case people on the quay thought more fishermen had been lost, but they soon got another call, an easy one, and the remaining crew started to settle down. Then, the day before Christmas, they were out again and picked up one of the bodies.

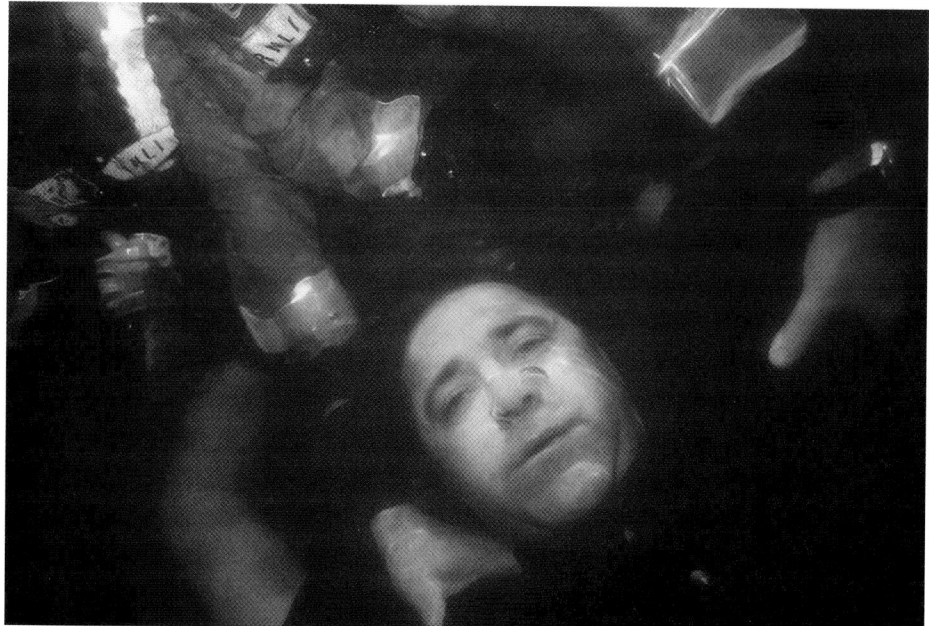

Survivor's view of being rescued. *(Jane Morgan)*

Alan remembers, 'It upset them all over again, just as they were beginning to get over it.' Two of the fishermen were never found.

Even the most hardened crews, who may have had the grim task of scooping the corpses of strangers into body bags, find dealing with drowned children an almost impossible strain.

The Sheerness crew had to bring back the body of a thirteen-year-old boy who had gone swimming, banged his head and drowned. By the time they reached him he was floating underwater. They took him back to the boathouse and covered him up. Already upset, the crew were shocked when a policeman came along, uncovered him and didn't even bother to put back the blanket.

Veteran coxswain Dick Evans also said his saddest rescue involved a child. A little girl had been in a boat with her sister and father and somehow caught her hair in the flywheel of the outboard engine as the boat sank. Dick and Evan Owen's sons, both called David, were on the scene within minutes of the alert and David Evans dived down some 20ft, surfacing again to help David Owen drag the boat to the surface, with the little girl hanging by her hair from the engine. The local doctor was in another boat. He came alongside, cut her free and all the way back to shore gave artificial respiration. The seven-year-old girl was gently laid on a bench in the boathouse and for two hours the doctor, Dick and a helicopter pilot worked on her, but to no avail. Dick said, 'I was very cut up indeed. I had a little granddaughter of my own. It really upset me and I'm not ashamed of saying that I wept for hours. To make matters worse her grandfather forced his way past the police into the boathouse. I shall never forget him. He said, "My darling little babby," and he put his arms around her and kissed her and hugged her. Oh my God, it was terrible. It was the most heart-breaking thing that happened to me since I've been in the lifeboat service. Everything humanly possible was done to save that little girl's life, but to no avail.'

The crews do find ways of coping. At Dunmore East, the crew had to deal with a double tragedy when two children drowned, not far from the lifeboat station, on a calm summer day. Divers found one body and the lifeboat picked up the second, a little boy. Luckily for the crew, Frances Glody, the first woman to be a regular crew member on an offshore lifeboat, was with them on the mission. Crew member Dermot Murphy said, 'You see some terrible things at sea – smashed limbs, people already dying when you haul them aboard – but a dead child is by far the hardest to take.' The men struggled with their feelings: 'After we'd got the little lad aboard and covered him up, the fellas stood there with our faces turned away, feeling awful for ourselves. But not Frances. She made the sign of the cross over him and said a prayer. I've never seen anything so cool and yet so soft-hearted.'

In spite of the tragedies, Dick Evans was clear about his motivation:

I've been asked on several occasions what did I get out of risking my life the way I have. I've had no financial benefit at all out of it but I have had tremendous satisfaction. I've gone out several times in the inshore lifeboat and plucked a drowning man out of the water. The wonderful gratitude in that man's eyes . . . or when I've picked up a little child and delivered it safely to its mother's arms . . . the gratitude in the face of the mother has compensated me for all the hardship I have had. It's only when it's all over, when you're sitting in your home on your own armchair, you go over these things. Sometimes I get terribly frightened, whereas in the lifeboat I wasn't; I was too occupied. And these things tell on you, you know. Yet I must say, I enjoyed it all. I would do the same thing over again.

When crews themselves come close to death, their own needs cannot be ignored. Counselling is the modern word that describes a long-standing and natural practice which has taken place in tight-knit lifeboat communities for many years. It was a word never mentioned or needed in Salcombe after the lifeboat capsized and righted successfully in 1983. The boat was exactly the same type as the Penlee boat which had been lost only two years before.

Salcombe lifeboat crew, safe only hours after their lifeboat capsized. Griff Griffiths is in the middle of the front row.

The Salcombe crew, wet but unscathed, got home safely and were told that the local doctor, honorary medic for the station, wanted to see them all for a drink in the yacht club that night. There, over a beer or two, they talked through the events of the day and went home with settled minds.

Griff Griffiths, the Salcombe coxswain that day, carried on as coxswain until he retired aged fifty-five. A few months later he was out in his fishing boat, single-handed, hauling his pots. A rope took a turn around his leg and dragged him into the sea. Inexplicably, he had no knife to hand, or could not reach one in time, and he drowned. A man who had saved so many lives lost his own in the cruellest way.

So crews, like other ordinary human beings, face very personal sadness, intensely close tragedy. They are not the mythical 'hearts of oak', heroic and impervious figures. That is what makes lifeboat crews remarkable. They are ordinary people doing an extraordinary job, which most of us could not – would not – do.

CHAPTER TEN

Diversification

In the 1990s, the Charity Commission began to take a close and ill-informed interest in the size of the RNLI's financial reserves. A routine visit to discuss annual accounts escalated to high-level meetings, which soon became acrimonious. The situation was exacerbated by new accounting regulations that demanded the removal of full capital costs from the annual accounts, for example, buying lifeboats or building lifeboat stations. The figure given instead was depreciation, so nowhere in the accounts could a reader tell how much the RNLI raised and spent each year!

However, the high level of reserves, amounting to almost four years' annual expenditure, which had been caused by a massive influx of multi-million pound legacies, remained an embarrassment. Unlike many other charities, the RNLI's needs are finite. Comprehensive rescue cover can be provided by a certain number of lifeboats and stations and there are only so many potential rescues every year. While the lifeboat service is expensive, it could not save double the lives if it had double the money.

So the question was, what could be done to spend this money responsibly? Brian Miles had already put in a capital spending programme to upgrade all lifeboat stations. There was a boat-building plan to provide a steady flow of new boats rather than the peaks and troughs of previous years. RNLI planners were spurred into action by a remark by trustee John Lunch. He urged them to look at the full picture of accidents at sea by moving away from the self-congratulatory habit of celebrating lives saved and analyse instead how many accidents and deaths still occurred.

The conclusions were that there was little more that lifeboats could do. The service was already comprehensive and efficient. But avoidable accidents were commonplace, especially on leisure craft, and lives were being lost close to the shore, off beaches.

Two initiatives were born from this study. The first, based on prevention rather than cure, was to launch a sea safety campaign. As with most things in the RNLI, this was not new; in Victorian times, the RNLI issued advice to fishermen and even installed barometers around harbours to help them forecast the weather. A small number of these barometers are still in place.

The lifeboat magazine of 1860 carried the following advice:

Public attention has frequently been called to the invaluable use of a barometer for indicating a coming storm. It not infrequently happens that a notice of a gale is given by a barometer two or three days before it actually takes place. It seems plain that with such powers placed providentially in our hands the calamities now endured by our fishermen and coasters might in many instances be avoided. A good barometer in a public situation would warn them in time what to expect and they could thus be frequently able to avoid the terrible consequences of storms, so often at present fatal to them.

Forty barometers had already been installed by Rear Admiral Fitzroy in 'our poorest fishing villages' and the Duke of Northumberland had similarly equipped villages on the Northumberland coast. The RNLI added barometers 'wherever found useful and practicable at the society's lifeboat houses' and twenty years later claimed: 'It is certain that the National Lifeboat Institution must have indirectly contributed to the saving of the lives of large number of fishermen.'

But the rather patronising, though doubtless accurate, attitude continued: 'At present it is notorious that the masters of our small fishing craft hardly ever think of carrying with them an aneroid barometer and thus, when in mid-ocean, they are without the most hopeful means of forecasting the disasters which too often overtake them when gales of wind suddenly spring up.'

The RNLI then decided to offer aneroid barometers at the bargain basement sum of 11s 6d – two-thirds off the retail price – but only for coasters and fishing boats over 100 tons.

A century later the RNLI launched its Sea Safety Campaign, this time involving national organisations, such as the RYA. The RNLI, as an independent neutral body, was in a unique position to bring together sports bodies, representing leisure sea users and government representatives from the coastguard. While there were already good links, there was some mutual suspicion from the users, who stoutly defended the freedom of the seas, and the government, concerned about accidents and deaths at sea. Michael Vlasto of the RNLI, who was given the job of setting up the sea safety initiative, had to muster all his diplomatic skills and back them with a steely determination to bring the parties together, not just to talk, but actually to produce agreed safety codes and advice. The success of his initial work can be seen in the number of sports now covered, which extends to personal water craft (jet ski is a trade name) divers, sail and power boat users, and now even kite surfers. Each code has been hammered out in detail, and if all were followed, accidents would inevitably reduce.

There are now ten sea safety coordinators working with over 600 volunteers, many of them retired lifeboat crew members, meeting boaters face to face on slipways, quaysides and beaches or visiting yacht clubs, boat shows and boat jumbles to give free safety advice and boat checks.

The most successful safety advisers share the same interests and experiences as those they are talking to; yachtsmen chat to yachtsmen, fishermen to fishermen, and so on. The most difficult area, commercial fishing, has been actively tackled. Even though fishing is in sharp decline, it is still the most dangerous industry in the UK and Ireland. The sea safety campaign has attacked the heartlands of fishing, such as south Devon and north-east Scotland. David Smith, RNLI fishing safety coordinator in Peterhead, was a fisherman all his working life, starting as a deckhand and ending up as a skipper. Then an accident with a high-pressure hydraulic pipe meant he had to come ashore and he now devotes his time to improving safety in the fishing fleets. Fishermen are notoriously reluctant to wear life jackets, which they find cumbersome and potentially dangerous as they can snag in gear, so the RNLI has asked them to try fifty different designs and identify the best and the worst, and has pledged to develop one they will wear. Another imaginative scheme, first proposed and pioneered by Pat Smith of Mousehole, who lost her son in the Penlee disaster, is a confidential position reporting system. Fishermen are secretive and don't want rivals to know where they are fishing, but if their boat founders it is difficult to know where to start a search. The new system relies on satellite technology to provide a position which is known only to the rescue services.

The difficulty with safety promotion is that it is almost impossible to trace the direct effect of sea safety messages, so this area of work is vulnerable if the RNLI runs into financial difficulties, though it is invaluable in countering the criticism sometimes heard that people enjoying the sea for recreation behave irresponsibly.

Drawing on experience from the US Coast Guard, another new service was introduced to make safety checks on leisure boats. In America, Coast Guard Auxiliaries have been checking the safety equipment on pleasure craft for many years. The RNLI copied this with its Sea Check programme, involving volunteer advisers. In the pilot scheme 50 per cent of them were from lifeboat crews. The checks, completely voluntary, cover safety equipment on the boat and are not a substitute for a proper survey but a reminder of the need to go to sea prepared for the unexpected. The combination of the advice and the checks should be a powerful reminder that things can go wrong – for example, many competent yacht skippers still put to sea with crews who do not know about emergency procedures, such as man overboard or how to make a distress broadcast on the radio, so if the skipper is the one that is knocked into the sea, the crew are helpless. Unfortunately, these things do happen and there have been a number of cases of husbands and wives sailing together where the man has had a heart attack and the woman has been left helpless. The man's attitude, considering himself invulnerable, is open to criticism, for the emergency procedures are easy to pass on and simple to learn. Nevertheless, this precaution is often ignored, and still in the majority of cases it is the man who is at fault.

Less competent people are exposed by tales which seem too ridiculous to be true, such as brand-new life jackets being left in the boot of the car, not taken to sea, or navigation from road maps rather than sea charts. It may take a long time for sea safety messages to reach these people, but some endeavours, such as offering sea checks at popular launching slipways in the holiday season, have helped. Once again, the RNLI's independence is invaluable as it can give the advice in a non-judgemental and supportive way, trying to win the hearts and minds rather than criticise or impose legislation.

WE WILL SAVE THEM ON THE BEACHES

As part of its 1990s review, the RNLI identified another gap in safety and rescue at sea – beach lifeguards. While some beaches had excellent, well-trained and organised lifeguards, often paid for by local councils, in other places there was a patchy service or no provision at all.

Once again a foreign model, this time from the French lifeboat service, Société National de Sauvetage en Mer, helped the RNLI in its plans to integrate beach lifeguards into the main lifeboat service.

Within days of the launch of the pilot scheme in May 2001, the beach rescue team at Whitsand Bay in Cornwall, saved a boy who had dived into the shallows and severely injured himself. Using a neck collar, spinal board and oxygen, the lifeguards then called an air ambulance. The hospital later confirmed that their prompt action had prevented the boy becoming a quadriplegic. A year earlier, there had been no lifeguards on that beach at that stage of the season.

Adopting a lifeguard service meant new ways of working for the RNLI. As lifeguard services expanded, the RNLI entered into agreements with local authorities to cover some of the costs. This in turn could mean that the proud claim 'supported entirely by voluntary contributions' will have to be dropped. Also, full-time lifeguards were needed, with extra cover from volunteers at weekends. Lifeguards also pushed the RNLI across the divide from a non-

An RNLI lifeguard plucks a swimmer from the surf. *(Gary Knight)*

judgemental reactive service to a 'policing' role, where, for example, swimmers may be encouraged to turn back if they stray too far out. This can be seen as a blurring of boundaries, moving into the territory previously occupied by statutory authorities. However, in the absence of a nationally coordinated approach to safety on beaches, the RNLI has seized the initiative and in 2005 launched new beach safety signs with the aim of having easily understood, standardised information available all around the coast.

Another positive aspect is that RNLI beach stations, lifeguards and boats bring a highly visible presence to thousands of holidaymakers and, crucially, save lives quickly in places that conventional lifeboats could not reach in time.

By 2005 there were fifty-nine RNLI beach lifeguard units, each costing around £70,000 a year to run with only a quarter of the funding coming from local authorities. Their value is beyond doubt, extending life-saving and giving safety advice. Off the gentle beaches of Bournemouth, one of the greatest risks is an irresponsible power boater hitting a bather, but off Cornwall, rip tides are an unseen menace. On a summer's day in 2005, the beach lifeguards at Perranporth rescued thirty-four people in one afternoon after warning flags had been ignored. Rip tides are caused by sandbanks building up underwater to form a bottleneck. As waves break on the shore, the water draining off the beach is forced through the funnel at speed, sweeping people off their feet and carrying them away. A flash rip tide, caused by the collapse of a sandbank, caught out dozens of swimmers and children on mini surfboards at Perranporth. The lifeguards had to wade in to pull them out, and further along the coast at Porthtowan their colleagues helped another thirty-five people in difficulties. The swift intervention of lifeguards, using oxygen on some bathers, undoubtedly saves the lives of the unwary and uninformed. On a busy beach there will always be those who have not read the safety notices, or who are swimming outside the designated zones because they are so crowded.

WORKING INLAND

At the same time as setting up beach lifeguards, the RNLI decided to extend its cover to large inland waters. It had been estimated that over 250 people drowned every year on inland waters, more than died at sea. The first inland lifeboat station was opened in May 2001 at Enniskillen in Northern Ireland, covering the 50 square miles of Lough Erne. Later, four lifeboats were placed on the River Thames at Tower Pier, Chiswick, Teddington and Gravesend.

RNLI River Thames rescue boats. *(Derek King)*

Teddington has a totally volunteer crew and the others always have two full time and at least one volunteer on duty to be able to give a ninety-second launch response twenty-four hours a day. It is essential to get the boats away quickly as they are mostly launched to people who are already in the water, having fallen or jumped in and many are injured, some traumatically. Among the early volunteers at Tower Pier was Bill Callaghan, a Beefeater ready quickly to swap his tunic for an oilskin. One of the most bizarre tasks for the River Thames boats was to help when a bottle-nose whale swam up the Thames in January 2006. They helped to keep other boats out of the way while specialist divers tried to save the whale but, sadly, she died.

The beach lifeguards and inland boats boosted activity enormously, though the number of lives actually saved, as a proportion of overall call-outs, was lower than in conventional lifeboating. There has been another fascinating development, which is literally halfway between land and sea rescue. This is the use of hovercraft in large tidal bays with extensive sandbanks or mudflats, such as Morecambe. The RNLI had flirted with hovercraft for years, employing Tony Course, a qualified hovercraft pilot, as a lifeboat inspector in the 1970s with the specific brief to watch developments and conduct hovercraft trials.

RNLI hovercraft, Hoylake. *(Graeme Sweeney)*

Hovercraft, versatile as they are, do not make ideal rescue craft at sea as they do not operate well in strong winds and it can be difficult to get survivors on board. However, their ability to skip over shallows and banks where boats would either have to take the long way round or simply never venture, give them a specialist role in a few places. Trials with hovercraft started in Poole Harbour in summer 2002. Tony Stankis, the trials manager, was only too happy to take scientists to remote mudflats in the harbour to help them with an ecological survey as it gave him invaluable experience in handling the craft, approaching people safely and working in, or rather just above, shallows and mudbanks. There are now operational rescue hovercraft at Hunstanton, to cover the Wash, Morecambe, to cover its extensive bay, Southend, to cover the Thames Estuary approaches, and New Brighton, looking after the mouth of the Mersey.

The final piece in the expansion jigsaw of the early twenty-first century was the building of a training college at Poole, opened in 2004. The idea had first been mooted by George Cooper, chief of operations in 1996. His vision was an international training college for lifeboat crews from around the world. As more

The training pool at the RNLI College, Poole. *(Chris North)*

work was done, it became apparent that the future of a high-quality rescue service demanded not only a training location but also new training systems.

Nowadays, only 10 per cent of lifeboat crews are seafarers, so training in all aspects of lifeboating, from basic seamanship to the use of complex electronic equipment is essential, together with a system of knowing how far each crew member has advanced. A trawl of occupations of a typical crew in 2000 included a photocopier engineer, a bookbinder, a project worker for the mentally handicapped, a foreshores inspector, a plumber and a solicitor. All won medals, which were presented in the following year.

Informal training, by more experienced crew members and lifeboat inspectors passing on their accumulated knowledge, had worked successfully for years but increasing demands to prove that crews had all the necessary skills were driven by the dramatic fall in the numbers of fishermen and concerns about litigation and health and safety challenges. A competence-based system, where different tasks are identified and skills demonstrated, allowed crews to build up their expertise and, in some areas, to gain useful qualifications.

Some greeted the system – and the college – with scepticism before they had tried them, but once in place they gained rapid acceptance throughout the lifeboat service. The college is now a vibrant place, with crews from all round the coast meeting staff and fund-raisers, bringing all elements of the service together. In its first full year of operation it has also saved the RNLI thousands of pounds in hotel bills for crews, thus more than justifying its initial cost.

CHALLENGES AHEAD

The RNLI is an historic institution and faces similar challenges to those of many other parts of society. In the last two or three decades, the media have shifted their interests considerably. Previously, every time lifeboat crews gathered in London to receive bravery medals there would be a crowd of photographers, camera crews and reporters. At least two national newspapers would carry photos and stories. Now, being brave is not enough to make national news. The news agenda centres more around created personalities, be they sports or entertainment stars or people who gain overnight fame from television reality shows. It now takes an unusual story of bravery, such as a woman winning a medal, to interest the papers. There is little the RNLI can do about this other than recognise it as a risk. Disasters, however, do make headlines and there is less unquestioning acceptance and more scrutiny of these events than ever before. Fortunately, although lifeboat disasters have been pivotal points in the lifeboat service and its development, lifeboating has become safer over the years.

Increasingly sophisticated and safer boats, better equipment and more training have all helped. The seas are as dangerous as ever and any sensible lifeboat crew will tell you that the first step to safety is to respect the sea. But, like it or not, disasters make news and even if an increasingly cynical world seeks to lay blame, it also responds generously to human suffering. Nevertheless, if the RNLI is no longer having either its dramas reported or experiencing disasters, it is in danger of slowly being edged out of the public consciousness.

It also faces what might be called a perception gap. All the big, long-established, national charities are finding that the public carry outdated stereotypes of what they do, that there is an increasing gap between their perception and reality. Barnardos have not run children's homes for years. Shelter has never provided houses for homeless people. The Royal Society for the Protection of Birds (RSPB) has transformed itself from a bird watchers club into one of the biggest land management and conservation bodies in Europe. And WWF, once the World Wildlife Fund and now the Worldwide Fund for Nature, cuddles very few pandas but is a worldwide lobbying organisation.

So where does the RNLI fit in this pattern of change? As there are far fewer merchant and fishing vessels around our coasts, most lifeboat rescues nowadays are in fair to moderate weather and to leisure craft. They involve inconvenience and sometimes discomfort to the crews, rather than danger, although one in ten will be in severe weather. The crews themselves no longer match the romantic image of gnarled weather-beaten fishermen, clad in yellow oilskins and a sou'wester, roaring commands into the teeth of a gale. In some places it is no longer even possible to form a crew. Tiny fishing villages, such as Runswick in North Yorkshire, lost their permanent populations and hence their lifeboat stations years ago. Now larger coastal communities are becoming dormitory settlements where people travel to nearby towns for work, leaving few potential crew members available during the day. The loss of affordable houses to outsiders as second homes exacerbates the problem. In parts of coastal Devon, Cornwall and Wales, young people are forced out of their own communities to live and work. In these places, recruiting lifeboat crews is now an acute problem.

One solution has been to pay two people full-time wages to look after the big lifeboats. Traditionally the mechanic was the only paid crew member but there are now substantial numbers of stations where the coxswain is also full time, eroding the tradition of having a fisherman or butcher, baker, or lobster pot maker in charge of the boat.

The River Thames lifeboats have paid crews, as do the lifeguard stations. While the majority of life-savers and lifeboat crew are still volunteers, the balance is shifting towards more paid hands.

A new problem is challenges over employment rights from volunteers. The old way of dealing with local disputes was for the coxswain or lifeboat inspector to have a quiet word in a corner of the boathouse, giving advice to step down, apologise or whatever was needed to resolve the issue. Private words are no longer good enough and more formal procedures are needed with witnesses present. It certainly does not solve the problems any more easily. Nonetheless, it would be a quaint and inaccurate simplification to believe that there never used to be disputes at lifeboat stations, or murky staff behaviour in the head office. Human nature being what it is means that there have always been rows, sometimes very serious ones, but they rarely reached the public domain. What is worrying now is that even volunteer crews are prepared to try and sue for unfair dismissal and to seek financial compensation in an adversarial way that is completely alien to the vast majority of their colleagues. Old hands regard this as heresy but for some younger people it's simply a question of exercising their rights.

As well as the potential difficulty in finding crews in some places, the RNLI perception gap may threaten future support; the issue of where future funding will be found is contentious. On the one hand is the argument that the 'me' generation, spawned in the 1960s, is more selfish and less charitable than previous generations. In this scenario the traditional charities will suffer from competing with campaigning organisations, such as Friends of the Earth or Greenpeace. On the other hand, the significant response by young people to the tsunami of 2004 or the Make Poverty History campaign of 2005 shows that giving is alive and well – if the cause is right.

Through careful research, the RNLI has tracked attitudes for over twenty years. It has shown that middle-aged and older people are the most aware of the RNLI and the most likely to give and that the bias towards older people is more marked than for most charities. Young people, when asked, respond just as well to the idea of brave lifeboat crews but unless they are water sports enthusiasts, the RNLI rarely impinges on their lives.

Several social changes help to explain this finding. Cheaper foreign holidays mean that there are fewer long domestic holidays, during which a trip to the lifeboat station used to be a highlight. The massive decline of the Royal Navy, the fishing fleet and the merchant navy means that the sea means less to modern Britons, most of whom have no contact with anybody who goes to sea for a living.

So the image of Britain and Ireland as maritime nations has changed radically, while the use of the sea for leisure has grown exponentially. While the huge upsurge in the use of small boats, sail boards and jet skis keeps the RNLI very busy, this is a double-edged sword. These new sea users are prepared to support the RNLI but tend to regard a subscription as a transaction rather than a gift. They have done their bit and are likely to resent further appeals. Furthermore, the public at large are unenthusiastic about supporting what they see as rich yachties or time-wasting sailboarders. They retain the image of the storm-tossed lifeboat battling out to haul a grizzled trawlerman from his sinking fishing boat.

Another significant competitor for the public's attention is the helicopter. Dramatic images of helicopter rescues are much more common than lifeboat rescues, as the helicopters get back to base far quicker. Difficult sea rescue is then seen as the domain of the helicopter, even though the earlier chapters of this book have conclusively dispelled this myth.

The RNLI's beach rescue services, with lifeguards and safety notices, have helped to make this area of the service more relevant to large sections of the public, but even this has potential problems. One well-informed commentator said that the lifeguards could be seen by some as 'a bunch of Aussie chancers poncing around on quad bikes or jet skis and pinching our girls'.

An imaginative response to these challenges is critical to the future of the RNLI. Have the core values of voluntary work, selfless public service and bravery lost their potency? There is plenty of evidence that young people's idealism shows that they have not. Will people change allegiances as they grow older, moving from trendier campaigns to more staid causes, such as medical research and lifeboats? They might, but the RNLI cannot afford to wait and see. It also cannot be sure whether multi-million-pound legacies from a generation that went to the seaside, lived through the war and has the old rather than a modern image of the RNLI, will continue in the future.

To ensure the RNLI's future, the fund-raising strategy that has been developed is ambitious; it aims to double membership to half a million people, reducing the dependency on legacies which have provided over half the charity's income for the last thirty years.

Ironically, it is the legacies which helped the RNLI into the strong financial position from which it was able to expand its services; but as soon as it is seen as economically strong, it is criticised for having too much money. Yet the RNLI provides a vital national rescue service, which, though costly, is tremendous value for money compared to anything the state could muster. It is important to be able to plan ahead with confidence to ensure that new boats, boathouses and equipment can be provided. In an uncertain world, financial reserves are needed to do this. When these reserves rise, usually because of large legacies, the public can become critical, though it is usually other charities that carp the most, perhaps out of envy. Then some donors turn away, income may stall, reserves drop and the charity has to renew its appeals. This could be seen as the free market at work but it is not necessarily a good thing, as the lag between, for example, a will being written and received, or a legacy within it cancelled, can be many years. The RNLI's challenge is to explain why it, uniquely among large charities, can quantify its future needs and must ensure that they can be met though not exceeded. It's a very difficult balancing act.

Another challenge is to balance the old-fashioned paternalistic humanity of the lifeboat service, caring for all its people who in turn care for others, with the stark reality of running a multi-million-pound organisation. As a national newspaper wrote recently, about another charity, 'It's a hoary cliché now that big charities are big business and have adopted many of the mannerisms and techniques of commerce; most are not persuaded they have left anything precious behind.'

In the RNLI, boats and equipment are supplied by commercial companies and they must be dealt with in a businesslike way. And, as a large organisation employing over a thousand paid staff, the RNLI has its computer systems, employment problems and other issues, commonplace in companies and costing hundreds of thousands of pounds, which have to be paid for from public donations. Being businesslike does not have to mean being ruthless but inevitably, as the organisation grows, it struggles to retain the ethos of valuing the individual.

FUTURE OUTLOOK

In 2005, the RNLI 200 project presented its findings. It had been set up to predict how the RNLI would look in 2024, its 200th anniversary. It was a root and branch study which anticipated significant changes as seafaring and hence rescue patterns changed. One conclusion was that the number and nature of lifeboat stations would change, a process described as a gradual reconfiguration of the service. There would be strategically located all-weather lifeboats available at all times; tactically placed inshore craft, subject to weather limitations; a beach lifeguard service on a seasonal basis; and safety education and accident prevention, all with the emphasis on volunteers. To put some flesh on these bones, the service aims to achieve an average launch time of ten minutes; to reach all casualties, where life is at risk, in all weathers out to a maximum of 100 miles; and to reach any beach casualty up to 300 metres from the shore, within the flags, on an RNLI-patrolled beach, within 3½ minutes. The immediate plans to help deliver these targets centre on fleet renewal with the Tamar slipway-launched boat, the Atlantic 85 and a new carriage-launched boat, currently codenamed FCB2 (Fast Carriage Boat).

The reconfiguration of lifeboat stations is almost certain to mean that some will be closed. For years, committees and staff planners have said that there are

The prototype fast carriage boat, FCB2. *(Tony Denton)*

too many lifeboat stations, too close together in parts of the north-east, east and south of England. The reason is that each fishing village needed its lifeboat when the only power was sail and oar. Engines and faster boats mean that one station can cover a much greater area than before, and many stations have been closed over the years, but each time a delegation visits, the stations mount a fierce defence of their interests and so closing stations or changing them from all-weather to inshore cover is a slow and painful process.

Another part of the plan recommended shedding 100 staff over six years. Again, this is bound to be a slow and painful process, if it is achieved. Successive chairmen and chief executives have tried to halt or reverse the rise in staff numbers but most have failed, as they then set about initiating new activities, which need more people. There may be a change in the type of staff but without dropping whole areas of work, overall numbers are more likely to rise rather than fall.

The RNLI, like any other large organisation, is grappling with the increasing pace of change while charting its future course. Whatever that course may be, its humanitarian mission and actions remain as worthy as they were at its foundation in 1824. The boats have changed. The casualties have changed. The sea remains as wild and unpredictable as ever. Lifeboat crews never know when they may be called or what they may face – but still, they never turn back.

Index

Abeille 10 31, 69
Aberdeen 124
Aberdovey 121–2
Aberystwyth 95
Admiralty, the 23, 127
Alcock, Thomas 46, 47
Aldeburgh 191
Alderney 189
Allen, Heather 'Mickie' 151
Angle 80
Anglesey 37
Appledore 123–4
Arbroath 125
Arun class lifeboats 12, 13, 17, 21, 85–7, 93, 97, 101, 146, 160–1, 173
Atlantic class lifeboat 85, 209
Atlantic College, South Wales 95, 97
Australia 170–1, 173

Baltic Exchange 83
Bangladesh 173–5
Barclay, Richard 27, 28
Barker, Roy 146–7
Barnett class lifeboat 75, 82
Barra 82
Beattie, Tom 125
Beaufort scale 111
Beaumaris 37, 80, 156
Belgium 163
Bembridge 158
Berriff, Paul 108–9
Bevan, Brian 1–4, 6–8, 13–17, 116, 139–40
Bewick, Amos 121–2
Birmingham 153
Blackpool 144
Blogg, Henry 24–8, 71, 116
Blue Peter 154–6
Bonita 64–70, 139
Borth 121–2

Bournemouth 168, 201
Bower, Keith 17–22, 160
Bowry, Charlie 84–5, 103–8, 119–20
Brede class lifeboat 99
Bridlington 1, 8–11, 15, 109
Brinton, Mike 174–5
Bristol Channel 95, 97
Brockman, Neil 51, 56, 57
Brooke Marine, Lowestoft 85
Broughty Ferry 53
Bryson, Bill 111
Buckie 80, 150
Buckingham Palace 16, 138

Caister 92
Calshot 87
Campbeltown 137
Canada 170
Cantonad 5
Cass, Eric and Jean 151
Castle, Robin 109, 116
Chile 87, 170–3
China 87, 167, 170
Churchill, Winston 142
City of Bradford IV 3–4, 6–8
Civil Service Lifeboat Fund 154
Clark, Hewitt 58–64, 110
Cleethorpes 182
Clemence, Dave 117
Clifford, Frank 149
Coastguard *see* HM Coastguard
Cockcroft, Barry 180
Cocking, Thomas 180–2
Compston, Peter 161
Couzens, Roy 112
Coventry 153
Cowes 96, 98
Cox, David 8, 11–12, 14–15, 115
Cromer 3, 24–8

D class lifeboat 100
Darling, Grace 72, 182
Deacon, Bill 58, 62–4
Denmark 164
Diana V 3–4, 6–7, 14–15
Dougan, Derek 153
Douglas 44–5, 127, 129
Dover 85, 111–13, 153, 168
Dudley 153
Dunbar 116
Dungeness 111, 151–3
Dunmore East 195
Dutch lifeboat service 98–9, 129, 141, 163–5, 167–8
Dutton, Gerard 94, 132

Edinburgh, Duke of 136, 141, 159
Edward Bridges 18–21
Enniskillen 202
Estonia 71
Evans, Richard 37–47, 71, 173, 194–5

Falkland Islands 173
Falmouth 190
Fastnet 2
Fernebo 25
Filey 136
Finland 168
Fish, Michael 110
Fishermen's Friend 135
Fishguard 80
Flamborough 8, 44
Fleetwood 135
Fogarty, Hugh 175
France 94, 164, 168, 200
Fraserburgh 76, 78–81, 161
FRC (fibre reinforced composite) 88–9, 91, 170

Georgia 26
Germany 101, 141, 167–70
Gorleston 92, 151
Gower Pride 183–4
Graham, Wilfred 53, 127, 132
Green Lily 58–63, 110
Griffiths, Griff 108, 196
GRP (glass reinforced plastic) 86–7
Guernsey 5, 30–7, 66–9, 86, 116, 138–9, 167
Guyana 176

Hartlepool 120, 185
Harvey, Harold 43–8, 95
Harwich 93, 124, 151
Hastings 119, 186
Hayling Island 97, 185
Herald of Free Enterprise 71, 163
Heseltine, Michael 161
Hillary, Sir William 72, 127–9, 132, 146, 149
Hindlea 37–42
HM Coastguard 51, 59, 77, 81, 92, 127, 159, 167, 198
Hoare, Desmond 95, 132
Holyhead 44–8
hovercraft 203–4
Howth 147
Hoylake 149
Hudson, David 87–9, 100
Humber 1–16, 109, 116, 148
Hunstanton 97, 204
Huq, Konnie 155–6
Hutchens, Maurice 57, 139

Iceland 87, 139, 141, 170, 173
Ilfracombe 117
Inshore Lifeboat Centre 96
International Lifeboat Conference 83, 163–4, 168, 173
International Lifeboat Federation 164, 170, 173, 176
International Maritime Organisation 141, 164–6
Ireland 163–4, 167
Irene 77
Islay 82–3, 85, 137
Isle of Man 44, 127, 167

James Burrough 151
Japan 164, 167
Jarman, Derek 152
Jersey 28–30, 34–5, 94, 146–7, 167
Johan Collett 30–2, 69

Kent, Duchess of 78–81, 137
Kent, Duke of 15, 53, 136–8, 141
Kenya 168
Kilmore Quay 177
King, Thomas 28–30, 37
Kirkpatrick, Dan 76–7
Kirkwall 77, 80

Le Bon, Simon 190
Lerwick 58–64, 103, 109–10
Leslie, Denis 51–3
Lethbridge, Matt 114–15
Lewis, Richard 131–2, 146
Lincolnshire Poacher 154
Littlehampton 94, 156
Liverpool 44, 48, 131, 143
Lizard 44, 57, 150
Lloyds of London 127, 153
London Boat Show 16, 96–7, 125, 156
Lone Dania 82
Longhope 53, 76–8, 81, 83, 161
Lovat 49–50
Lymington 149–50
Lyrma 18–21
Lytham 131, 144–5

Mabel Alice 150
Macara, Charles 144–6
Madoc, Philip 108
Manchester 145
Martin, Joe 119, 186
Matthews, Lord 16
Maurice George 29
McKay, Donald 117
McLachlan class lifeboat 85
Medina class lifeboat 73, 98–9
Mersey class lifeboat 90–1, 101, 125, 135
Mexico 143–4
Mi Amigo 105–7
Michael and Jane Vernon 59–63
Miles, Brian 77–80, 132, 150–1, 197
Milligan, Spike 157
Mitropoulos, Thimio 141, 165
Moelfre 37–42, 45–8, 116
Morecambe 203–4
mountain rescue 187–8
Mozambique 175
Mumbles 53, 108, 177–9, 183–4

Nafsiporos 44–8
New Brighton 204
Newquay 149
New Zealand 170–3
Newhaven 133–4
Newman, Paul 69
Nicol, Phil 121–2

North Berwick 156
Northumberland, Duke of 131–2, 146, 198
Norway 32, 101, 164, 167–8, 170
Nutman, Tom 6, 11

Oakley class lifeboat 8, 11, 75, 87–8, 101
Oakley, Richard 74–5, 94, 132
Oban 126, 185
Opel 78–9
Orion 35–6

Padstow 119, 151, 185, 191, 193–4
Pegg, Brian 125
Penarth 136
Penlee 49–58, 70, 103, 115, 137, 140, 150, 195, 199
Perks, Dick 151, 174
Perranporth 201–2
Petit, Hubert 30–2, 37
Petit, John 5, 30, 32–7, 66, 116
Pionersk 59–60
Piper Alpha 109
Poole 188
Portchmouth, Roy 98, 141
Porthcawl 182–4
Porthtowan 202
Portpatrick 136–7
Prince Charles 53
Princess Alexandra 136, 138
Princess Diana 136
Princess Marina 136
Pritchard, Aileen 182–4

Queen Mother, HM 29, 133–4, 186
Queen Victoria 30, 158
Queen Elizabeth II, HM 16–17, 53, 133, 141

Radio Caroline 105
RAF 167
Ramsgate 168, 179
Red Cross 129, 174–5
Redford, Robert 69
Rescue Lima Charlie 59
Revi 6–8, 15
Rhyl 44, 185
Richards, Alun 108
Richards, Mary 55, 140
Richards, Trevelyan 49–52, 55, 58

RNLI Headquarters 85, 150
Robinson, David 150–1
Royal Humane Society 42
Royal Navy 127, 167, 207
Royal Yachting Association (RYA) 185, 198
Russia 167
Rye Harbour 53

St Agnes 156
St Annes 144–5
St Ives 53, 179–82
St Marys 57, 114–15
Salcombe 83, 108, 195–6
Saltoun, Lord 80
Santampa 177
Sargent, Derek 109
Savinesti 8, 11, 13, 15
Scales, Mike 55, 66–70, 138
Scarborough 120
Scott, Derek 108, 177–9
Sea King helicopter 19–20, 49, 51, 65
Selsey 140–1
Sennen Cove 57, 139
Severn class lifeboat 59, 61, 92–3, 100
Sheerness 84, 103–12, 116, 119, 194
Sheringham 125
Sikorsky helicopter 59, 62
Sir William Arnold 67–8
Skegness 191
Slater, Jock 141
Solomon Browne 49, 50, 53–4, 57
South Africa 99, 170–1
Southend 204
Southport 143–5
Spain 164
Spurn 1–4, 17, 109
Stogdon, David 94–6, 98–9, 132, 174
Stornoway 93
Stranraer 137
Stromness 78
Stronsay 78
Stultiens, Jeff 37
Sumnia 111–12
Sunnahavan 8–9
Sutherland, Albert 192–3
Swanage 190

Swann, Ralph 161
Sweden 141, 164–5, 167

Tamar class lifeboat 73, 101–2, 209
Tarby, Alan 119, 185, 193–4
Tate, Alan 133
Teare, Harry 83
Teesmouth 120
Thames class lifeboat 82–3, 85, 161
Thames, River 202–3, 206
Thelwall, Kenneth 147–8
This is Your Life 16–17, 37, 115
Thompson, Peter 157–9
Thompson, Tim 37–8
Thurso 78
Torbay 17–22, 69, 114
Trent class lifeboat 92–3, 100–1
Truro Cathedral 57
Tyne class lifeboat 140–1

Union Star 51–2, 54, 59
United States Coast Guard 83, 89, 164, 166–7, 170, 199
Uruguay 170, 172–3

Valentia 44
Vlasto, Michael 99, 198

Walker, Graham 11–12, 125
Walkington, Fred 1, 8, 10, 11, 15
Walton and Frinton 44, 188
Ward, John Ross 131
Watson class lifeboat 80, 83
Watson, George 74
Waveney class lifeboat 84–5, 92
Wells 8–12, 14–15, 115, 125
Wessex helicopter 20, 124
Weymouth 109, 115
Whitby 157–9
Whitesand Bay 200
Wick 117, 147
Wilberforce, William 129, 131
Withernsea 139
Wolverhampton 153

Zeebrugge 71, 163